禅学への道

An Introduction to
Zen
Buddhism

鈴木大拙
DAISETZ T. SUZUKI

坂本弘 訳

アートデイズ

晩年の鈴木大拙

鈴木大拙の英語──序にかえて

私は三十歳をこえたばかりのころ、仙台を離れて、東京に出てきた。いまの護国寺のあたりにあった鈴木学術財団というところに就職したのである。これは鈴木大拙さんを会長にいただいて、インド学や仏教学にかんする学術書を編集したり出版したりするところだった。

そこで私は編集者のような、校正者のような仕事をしていた。梵和辞典の編纂(へんさん)に従事したのもそのころのことである。

そういうことがあって、私は晩年の鈴木大拙さんに何度かお目にかかる機会があった。北鎌倉にお住いだったので、そこまで出かけていったこともある。そこは松ヶ岡文庫といって高台にあり、道を登っていくのが大変だったが見晴らしがとてもよかった。さきごろ亡くなった古田紹欽さんがいっしょに住んでおられたのである。

松ヶ岡文庫の高台の麓には東慶寺があり、そこにも何度も行った。この寺は江戸時代、女人の駆け込み寺として知られたところで、そこの墓地には西田幾多郎や和辻哲郎の墓石が立っていた。

その東慶寺で、あるとき鈴木大拙さんがお話をされるというので、東京の池袋からはるばる出かけていった。著書の方はかなり読んでいたのであるが、直接お話をうかがうのはそのときが初めてであった。

聴衆はお寺の奥の座敷に四、五十人もいたであろうか。大拙さんは終始くつろいだ雰囲気のなかで、雑談風に話をすすめていった。前後の脈絡はすっかり忘れてしまったけれども、アメリカ時代のことが話題にのぼった。たまたまインドのタゴールがノーベル文学賞をもらった直後に太平洋を渡り、サンフランシスコにやってきた。そのとき大拙さんも、何かの仕事でその地に滞在していた。それでタゴールの講演会に出席し、そのあと面会に行ったのであった。

挨拶を交わし、辞去するとき、タゴールが大きな手を差しだしてきた。それで思わず、その手を握りしめることができた。ところが驚くべきことに、そのタゴールの大きな掌がじつに柔らかだった。大拙さんは、そのときの情景をなつかしく想い出すように目を細め、何度も何度も、タゴールの掌は優しく柔らかだった、とくり返しいわれたのである。

だが私の方は、その講演会が果てたあと、大拙さんの掌にふれる機会を逸してしまった。もしもそのときふれていれば、大拙さんの掌の感触を通して、タゴールの柔らかい肌にふれるような気分を味わうことができたのではないだろうか。大拙さんに握手を求めなかったことが、いま思い返して残念でならないのである。

そのときから、ずい分経ってからだった。十五年ほど前に、たまたまロンドン大学を訪れる機会があった。そこの日本研究をしているスタッフの方々と懇談をしているときだった。ある教授があらたまった面持ちで、明治以降の日本の思想家で西欧世界にもっとも深い影響を与えた人物は誰か、と質問をぶつけてきた。しばらくしてそれは鈴木大拙ではないか、という言葉が返ってきた。なぜかというと、知的なレベルで西欧世界に刺激や影響を与えた日本人はその外にも何人かいるけれども、しかし西欧人

2

の感性のレベルにまでとどくような深いメッセージを発したという点では鈴木大拙をしのぐような哲学者や思想家はいないと思うからだ、というのである。

私は、なるほどとうなずかざるをえなかった。鈴木大拙は東洋の文化や禅の仏教をわかりやすい英文で書き、日本文化の啓蒙という仕事にも積極的にとりくんだ思想家だった。それらの作品は今日なお、海外で高く評価され、日本の文化や社会に関心をもつ人々の基本的なテキストになっているのである。

ここに、新たに出版されることになった『禅学への道』も、鈴木大拙の重要な仕事の一つであった。本書は、一九三四年、海外の読者のための禅の入門書としてロンドンで出版されたものだが、おそらく、今日にいたるまで欧米で最も広く読まれてきた鈴木大拙の著作といえるかも知れない。今回は、鈴木大拙の英文による原文と坂本弘氏の訳文を併録した初めての出版であるという。

さて、その鈴木大拙の文章であるが、面白いことに彼は、日本語で自説を展開するときはつとめて論理的に書こうとしているけれども、その同じ内容のことをひとたび英語で表現しようとするときは、いつのまにか心理学的な用語を多用している。日本文と英文とにおいて、どうも使い分けをしているらしい。そこに鈴木大拙の工夫があり、明白な意図がこめられているのではないだろうか。

日本文で書くときの彼の「論理」というのは、いわゆる禅の論理であったり、西田哲学流の論理であったりする。

鈴木自身の言葉でいうと、「即非」の論理ということになる。彼の主著の一つである『日本的霊性』には、こんな「論理」的な文章が出てくる。

山は山で川であると云う。また桜は紅くてそのまま紅くないと云う。黒は黒でない、白でない、そして黒に

もなり、白にもなる。そして黒は黒であると云う。

要するに、AはAであり、Bであると、一方ではいう。と同時に、AはAではない、Bではない、そしてただちにAであり、Bである、といい返す。何の理由や因果も説くことなしに、AはAでありBである、といいつつ、ただちにAはAではないBではないと否定し、そう言った舌の根の乾かないうちに、AはAでありBである、と言明する。否定すなわち「非」の言明が、間髪を入れずに宣言される。万物はそのようにしてこの世界に存在しているのだ、というわけである。そしてそれを「即非」の論理と、鈴木大拙は称したのである。そのまま否定し、そのまま肯定するということだ。

分かったような、分からないような話ではある。こういう議論の立て方というのは、かならずしも西欧流の「論理」ではないであろう。鈴木はしばしば論理を超越するといったり、論理そのものを空無化したり否定したりもする。かと思うと、そのことを説くために他方でメタファーやアレゴリーを多用したりもする。論理であって論理でないような、そしてまたその逆であるような融通無礙(むげ)の論法を用いている。しかし考えてみると、それは日本の禅者たちがみんなやってきたことではないか。いわゆる禅問答といわれるものだ。それだけではない。そもそも西田哲学の「絶対矛盾の自己同一」という独特の「論理」もまた同じ伝統に発するものだったのではないだろうか。禅的体験という、そもそも西欧流の論理によっては論理化できないものを、何とか論理化しようとするときに出てきたのが「絶対矛盾の自己同一」という非西欧的な論理だったからである。それがいってみれば、同一化しようとする日本の近代哲学が西欧の哲学と出会うことでつきつけられた最大のジレンマ、すなわち論理的なジレンマであったのだと思う。おそらく鈴木大拙もまた、そうした時代の影響をうけて、さきの「即非」の論理をあみ出すことにな

ったのである。
　ところがその鈴木大拙が、さきにもふれたように「東洋的」ともいうべきそうした「反」論理の禅の世界を英文にしようとするときは、こんどは徹底的に心理学的な用語を用いるようになる。論理主義者がたんに心理主義者に変身してしまっているといっていい。日本語の仮面をかぶるときは言葉の論理的な側面に照明をあてているのにたいし、英語の仮面をかぶるときは、替わり身も早く言葉の心理的な内面に重心を移しているのである。彼の英語で書かれた禅の研究書とか解説書をみると、そこに心理学的な考え方や説明が自由自在に活用されていることがただちに分かる。もともと英文で書かれた本書もまた、その原則でつらぬかれているのである。
　ちなみに、鈴木大拙は、一九五七年八月、メキシコ自治国立大学医学部精神分析学教室の主催で開かれた、「禅仏教と精神分析学」の研究会議に出席し、講演をおこなっている。それが機縁となって、一九六〇年一〇月に、鈴木の講演内容がエーリッヒ・フロムとリチャード・デマルティーノの寄稿論文とともに翻訳され、『禅と精神分析』と題して創元社から出版された。このときの翻訳者の一人である佐藤幸治氏によると、禅と心理学にかんするそれまでの研究蓄積にはすでにかなりの成果があがっていたのだという。すなわち禅経験の研究（現象学的研究）、禅にかんする心身両面にわたる研究（生理心理学研究）、禅者の行動・人格の研究（性格学的研究）、精神神経症の治療と禅との関係の研究（精神治療学的研究）、そして言葉と禅の関係についての研究（一般意味論的研究）などの多岐にわたっていた。そしてこれらの領域のなかでも、とりわけ精神治療学方面からの関心が高く、フロイト学派、ホルナイ、フロムなどの精神分析新派、そしてとりわけユングの分析心理学派が深い興味を寄せていた。この『禅と精神分析』の冒頭にそのユングの序文が付されているのも、右に記したような背景を考えるときうなずかれるの

である。

これまで鈴木大拙の仕事が、主に心理主義的な回路によって「翻訳」され伝達されてきたということをのべたのであるが、それにたいして西田哲学についていえば、これはむしろ「哲学」として「翻訳」され伝達されてきたのではないだろうか。ここでは詳しくは論じられないけれども、西田幾多郎の哲学はもともとは心理主義の立場から出発していて、最後になって論理主義（無の弁証法）に行きついたのだったと思う。つまり西田の最初期のデビュー論文である『善の研究』は「純粋経験」というものにかんする心理主義的な研究なのであって、作品の完成度からいっても面白さからいっても抜群のものだと私は思っている。文章も練りに練られた、ひじょうにすぐれた作品ではないであろうか。

その西田の『善の研究』が心理主義的な方法で書かれていることで、日本の青年たちの多くの心を惹きつけたというのは、ちょうど鈴木大拙が自分の禅にかんする思想や考え方を西欧に紹介するときに主として心理主義的な方法によったということと、まさにそのまま対応しているように私の目には映るのである。

平成十五年七月

山折哲雄（国際日本文化研究センター所長）

禅学への道

目 次

鈴木大拙の英語——序にかえて……………………山折哲雄 一

序 …………………………………………………………………… 二

原序 ………………………………………………………………… 一四

第一章 緒 論 ……………………………………………………… 一七

第二章 禅とは何か ………………………………………………… 二七

第三章 禅は虚無主義か …………………………………………… 四三

第四章 禅の没論理性 ……………………………………………… 五九

第五章　大肯定の禅 ……………………………… 七一

第六章　禅の日常性 ……………………………… 八五

第七章　悟り──新見地の獲得 ………………… 一〇七
　　一 ……………………………………………… 八六
　　二 ……………………………………………… 九五

第八章　公案 ……………………………………… 一三三

第九章　禅堂と雲水の生活 ……………………… 一四七

訳者後記 ……………………………………… 坂本　弘　一六七

序

禅入門書とも云ふべき此書は今までに度々邦訳せられたが、坂本君のやうに、わが意を得たものはない。君は多年の交際でよく著者の思想を呑み込んで居られる上に、英語を解する点においても今までの邦訳者のやうではない。これがこの訳書のもつ強味である。しかし今になって見ると原書其物が未熟だ。改めて筆を執るとすれば、大分違つたものになると信ずる。それ故、此書を読まれる人は、更に進んで著者のその後の邦文の書を読んで戴きたい。邦文の外に、最近英文で "Living by Zen"（東京三省堂、及びロンドン、ライダー出版社発行）と云ふのを書いたが、これを原文で読んでほしいと思ふ。今度渡米したら此書の思想を本として彼地の知識人と話して見たいのである。

坂本君邦訳の原書はもとく〜外国人を目標において書いたものであるから、必ずしも邦人向きとは云はれぬ。併し或る面から見ると、近頃の邦人——殊に若い人達——は、自分等が本来持って居るものを、どこかに置きわすれて、ひたすらに、外国輸入の思想にあこがれて居る。それもわるいとは云はぬ。世界の政治的、社会的情勢は若い人達における此動きかたを促進せしめるものがある。さりながら邦人は邦人である。歴史的にその条件から遁れるわけに行かない。これを忘れると、どこかで思はぬ蹉跌を行ずる。悲劇は成るべく避けたがよい。その一方法とし

て、外人向きに書いた拙著も邦訳せられて若い人に読まれてよいと信ずる。
東洋伝来の思想としての禅には、今世界に荒れ狂ふ思想と、甚だそぐはぬやうに考へられる面もあると云へば、云はれぬこともあるまい。が、実際は、人間生活の両極端であると見てよい。さうして相互に扶ぎょうして居るのである。
東洋の思想は大凡直観から出発する。西洋のはこれに反して論理から深まつて行く。それで直観は重視しない。たとひこれを認めた場合でも、それを論理の解剖台上で分析し尽さんとする。東洋は然らずして直観を弥が上に奥深めんとの努力にいそしむ。そして其方法論が立派に出来て居る。公案禅がそれである。所謂る「定より慧を生む」のである。
禅的方法論は漢民族の中から発展したものであるが、印度的と云ふべきものもある。それは『華厳』などで見られる華蔵荘厳法界の様相描写である。浄土の荘厳も亦此面における方法論的なものと見たい。海印三昧の直観は抽象的空虚でなくて、一切の有を包んだ豊富此上もなく、また絢爛けんらん目を奪ふものである。それで極楽は光耀に充ちて居る。法界は恒沙ごうしゃ無尽の仏刹ぶっせつで出来て居る。何れも兆載永劫の連続体である。これが経典の中で方法論的に記述せられて居る。限りなき論理の連鎖でなく、窮りない形相フォームイメージ又は想念の累積である。「無」の事事無礙界じじむげかいが此方法で作り出される。華蔵界や極楽世界はこれでないと了解せられない。
話がいくらか横筋に這入つたが、般若の「空」を本体とする禅研究の窮極に華厳的なもののあることを忘れてはならぬと云ふのが主旨なのである。現代の社会思想も決して如上を閑却してはならぬ。
坂本君の邦訳につづいて、英文の拙著が次から次へと日本文になるやうだが、何れも大分以前のもので、必ずし

序

も我意を得たとは云はれぬ。ロンドンではもとの英文を重刊して居る。新しいものも附け加へられる。それがまた既に仏訳や独訳になつたのもあり、まさにならんとするのもある。そのやうなものからまた何か生れるかも知れない。自分もます〴〵精進して深められるものを深めて行きたいと思ふ。訳者の労を多とする序でに思はず多言した。

昭和二十四年四月

湘南の一草庵にて

鈴木大拙

原　序

ここに集めた数篇の論文は、もと、第一次大戦の頃ロバートスン・スコット氏編輯のもとに日本で発行されてゐた英文雑誌『ニュー・イースト』の為に書いたものである。氏はそれらを一書にまとめて出版するやう勧めたが、当時は気が進まずそのままになつた。やがてそれらは英文『禅論』第一巻（一九二七年刊）の素地となつた。したがつて『禅論』第一巻は略ぼ同様の領域を取扱ふといふ結果になつてゐる。

ところが最近、やはり此等旧稿を一書にまとめるのもよからう、といふ気持が動いてきた。おもふに、『禅論』の方は浩瀚に過ぎて、禅についてごく予備的な知識を得たいといふ人々には取りつきにくいところがある。とすれば、海外の友人の間では入門書のやうなものもまた喜ばれるのではなからうか。こんな考へからであつた。

これを念頭に置いて私は改めて旧稿の全部に眼を通し、依用の文献はもとより、措辞・用語についても不正確と思はれるものはすべて訂正した。中には今になつて見るとむしろ表はし方を変へた方がよいと思はれるところが二、三あるが、そのままにしておいた。それを改めようとすれば、どうしても全然初から書き直さねばならぬからである。

誤謬に亙らぬ限りそれらには強ひて手を加へないことにした。

この書が、禅への入門書として実地に役立ち、自分の他の諸著作を研究する手引となれば、目的は達せられたと

原序

いつてよい。ここでは問題の学的な取扱ひを任としてゐないのである。なほ本書の姉妹篇として"The Training of the Zen Buddhist Monk," 1934（邦語版『禅堂の修行と生活』）、"Manual of Zen Buddhism," 1935 が出てゐる。禅入門の三部書として併せ用ゐられるならば、さらに読者の便宜に資するところがあらうと信ずる。

一九三四年八月

鎌倉にて

鈴木大拙

第一章　緒論

仏教はその発展につれて、いわゆる原始仏教或は根本仏教とは判然と異る一つの形式を作りあげた。その相違はいかにも判然たるものであって、我々が仏教の大乗・小乗二派への歴史的分裂を重視するのも当然といわなければならぬ。ところが事実上、大乗仏教はその様々な教説をも含めて仏教の発展した形式に過ぎず、またその窮極の権威を遡って開祖釈迦牟尼に求めるのである。この発展的仏教としての大乗仏教は、シナに、次いで日本に移入されるに及んでさらに一層の発展を遂げた。これは疑いもなくシナ・日本の指導的仏教者たちに負うものであって、彼等はその信仰の諸原理を絶えず変化する生活条件や民衆の宗教的要求に適合させる術を心得ていた。彼等のこのような努力と適合とは大乗仏教をより原始的な形態との間に生じていた裂け目をいよいよ大きくしたのである。現在大乗仏教は、少くとも表面的には、根本仏教を最もはっきりとしるしづけていた諸特色を何等発揮していないということができよう。

この理由から、この派の仏教は実際上一般に理解されている意味の仏教ではないと断定する人もある。しかし私

第一章　緒論

のいいたいのは次の点である。すなわち何物にもあれ生命を有するものは生き物である。そして、決して同じ状態にじっとしていないのが生き物の本性である。樫の実は、よしそれが丁度殻を破って柔かな葉芽をつけ、どうやら樫らしい恰好になっていても、十分成長して亭亭として巨人のように聳（そび）え立つ樫の大樹とは全く趣を異にしている。しかし此等の移り行く変化の相を通じて一すじに成長して行くものがあり、紛れようのない同一性のしるしがある。そこからして我々は、同一の植物が多くの生成の段階を通って行ったことを知るのである。いわゆる原始仏教はその種子にあたる。その種子から極東の仏教も生じたのであり、それは又さらに一層の生成を約束しているのである。学者は歴史上の仏教を説くかも知れないが、目下の私の意図は仏教を歴史的発展の上からのみではなく、それが極東に於ける霊活なる精神的動力として常に活き活きと我々に作用しているところに著眼して仏教を見よう、という にある。

特にシナ・日本に於て成長した仏教諸宗派の中には、仏教の本質と精神とを創始者より直接に受け伝えていることを、そしてそれは如何なる秘伝の文書にも密儀的行事にもよるものではないことを主張するユニークな僧団がある。この僧団こそ、その歴史的意義や精神的意義からのみならず、その最も独創的で刺戟に富む実地指導の方法から見て、仏教の最も意味深い部面のひとつである。「仏心宗」というのがその学的な名称であるが一般には「禅」として知られている。禅が言葉の上ではサンスクリットの原語 dhyāna の音を漢語に移した「禅那」に由来しているにもかかわらず、dhyāna と同一のものでないことは後程説明するであろう。

この派は色々な点で宗教史上に独自の意味をもっている。その所説は、思弁的に述べるならば思弁的神秘主義の所説に通ずる、ということができよう。だがそれは、久しく練磨工夫を重ねて親しくその何物なるかを体得した参

学の人にして初めてその窮極の意味をも理解し得るものであると提示し、且つこれを事実を以て示すところに独自の面目があるのだ。この洞察は全くしないもの、すなわち自家日常の実生活に触れて禅を体験していないものには、その教え、否その表現は全く奇異・奇矯、さらにいえば全く不可解なものとしか思われない。このような人々は、勢い禅を概念的に見て、全然荒唐無稽であるとか、或はその深さらしいものを外部の批評から護るためにことさらに不可解なものにしているのだ、と考えるのである。しかしながら禅者によれば如何にも逆説的(パラドキシカル)なその説き方は何等自身を包み隠そうとする作為ではない。ただ人間の言葉が禅の深い真理を表現するに相応わしくないために、その真理性はどうしても論理的解明の問題とはなり得ないのである。それは魂の内奥に於て体験されるとき初めて知り得るものとなるのである。事実、人間経験の他のどの方面に於ても禅の表現以上に平明直截な表現は甞て見られなかった。「炭は黒い」——これは明明白白である。ところが禅は主張する、「炭は黒くない」と。これもまた明明白白なのである。いや実は、這箇の消息が手に入るときは、先の肯定的論述にもまして一層明明白白でさえあるのだ。

このように禅に於ては個個人の経験がすべてである。経験の裏づけのない人には如何なる観念も通じない。これは分り切った話である。嬰児はどんな観念をも持ち合さない。それはその心性が何事をも観念を介して経験するまでになっていないからである。仮に持っているとしても、その観念はきわめて曖昧模糊として事実そのものとは対応しないものであるに相違ない。このように、或る事物について最も明確で充実した理解を得るためには、それを個人的に経験するところがなければならぬ。殊にその事物が生そのものに係わる場合、個人的経験は絶対に必要である。この経験がないならば、その深いはたらきに関する何事も決して的確に、したがって有効に把握されるものはない。

第一章　緒論

ではない。あらゆる概念の基礎となるのは単純素朴な経験である。禅はこの基礎経験を最も重んずる。禅がその「語録」に見出されるような言語上・概念上の足場を構築しているのはすべてこの基礎経験をめぐってのことである。その足場は深奥の実在に達するための極めて有用な手段ではあるが、やはり一つの技巧であり作為である点にかわりはない。それを窮極の実在に解する時その意義はことごとく失われてしまう。人間的悟性はその性質上、上部構造にあまり重きを置かないように動くものである。神秘化などということは禅そのものからいえば凡そ目標どころではないのだが、生の中心的事実に触れたことのない人にとっては禅はどうしても神秘化としか思われないのである。だからその概念的な上部構造を突破するがよいのだ。そうすれば神秘化と思われたものはたちどころに消滅するであろう。同時に心機開発、すなわち悟りがそこに現成するであろう。

かくして禅は内的な霊的経験を最もつよく且つどこまでも主張するのである。聖典や賢哲によるその論釈には何等本質的な意味を認めない。権威や外的啓示には個人的経験を以てつよく対抗する。霊的知見を得る最も実践的方法として禅者の提示するのは禅那（日本語では坐禅、禅は語原的にはその略語である）の実修である。

ここで、曩に禅の基礎経験として言及したかの霊的洞察を得るために禅者たちが行う組織的訓練について少しく言葉を費さねばならぬ。何故ならばこれは禅が其他の神秘主義の諸形式に優越する特色をなしているからである。大抵の神秘家にはかくも強度に個人的な霊的経験は、散発的、孤立的な予期しない何物かとしてしかやってこない。基督者はこの経験を自身にもたらす方法として祈り、或は苦行或はいわゆる凝心を用いるが、その成就は神の恩寵に委ねる。ところが仏教は元来かような事柄に超自然的な力を認めないのであるから、禅の精神訓練の方法はいたって実修的であり組織的である。シナに於けるその歴史の発端からしてこの傾向は実にはっきりと認められるの

であるが、時代の移るに従ってついに規則的な体系を生じ、かくして禅宗はその修行者をして目的達成のため、自己訓練せしめる周到な方法を有するに到ったのである。ここに禅の実践的長所があるのだ。それは一面高度に思弁的でありながらも、他面その組織的訓練は品性の上に豊富かつ有益な結果を生み出している。我々はそれが日常実生活の事実に触れて表現される場合、その高度の抽象性を忘れがちであるが、禅の真価を味わうべきはまさにこの点なのである。何故ならば禅は、一本の指を挙げ或は偶ミ路上に遇う友に「お早う」という、只それだけのことにも尽しがたい深い意味を見出すものだからである。禅の眼には最も実際的なものが最も深いものであり、その逆もまた真である。禅の採用する規律の全体系はこの根源的把握から出たものといってよい。

自分は、禅は神秘的である、と語った。これは禅が東洋文化の基調をなす以上当然といわねばならぬ。西洋が屢々（しばしば）東洋的心情の深みを測ろうとして得ないのもこのためである。何故ならば神秘主義はその性質上論理的分析を拒むものであるのに、西洋の思想は論理を以て顕著な特色とするからである。東洋の考え方は綜合的である。それは全体の把握を先とし、細部の精究にはそれほど意を用いない。そしてこれは直観的におのずとそのようにはたらくのであり、だから、今かりに東洋的心情というようなものを考えるならば、それは必然的に茫漠としてさだかならぬものであり、その内容を即座に外部の人に示し得るような索引はありそうもないのである。しかしそれをより精密により系統的に吟味するために我々の手にとらえようとする途端にそれは逃れ去り、その跡をも止めぬのである。禅は腹立たしいほど逃げ上手である。

以上、そういうものが目前にあることは疑われない。無視することを許さぬ以上、東洋的心情が他者の穿鑿の眼ざし（まな）を避けるために案出する意識的、計画的な術策に基くものではない。これは、勿論、東洋的心情の謂わば本質そのものに根ざしているのだ。従って東洋を理解するためには、神秘い。その測り難さは東洋的心情の謂わば本質そのものに根ざしているのだ。

第一章　緒論

主義、すなわち禅を理解しなければならぬ。

しかし神秘主義にも様々な類型のあることを記憶しなければならぬ。合理的なものもあれば、非合理的なものもある。思弁的なものもあれば秘義的なものもある。また理解可能なものもあれば怪奇的なものもある。東洋が神秘的であるというのは、東洋が怪奇的、非合理的で、知性的把握が全然不可能だ、という意味ではない。私のいうとするのは、東洋的心情のはたらくところには、恰（あたか）も常に永遠を観ているかのような穏やかな静かな擾（みだ）すことのできぬ何物かがある、ということである。しかしこの静寂と沈黙とは単なる無為と沈滞とを指すものではない。その沈黙は、如何なる植物も育たぬ沙漠の沈黙でもなければ、もはや永久の眠りに就いて朽ちるに任せた死者の沈黙でもない。それはあらゆる対立と条件とを亡じつくした「永遠の深淵」の沈黙である。それは過去・現在・未来にわたる自身のはたらきに深く思いを凝らして絶対的一即全の王座に静かに坐する神の沈黙である。それはまた相反する電流の撃ち出す閃光と轟音とのさ中に得られる「雷鳴の沈黙」（ほとばし）である。こうした沈黙が東洋の事物物に充ちわたっているのである。これを頽廃や死と解するものこそ禍いである。かかる人は永遠の沈黙のこの意味に於出る圧倒的な大作用によって気死せしめられるだろうから。私が東洋文化の神秘主義を云々するのもてである。そして私はこの種の神秘主義の教養が主として禅の影響によることをはっきりと認めるものである。仏教が極東に発展してその民衆の霊的渇望を潤おそうとするならば、どうしても禅にまで成長しなければならなかった。印度人は神秘的ではあるが、その神秘主義はあまりにも思弁的、瞑想的で、また余りにも煩瑣にわたり、その上、我々のすむ実際的な個々特殊の世界に活き〴〵と切実に触れ合う何の関係をも有していないように思われる。これに反して極東の神秘主義は直接で、実践的で、単純なること実に驚くばかりである。その発展の方向は禅以外

にあり得ぬであろう。

シナ・日本に於ける仏教の他のどの分派も紛う方なくその印度的起原を示している。その形而上学的煩瑣、冗長な措辞、極めて抽象的な推理、存在の実相についての深遠な洞察、生に係わる問題の抱擁力に富む解釈、等は明かに印度的であって全然シナ的でも日本的でもない。極東仏教をよく知っている人ならば、即座にこれを認めるであろう。例えば真言宗の行う極めて複雑な儀式やその宇宙解釈の依拠としている「曼陀羅」の彫琢をこらした諸体系を見るがよい。先ず印度思想によって影響されるということがなかったら、シナ人や日本人の心情にはこのような複雑な構造をもつ哲学は到底思いも及ばなかったであろう。また中観・天台・華厳の哲学が如何に高度に思弁的であるかを考察するがよい。その抽象力と論理の鋭さには真に驚歎すべきものがある。以上によっても此等極東仏教の諸派が畢竟外来底であることは明かである。

しかしながら仏教全般を見渡してから禅に眼を転ずるとき、我々はその単純性、その直接性、そのプラグマティックな傾向、その日常的生との密接な聯関が他の仏教諸派と著しい対照をなしているのを認めずにはいられない。疑もなく禅の中心観念は仏教から出ている。それは仏教の正当な一発展であると考えざるを得ない。只この発展は極東民衆の心情に固有な要求に応えようとして成就されたものであることを見落してはならぬ。仏教の精神は実践的な生の一規範となるためにその高度に形而上学的な上部構造を捨て去ったのだ。そこに生れたものが禅なのである。故に私は思い切って率直にいう。具に見れば禅の中には極東民衆の、特に日本人の、哲学・宗教のすべて、さらに生そのままがあまりなく体系的に統摂されている、否むしろ結晶しているのだ、と。

第一章　緒論

原　註〔坂本弘訳〕

(1) 正確にいえば、大乗の基本的諸観念は般若部経典に説述されている。その最も初期のものは仏滅後三百年近くになって現われたに相違ない。その萌芽は疑いもなくいわゆる原始仏教系統の述作に見えている。只その発展、すなわちそれらを開祖の教説の最も本質的なものとしてはっきりと把握するということは、その弟子たちが様々に変化する生活条件の中を或る期間身を以てその教説を実践して行くということによって初めて実現したのである。このように経験によって豊かさを増し、反省によって円熟した印度の仏教者たちは、小乗的或は根本的形式とは異った仏教の大乗的形式を有するに到ったのである。印度に於ては二派の大乗が知られている。すなわち龍樹の中観派と無著・世親の唯識或は瑜伽唯識派である。シナに於てはさらに数派が発展している。すなわち天台・華厳・浄土・禅等である。日本に於てはその外に法華・真言・真宗・時宗等がある。すべて此等の分派・宗派は仏教の大乗系に属している。

(2) 坐禅は略ミ「瞑想裡に坐すること」と考えてよい。その正確な意味については第九章「禅堂と雲水の生活」に関する記述参照。

第二章　禅とは何か

以下幾分詳細に禅の教えを解説するに先立って、よく批評家が禅の本質について持ち出す質問のいくつかに答えておきたいと思う。

大方の仏教教説がそうであるように、禅もやはり高度に知性的なまた深く形而上学的な哲学の一体系であろうか。禅の中に東洋のあらゆる哲学が結晶していることは緒言に述べたとおりであるが、これを、禅が一般にいわれているような意味で一つの哲学である、と取られては困る。禅は論理と分析とに依拠する体系とは全然別物である。むしろ、二元的思惟の方法としての論理の対蹠物(たいしょ)である。禅が全心情であり内に数々のものを蔵するところからすれば禅にも知性的要素があるといってもよかろうが、心情というものは、数々の能力に分離することができ解剖が終ればあとに何も残らぬような集合体ではない。禅は知性的分析という点では何も我々に教えるところはないのだ。この点に於て禅はまたその弟子たちに信じさせねばならぬような型にはまった教義は一切持ち合せていないのだ。謂わば全くカオス的である。恐らく禅者はそれぞれ一定の教説を持っているであろうが、それは各人の好尚と便宜

第二章　禅とは何か

によるのであって禅そのものによるのではない。従って禅には如何なる聖典・教理もなければ、禅の真義に近づくよすがとなるような如何なる象徴的方式もない。そこで、禅は何を教えるのかとたずねられたら、自分は答えるであろう。禅は何も教えはしない、と。禅にどんな教えがあろうと、それは人々自身の心情から出たものである。我々を教えるのは、我々自身である。禅はその途を示すに止まる。この示すということを教えだといわない限り、禅には基礎教義もしくは基礎哲学としてことさらに標榜するものは何一つとしてないのである。

禅は自ら仏教であることを主張するが、経論所説底に対しては悉く知性の不浄を拭い去る以外に用のない故紙と断じて憚らないのである。さりとて禅を虚無主義と考えてはならぬ。すべて虚無主義は自己破壊的であってその止まるところを知らぬ。否定の立場に立つことは方法としては堅実であるが、至高の真理は一箇の肯定でなければならぬ。今、禅は哲学を持たないといい、禅はあらゆる教説上の権威を否定するといい、禅はいわゆる聖典の類いを一切無価値として顧みないというとき、実は禅が外ならぬこの否定を通じて全然積極的な、そして永遠に肯定的な或る物を打ち出していることを忘れてはならぬ。このことは次第を逐うて明かにせられるであろう。

抑々禅は宗教であろうか。普通に理解されているような意味では宗教であるとはいえない。何故ならば禅は、礼拝すべき神をも、執行すべき儀礼的行事をも、死者の生れ行く未来の国土をも、そして最後に冥福祈念の目あてで人によってはその滅不滅に強烈な関心を寄せる霊魂そのものをも有しないからである。禅はすべてそのような教義的、「宗教的」な羈絆を脱しているのだ。

禅に神なし、といえば敬虔な読者は定めし驚くことであろうが、これは神の存在を否定するものではない。否定・肯定、ともに禅者の与り知らぬところなのだ。一物の否定されるとき、否定そのものには否定されない何物か

がある。同じことが肯定についてもいえる。これは論理の宿命である。禅は論理を超出し、対立を容れない一箇高次元の肯定を見出そうとするのだ。従って禅に於ては神は否定もされなければ主張もされない。只、禅にユダヤ人や基督者の懐き来ったような神観念のないことは事実である。禅は哲学ではない、というその同じ理由によって禅は宗教でないのだ。

禅寺で出会す様々な仏・菩薩・天人その他の像についていうならば、それらはそこばくの木材・石材・金属のとり合わせに外ならぬ。わが庭園の椿・躑躅・石燈籠と同様である。思召しのままにそこなう満開の椿を拝み給え、と禅者はいうであろう。諸天諸神を拝し或は浄水を灑ぎ或は聖餐式に列する底の宗教味もこの一挿一拝を出づるものではないのだ。のみならず、大抵のいわゆる信心深い人々が功徳あり神聖であると考える此等の敬虔な行為のすべては、禅の目を以てすれば却って余計なわざである。禅は大胆にも「清浄の行者涅槃に入らず、破戒の比丘地獄に落ちず」と宣言するのだ。これは普通に考えるならば道徳的生活に関する不文律を真向から否定するものがあるが、禅の真理と生命は実はここにあるのである。禅は一人間の精神である。禅はその本来清浄であり本来善であることを信ずる。何によらず附加せられたり、或は不当に切り取られたりするものがあれば、それは精神の健全性をそこなう。かくして禅はあらゆる宗教的因襲に力づよく反対するのである。

とはいえ、禅の非宗教性は外観上のことに過ぎぬ。真に宗教的な人々は結局禅の野蛮な宣言の中に豊かな宗教性のあることを見出して驚くであろう。しかし基督教やマホメット教と同じ意味に於て禅が宗教であるというのは誤りである。この点を明らかにするため、次の例を引こう。釈迦は生れ落ちるや否や片手で天上を指し、今一方の手で大地を指して「天上天下唯我独尊」と叫んだといわれているが、禅の雲門宗の祖、雲門文偃はこれを評していうに

第二章　禅とは何か

は、「もし自分がそこに居合わせたら、一撃の下に打ち殺して飢犬の胃袋へ投げこんだであろうものを」と。一箇の精神的指導者に対して如何なる不信の徒と雖も、かかる狂気の批評は思いも及ばないであろう。しかも一禅匠は雲門に続いていう。「これこそ正しく雲門が、身心を問わず自分の一切を犠牲にして世間に仕えようとするやり方なのだ。」彼の仏恩を憶う心の深さは推して知るべきである」と。

禅を、「新思想（ニュー・ソート）」或はクリスチャン・サイエンスを奉ずる人々、或は印度教の遊行僧（サンニャーシン）、或は一部仏教者によって行われる或る形式の瞑想と混同してはならぬ。禅は言葉の上からは禅那（ディヤーナ）ということになるが、それは禅における修行の実際と合致するものではない。禅の修行中、宗教上或は哲学上の問題について想いふけることもあろうが、それは偶然以上の意味を有するものではない。禅の本質は全然そういうところにはないのだ。禅は心そのものを鍛練し、その本来の性質を徹見することによって外ならぬ心自身の主たらしめようとするものなのである。このように禅はいわゆる瞑想や禅那以上の真性質に徹するということこそ、禅仏教の根本目的をなすものである。この自己心霊のものである。禅の訓練は霊の眼を打ち開いて存在理由そのものに観入せしめるところにあるのだ。

瞑想しようと思えば、どうしても自分の思念を何か或る物、例えば神の一者性とか、その無限の愛とか存在の無常とかの上に集注しなければならぬ。ところが、これこそ正しく禅の避けようとするものなのだ。禅に力強く主張するものありとすれば、それは自由、すなわち不自然な絆からの自由、の実現である。瞑想というは人為的に装著した何物かである。空飛ぶ鳥は何を瞑想するだろうか。水中を行く魚は何を瞑想するだろうか。鳥は飛び魚は泳ぐ。それで十分ではないか。心の本源的なはたらきには属しない。神と人との一者性に、或は現在のむなしさに思いを凝（こ）らす必要がどこにあるというのか。日々展転してやまぬ生活活動を神の善とか地獄の永劫の炎とかいう瞑想によ

って阻止する必要がどこにあるというのか。

基督教は一神論的である、ヴェーダンタは汎神論的である、というもよかろうが、禅について同様の主張をすることはできない。禅は一神論的でもなければ汎神論的でもない。禅はこのような称呼を一切受付けないのである。従って禅には思念を集注すべき対象ということもできない。禅は空にただよう一片の雲である。釘でとめることも紐で捉えることもできない。おのが好むままに動いて行く。どれほど瞑想を凝らしても禅を一所に止めることはできない。瞑想は禅ではない。汎神論も一神論も、禅に集注すべき主題を与えはしないのだ。もし禅が一神論的であるならば、禅はその学人に対して、神的光明の遍照裡にあって一切の差別相の亡ぜられる万法一なるところを瞑想するように教えるかも知れぬ。また禅が汎神論的であるならば、野に咲く名もない草花も神の栄光を宿しているのだと説くことであろう。ところが禅の説くところは次の如くである。

「万法が一に帰するものならば、その一はどうなるのか」。禅は各自の心を自由無礙ならしめようとするものである。一とか一切とかの観念すら、精神の本源的自由を脅かす障礙であり陥穽である。

それ故に禅は、一狗子も神であるとか、麻三斤も神的なるものであるとかいう観念に思念を集注せよと教えはしない。それを敢てするならば、禅は失われているのである。禅は端的に火は暖いと感じ氷は冷いと感ずる。我々が凍てつくような日には身震いをして火の傍をよろこぶ、そのままである。ファウストの道破するように感情こそ一切である。すべて我々の論議は実在に触れることはできない。ところでこの感情という言葉は、ここではその最も深い意味に於て或はその最も純粋な在り方に於て理解されなければならぬ。「これは感情である」といってさえ、もはや其処には禅はないのだ。禅はあらゆる概念構成を排する。禅の把捉しがたい理由は此処にある。

第二章　禅とは何か

そこで、もし禅の提唱する瞑想ありとすれば、それは、事事物物をあるがままにとらえよ、雪は白く鴉は黒いところを見とどけよ、ということになる。瞑想とは何か或る高度に一般化せられた命題に精神を集注することである。そしてそのような命題はその性質上必ずしも具体的な生活に密接なつながりをもつものではない。禅は徹底してはたらきそのものであり、そこにはもはや見るものも見られるものも存しないのである。これに反して瞑想は明かに二元論的であり、したがって皮相的であるを免れない。

①一批評家は禅を「聖イグナチウス・ロヨラの『霊的訓練』の仏教版」という風に見ている。この批評家はどうも仏教的な事物に基督教的類似点を見たがる傾きがあるが、これなどもその一例である。禅について一見識を有する者からすれば、この比較が見当外れも甚しいことを直に気付くだろう。外見からして禅の修行とイエス会創始者の提唱する修行との間には類似点らしいものは何ひとつないのである。聖イグナチウスの凝心と祈禱は、禅の見所からすれば、敬虔な人達のために丹念に織りあげた数々の想像の織物に過ぎない。実際それは頭上に瓦を積み重ねたようなものであって、精神生活の上に何等真の利益をもたらすものではないのだ。只、此等の「霊的訓練」が五停心・九不浄観・六随念・十徧処等の小乗仏教の観法に通った点があることは認めることができる。

禅は「精神の謀殺、呪うべき無為の瞑想」を意味するものと考えられることがある。彼が「精神の謀殺」という真意は知る由もないが、禅は思念を一事に集注せしめ或は催眠せしめることによって精神のはたらきを封殺するとでも考えているのだろうか。ライシャウアー氏はその著書に於て、③禅は「神秘的自己陶酔」であることを主張し、このグリッフィスの見方をほとんど
者として知られているグリッフィスの言葉である。これは②『日本の宗教』の著

裏書している。彼はスピノーザが神に陶酔したように禅はいわゆる「大我」に陶酔するとでも考えているのだろうか。ライシャウアー氏の「陶酔」という意味はあまり明瞭ではないが、禅は不当にも個別の世界に於ける窮極の実在としての「大我」の思念に没頭していると考えているのかも知れぬ。批判の眼なき禅の観察者の浅薄さ加減いたっては只ゝ驚くの外はないのだ。実のところ禅は謀殺するにも「心」を有しないのだ。禅はまた隠れ家として執著することのできるような「自己」というものも有り得ない。従って禅にはまた「精神の謀殺」などというものは有り得ない。実際、禅はその外に現われた相に関するかぎり極度に把捉しにくいのである。遠くから見るといかにも近づき易く思われるが、近寄って見ると一層遠いようにさえ思われるのである。従ってその根本原理を会得するために幾年月を捧げて熱心に参学するのでなければ、禅について概ね公正な理解を有することは期待できない。

「神へ上昇する道はおのが自己に下降するにある」。――これはユーゴーの言葉である。「もし神の秘義を探ろうと思うならば汝自身の精神の深みを探求するがよい」。――かくいうのは聖ヴィクターのリチャードである。ところがこれらの秘義が究尽されるときには「精神」なるものはもはや存しないのだ。諸君が下降し得るところには、もはやその深さを測られるような「精神」も「神」も存しない。何故か。すなわち禅は底なき深淵であるからだ。「三界を通じて真に存在するものは何一つとしてない。何処に心を見ようというのであるか。四大は畢竟空であるとすれば、仏の住所は抑ゝ、何処に求め得るのであるか。――しかも見よ、真理は紛う方なく汝の眼前に全現しているではないか。これこそ真理の全分であり、正しくそれだけなの

第二章　禅とは何か

だ」。一瞬も躊躇するところがあれば禅は既に失われて取り返す術もない。三世の諸仏が寄ってたかって今一度それを取り返させようとしても既に遠ざかること千万里である。「精神の謀殺」「自己陶酔」も結構だが、禅はそんな批評を一一気にしている暇はないのだ。

批評家の中には次のように考える者があるかも知れない。すなわち、禅によって精神は無意識の催眠状態に引入れられ、そこに仏教徒の得意とする空（śūnyatā）の教説が体験される。この状態に於ては、主体は或る茫漠とした空無――それが何であるにもせよ――の中に没し去って客体的世界をも自己自身をもさらに意識しなくなるのだ、と。この解釈もまた禅の核心を逸している。尤も禅にはこの種の解釈を示唆するような表現がないではないが、禅を理解するためにさらに一歩を進めなければならぬ。すなわちこの「茫漠たる空無」は横断されなければならぬ。主体は、生き埋めにされることを欲しないならば無意識の状態から覚醒するところがなければならぬ。精神が「謀殺」が放棄せられ、「酔っぱらい」は目覚めきたってより深い自己に触着するところがなければならぬ。さるべきものであるならばその仕事は禅の手に委ねるがよい。何故ならば殺されて生命なき存在を再び蘇らしめ永遠の生命を与えるのは正しく禅だからである。「生れ変るのだ。夢から醒めるのだ。死から起ち上るのだ。おお汝酔漢たちよ」。禅はかく叫ぶであろう。目隠しをして禅を見ようとしてはいけない。それでは手許が狂って確実に把握することができないだろう。そしてかくいう私の言葉には何の誇張もないということを記憶して貰いたい。

このような批評を挙げようと思えばまだまだいくらもあるが、読者諸君が以下のさらに積極的な禅の論述へ進むための準備はこれで十分できたことと思う。禅の目指すところは我々存在の内的なはたらきに親しく触れるに在る。従って禅はそしてこのことを何等外部的、追加的存在にたよることなく、できる限り単刀直入に遂行するにある。

外部的権威を思わせるようなものは悉く斥けるのである。絶対信は一個人自身の内的存在に置かれる。何故ならば禅に於ける如何なる権威も内から現われるのである。これは最も厳密な意味に於て真実なのだ。知性のはたらきですら窮極のものとも絶対のものとも考えられてはいない。それどころか却って心それ自身との直接の感応を妨げるものである。知性は媒介的にはたらくときにその使命を全うするのであるが、禅は他人に自らを伝えようとする場合以外は、何等媒介的なものに交渉をもたないのである。かく見来るとき、一切の聖典は単に試図の範囲を出ず、条件つきのものに過ぎず、何等の窮極性を持たないのである。現に生きつつある生の中心的事実こそ禅の把握しようと目指すところのものであり、且つ、これを最も直接に最も生気ある仕方で行おうというのである。禅は自ら仏教の精神であることを表明するのであるが、事実上それはあらゆる宗教あらゆる哲学の精神でもあるのだ。禅が徹底して体験されるとき、もはや揺らぐことのない心の平和が得られ、人は計らわずして如法の生を生きるのである。それ以上の何を望むことができようか。

或はいう、禅は明かに神秘主義の一形態と見られる以上、宗教史上にユニークな位置を要求することはできない、と。恐らくそうも見られようが、禅は自己自身の秩序をもつ神秘主義であることを見落してはならぬ。それは、太陽が輝き、花が咲き、私が丁度今、誰かが街路上で太鼓を鳴らしているのを聞くのと同じ意味に於て神秘的なのである。此等が神秘的事実であるならば、禅は神秘に充ち溢れんばかりである。禅はいかなる宗派根性とも没交渉である。基督者も仏教者と相携えて禅を行ずることができる。それは大小の魚類が共に満足して同一大海中に棲むのと全く同様である。曰く、「平常心（びょうじょうしん）」。如何にも平明で核心を衝いているではないか。禅は大海である。禅は大気である。禅は山岳である。禅は雷鳴であり、閃光であり、

第二章　禅とは何か

春咲く花であり、夏の炎熱であり、冬の雪である。否、それ以上のもの、すなわち禅は人間なのだ。禅はその長い歴史を通じて累積し来った形式的行為・因襲、その他の附加物にも拘わらず、その中心的事実に於て潑剌として活きている。禅独特の長所は、今日依然として何物によっても偏らしめられることなく能くこの窮極的事実を体認せしめ得るところにあるのである。

既に述べたように日本に行われている禅のユニークな特色はその秩序立った心の訓練方法にある。従来神秘主義といえばその赴くままに余りにも日常実地の生活と懸け離れたところがあったが、禅はこれを根本的に転換せしめた。禅の発展と共に神秘主義はもはや神秘的でなくなり、また異常な天分を有する者の発作的な所産ではなくなったのである。何故ならば禅は、現に生きるがままの生の只中に生きるという事実を認得することによって一市井人の最も目に立たぬありふれた生活の裡に自身を啓示するからである。禅は組織的にこれを見させるように訓練する。胸宇を広闊にし、その一鼓動毎に永劫の時間、無限の空間を包容せしめる。我々の実世間に生きるそのままがエデンの園を歩むが如くならしめる。禅は人間の眼を打ち開いて日日時時刻刻に演ぜられる最大神秘を直視せしめる。そしてこの霊的な離れ業の数々は、何の教説をも恃みとすることなく、只我々の内的存在に横わる真理を直に指すことによって成し遂げられるのである。

ともかく禅はどこまでも実際的であり、日常的であり、同時に最も潑剌としている。昔或る禅匠は禅の何たるかを示そうとして一指を竪て、今一人は毬を蹴り、さらに今一人は問者の顔に一掌を与えた。我々の内奥に横わる内的な真理がかくのごとく実地に証明されるとすれば、禅こそ、如何なる宗教も依用することを知らなかった最も実際的で直接な心の訓練方法ではなかろうか。事実、禅は、概念に渉ることを拒んでひたすら生の活事実を取扱

おうとするところからすれば、只こ独創的、創造的というより外はないのである。概念的に理解するならば一本の指を竪てるということは日常茶飯事のひとつである。しかしそれは禅の目を以て見るとき、霊妙な意味と創造的な活気とに脈脈生動しているのだ。禅がこの真理を我々の因襲的な概念に縛られた生活の只中に指摘する限り、正しく存在理由ありといわねばならぬ。

次に引用する圜悟（西暦一五六六―一六四二）の一書翰中の言葉は、本章の冒頭に置いた「禅とは何か」の問に或る程度まで答えるものということができよう。

覿面相呈即時分付了也。若是利根一言契証已早郎当。何況形紙墨渉言詮作路布。転更懸遠。然此段大縁人人具足。但向己求。勿従它覓。蓋自己心無相虚閑静密鎮長印定六根四大光呑群象。若心境双寂双忘絶知見離解会直下透徹即是仏心。此外更無一法。是故祖師西来只言直指人心教外別行単伝正印。不立文字語句要人当下休歇去。若生心動念認物認見弄精魂著窠窟即没交渉也。石霜道。休去歇去。直教唇皮上醭生去、一条白練去、冷湫湫地去、古廟裏香炉去。但信此語依而行之。放教身心如土木如石塊。到不覚不知不変動所靠教絶気息絶籠羅。一念不生驀地歓喜如暗得燈如貧得宝。四大五蘊軽安似去重担身心豁然明白。照了諸相猶如空花了不可得。此本来面目現本地風光露。一道清虚便是自己放身舍命無為快楽之地。千経万論只説之。前聖後聖作用方便妙門只指此。如将鑰匙開宝蔵鎖門。既得開触目遇縁万別千差無非是自己本分合有底珍奇。信手拈来皆可受用。謂之一得永得尽未来際。於無得而得。得亦非得。乃真得也。（圜悟心要、巻下）

それはおんみの面前に放り出されている。全体は即今そのままおんみに手渡されているのだ。利根のものなら

第二章　禅とは何か

ば一言でその真実を肯うことができる筈だ。だが、この時すでに差違が忍びこんでいるのである。それが紙墨に附せられ言詮に渉るとき、逸脱は愈こ大きくなるばかりである。禅の偉大な真理は各人各人の所有である。直ちにおんみ自身の存在を洞見せよ。他によって求めてはならぬ。おんみ自身の心はあらゆる形相を超え自在であり、静寂であり、充足している。しかもそれはどこまでも六根四大に自己を印するものである。その光の中にすべては呑み去られる。主観・客観の二元論を沈黙せしめよ。双ながら忘れ去れ。知性を越え悟性を離れ、直下に透徹するところがなければならぬ。そこに仏心がある。これを他所にして何の実在もないのだ。さればこそ菩提達摩が西方より渡来したとき、只次のように説いたのである。「直ちに人心を指すわが立場は独特なものであっていわゆる教えに囚われることがない。直ちに真実を肯うて安心し去れ、正しく心印を単伝するものである」。禅は文字・言葉乃至経典とさらに係わるところはない。一念の動くところ、やがて対象を分別し、悟性の作用を分別し、いろいろに妄想を逞しうし、迷執に身動きの取れなくなるものだ。そこにはもはや禅の片影すらも見当らない。

賢者石霜は語っている。「すべて心の喘ぎを止めよ、唇皮上に黴が生えるようにせよ。一筋の白練の糸のようになれ。この一念を永劫に漉らしめるな。冷く生命のない死灰のようになりはてよ。さびれた村廟の香炉のようになりはてよ」。

この言葉を一途に信じて、どこまでも修行に励むがよい。身心を土木とし石塊とし、完全に変動なく覚知もない状態に達すれば、あらゆる生の徴は消失しあらゆる限界は跡形もなくなる。もはや意想の片影もおんみの意識を擾すことのないときに当って、思いがけなくおんみは充ち溢れる歓喜のうちに一道の光明に照破されるの

を覚えるだろう。それは闇中に燈を得、貧窮に財宝を得るにも似ている。四大五蘊のこの身ももはや重荷とは感じられなくなる。それほどに軽く安らかで自在である。おんみの真の存在はあらゆる限定から解放されたのだ。おんみは今や身心豁然とひらけ軽安になり、障礙を知らなくなったのだ。またおんみは物の真性質についての瞭瞭たる洞察力を得るようになる。諸この存在は今やおんみの前に、何等実在として捉えることのできぬ数々の空華として映ずるようになる。ここに戯論の瞞著し得ない自己が現われる。これこそおんみの本来の面目である。またここにおんみの本地の風光が何のかくれもなく現われる。道は只ひと筋、但しあくまでひろびろと何の礙(さまたげ)もなく直通している。すべてを捨てるということ——一体も生命も内奥の自己に属する一切のものをも——そこにその道があるのだ。ここにおんみは平和・安住・無作、さらに、いいがたい歓喜を得ることができる。一切の経論は只この事実を知らしめようとするに外ならぬ。古今すべての聖者がその能を尽し構想の妙を尽したのも只このためであるのだ。それは鍵を以て宝庫を開けるにも似ている。一度開けることができたら、現じ来る機会は一としておんみのために役立たぬはない。何故ならば、それらはすべて、如何に千差万別であろうとも、おんみ本来の自己の内にあって自由自在に得られるものではないか。そこにあるほどの宝は只管おんみ(ひたすら)の享受と利用とを待っている。「一得永得尽未来際」とは正にこのことだ。おんみの所得は所得ではない。しかもここに真に得られた何物かがあるのである。

第二章　禅とは何か

原註

(1) Arthur Lloyd: *Wheat Among the Tares*, p. 53.（『毒麦の中なる麦』）
(2) William Elliot Griffis: *The Religions of Japan*, p. 255.
(3) August K. Reischauer: *Studies of Buddhism in Japan*, p. 118.（『日本仏教研究』）

第三章　禅は虚無主義か

シナ禅宗の第六祖と伝統的に考えられている慧能（西暦六三八―七一三）は禅史上極めて重要な人物である。事実上、彼は当時シナにあった仏教諸宗に対する独立の一宗、すなわち禅宗の開祖なのである。彼が禅的信を端的に、旗幟(きし)鮮明に、打ち出しているのは次の一偈である。

　　菩提本無樹

　　明鏡亦非台

　　本来無一物

　　何処惹塵埃(じんあい)

　　菩提、すなわち真の智慧は樹木に擬せらるべきものではない。

　　また明鏡があってどこかに輝いているのでもない。

　　本来無一物なのだ。

　　塵埃を惹こうにも惹きようがないではないか。

これは、自ら禅的信を純粋に体得したと信ずるいま一人の禅者の偈に応じて発表されたものである。その偈は次の通りである。

　　身是菩提樹　　この身は菩提の樹である。

44

第三章　禅は虚無主義か

心如明鏡台　　心は明鏡の如きものである。
時時勤払拭　　不断に心して払拭し、
莫使惹塵埃　　塵埃を惹かしめるようなことがあってはならぬ。

この両人は共に第五祖弘忍（西暦六〇二―六七五）の弟子であった。弘忍は、慧能こそ正しく禅の精神を体得し衣鉢を継承するに足る人物であると考えたのである。前掲慧能の偈の意義をその師がかく認めたということは、禅的信の正統的表現として印可したことに外ならぬ。ところが、この偈が一見無の精神を気息に感じさせるところから、禅を虚無主義に与するかのように考える人が多い。本章の目的とするところはその論駁にあるのだ。

尤も禅の文献には、例えば、空（シューニヤター）説のように虚無主義的教説を伝えるかとも思われる箇所が多い。大乗仏教一般に通暁している学者の中にも、今もって禅は三論哲学もしくは中観派教説の実践面への応用だと考えているものもある。因に三論とは龍樹の『中論』・『十二門論』及び提婆の『百論』であって、いずれもこの派の主要教説を形造るものである。龍樹はその開祖とされている。この派の哲学は、いわゆる般若系大乗経典と相通ずる見地に立つところから、屢と般若系教説として指称されている。そこで、彼等は考える、禅は実際上この部類に属する。換言すれば禅の意義は詮ずるところ空の体系（システム）を挙揚するに尽きるものである、と。

或る程度までは、少くとも皮相的には、この見解は当っている。例えば次の如きを見るがよい。或る弟子が師に問うた、

「私は仏教の真理を求めて此処まで訪ねて参りました。」

師は、答えた、

「此処にそんなものがあると思っているのか。自家本来の財宝を忘れて一体何処をうろつき廻っているのだ。お前に与えるようなものは何もない。この庵室に一体どんな仏教の真理を見付けようというのか。無い、と言ったら全く何も無いのだ。」

或る禅匠は何かというと次のように語った、

「自分は禅などというものは知らぬ。こうだと示すものもない。ぼんやり突立っていても何も無いところからは何も出てこないぞ。どうしても悟りたければ自分で悟るがよい。捉うべきものがあるなら自分で捉えるがよかろう。」

また曰く、

「真の知（菩提）はあらゆる表現を超越している。求め得て悟りとすべきものは本来存在しないのだ。」

また、

「禅には言葉によって説き得る何物もなく、神聖な教説として宣布すべき何物もない。道い得るも三十棒、道い得ざるも三十棒だ。沈黙を守るな、言説に亘るな。」

「どうしたら何時も仏とともに在ることができましょうか。」

という問に応じて或る師匠は次のように答えている、

「念を動かすな。境に対してどこまでも澄明であれ。このように常に絶対の空寂に住するのが、仏とともに在るその在り方なのだ。」

また時として次のような言葉に出会す、

第三章　禅は虚無主義か

「中道とは中間も両辺もともに存せぬところにある。対象的世界に束縛されるのがその一辺、自心に迷うのが他の一辺だ。両辺ともに存せぬところ、ひとり中間のあろう筈がない。これがすなわち中道なのだ。」

数百年前盛名を謳われた日本の一禅匠は、生死の問題について指教を乞う弟子たちに対して次のように答えるのが常であった、

「此処には生死（しょうじ）というものがないのだ。」

シナ禅宗の第一祖菩提達摩は、梁の武帝（在位五〇二―五四九）に仏教の第一義を問われて、「廓然無聖（かくねんむしょう）」と答えたと伝えられている。

此等は厖大な禅の文献から任意に引用したものであるが、いずれも空（śūnyatā）・無（nāsti）・寂静（śānti）・不思議（acintya）等の観念が滲透しているように思われ、見様によっては虚無主義的に、或は消極的な寂静主義（クヮイエティズム）に与するようにも考えられるのである。

次に引用する『般若波羅蜜多心経』中の章句は上掲のいずれにもまして驚くべきものがあろう。事実般若系大乗経典のいずれにも空の思想が徹底的にしみわたっている。従ってこの思惟方法に慣れない人々が、これに面喰うのは必定であるし、その印象をどう言い表わしてよいかにも困るかも知れぬ。この『心経』は般若系経典中最も簡潔にして要領を得たものと考えられ、禅堂では日々読誦（どくじゅ）されている。実際禅僧たちが晨朝（じんちょう）にまた食前に先ず第一に読誦するのはこの経典なのである。

舎利子。是諸法空相。不生不滅。不垢不浄。不増不減。是故空中。無色。無受想行識。無眼耳鼻舌身意。無色声香味触法。……無無明。亦無無明尽。乃至無老死。亦無老死尽。無苦集滅道。無智亦無得。以無所得故。

47

菩提薩埵。依般若波羅蜜多故。心無罣礙。無罣礙故。無有恐怖。遠離一切顛倒夢想。究竟涅槃。

舎利弗よ。すべての存在はかくの如く空を性格としている。生もなければ滅もない。垢もなければ浄もない。増もなければ減もない。されば、空なるところ形相もなく、知覚もなく思想もなく造作もなく意識もない。眼・耳・鼻・舌・身・意すべてなく、これに対応する色・声・香・味・触・法もすべてない。……無明もなく無明の尽きるということもない。涅槃の智もなければこれを得るということもない。かく所得とすべきものは何一つないのだ。菩薩は般若波羅蜜、すなわちこの体認に立脚する故に無礙の心境に住するのである。無礙である故にもはや恐怖というものがなく、一切の顛倒妄想を遠離して窮極の涅槃を享受するのである。

これらの引例を通読するとき、禅を以て純然たる否定の哲学の弁護として非難する批評家の立場も一応尤もと思われるかも知れないが、この批評ほど禅の実際から遠いものはないのだ。何故ならば禅はつねに、生の中心事実を把握しようとするものであり、この生の中心事実たるや絶対に知性の解剖台に載せることのできないものである。これを把握するために禅はどうしても否定に次ぐに否定を以てしなければならないのだ。だが、単なる否定は固より禅の精神ではない。しかしながら二元的な思惟の方法は、習性となって深く我々に滲みこんでいるために、どうしてもこの知性的誤謬を根本から剪除してかからねばならぬ。かく見るとき禅が「これでもない。あれでもない。」と言明するのもまさに然るべきところである。ここでもし我々が、かく否定を尽して最後に残るものは何かと喰い下ろうものなら師匠は我々の頬に一掌を与えて、「この瘋癲漢、これは何だ」と叱呼するだろう。人或はこれを窮余の一策とし或は身の粗放を暴露するに過ぎぬ、とするかも知れない。が、禅の精神を純粋に把握

48

第三章　禅は虚無主義か

しているものには、その一掌が如何に切実なものであるかが分るのである。何故ならば此処には、否定もなく肯定もなく、唯一箇の紛れなき事実、一箇の純粋経験、我々の存在と思想との依拠そのものがあるからだ。我々が動いてやまぬ心の只中にひそかに願い求めるしずけさと虚しさとはすべてここにあるのだ。苟且にも外的なもの因襲的なもののために道を踏み迷うことがあってはならぬ。禅は、套を脱して赤手を以て直接に捉えなければならぬ。禅が否定によらなければならぬのは、我々の生れもつ無明（avidyā）の故である。それは濡れた衣服が体に密著するようにしっこく心にまつわって離れないものである。無明はその分限内に於ては何等不可とすべきはないが、その分限を越えてはならぬものなのである。無明とは論理的二元論の別名である。雪は白く鴉は黒い。しかしかくいうのは世間に属することであり、その無明的な物の言い方に属することである。もし事物の真理そのものに参到しようと思うならば、その事事物物を、世界も未だ創造されず彼此の意識も未だ呼び醒まされず心はその本来底すなわちその浄らかさとむなしさに安らう、まさにそのところから見なければならぬ。これは否定また否定の世界である。但しこの否定は、より高いむしろ絶対の一肯定、否定の只中の一肯定を打ち出さんがためのものである。雪は白からず、鴉黒からずである。しかも依然として雪は白く鴉は黒いのだ。ここらが我々日用底の言葉では禅の真意を伝えにくいところである。

紛れもなく禅は否定する。だが、その実禅は、瞭瞭として我々の眼前にあるところのものを我々に、さあ手に取って見よとばかりに突きつけているのだ。それをわが手に取ろうとしないならば、それは我々の過ちである。無明の雲に心眼を曇らされた大方の人々はそれを素通りして眼にとめようともしない。彼等にとっては、如何にも禅は虚無主義である。それもその筈、正しく彼等は禅を見ていないのであるから。

黄檗（西暦八五〇または八五五歿）が仏殿にあって仏陀に礼拝していると一弟子が問うた、

「仏に著いて求めず、法に著いて求めず、僧に著いて求めず、というが今師が何かを求めるかのように仏を礼拝せられるのはどうした訳ですか。」

「仏に著いて求めず、法に著いて求めず、僧に著いて求めず、唯いつもこうやって礼拝するというだけのことだ。」

弟子は承服しかねて言った、

「礼拝してどうしようというのですか。」

師はすかさず一掌を与えた。これには弟子も驚いて思わず叫んだ、

「太麤生！」
らんぼうな

「そういうお前の所在はどこだ。細とか麤とかほざき居って。」
そ

こう叫ぶなり師はさらに一掌を加えた。

聡明な読者諸君は黄檗のこの態度の中に外見上の粗放さにも拘らず彼が何とかしてその弟子に伝えようとしている或る物を看取するであろう。外見上奪うが如く見えてその実精神に於ては与えているのである。このことが理解されなければ禅はなかなか分るものではない。

形の上の礼拝に対する禅の態度は、仏前礼拝の一僧に与えた趙州（西暦七七八—八九七）の言葉の中に一層はっきりした形で見出すことができる。趙州が件の僧を掌打したとき僧は問うた、

「仏を拝するのは讃むべきことではありませんか。」

50

第三章　禅は虚無主義か

「その通り、だがその讃むべきことすらないのがなお結構だ。」

この態度に虚無主義的な或は偶像破壊的なところがあるかどうか。皮相的にはそうも見られよう。だがこの言葉を発した趙州の精神の深みに身を躍らせるとき我々は、全然分別的理解を越えた一箇絶対の肯定に直面していることを覚えるに違いない。

近代日本禅の創始者白隠（西暦一六八五―一七六八）が未だ年若く禅の修行に傾倒していた頃、正受老人に面会の機を得た。白隠は、既に自分は十分禅を体得していると考え、ひそかに心驕っていたのである。この正受との会見も、実は自分自身のすぐれた見解を実地に証拠てるためであったのだ。正受は直にその見得底を求めた。白隠はさも疎ましげに、

「もし見得底として手脚を著け得るものがあったらすっかり吐き出してしまいましょう。」

と答えて嘔吐の恰好をして見せた。正受は白隠の鼻頭をしっかりと捉えて問うた。

「これは何だ。とにかくこうして手脚を著け得るものがあるじゃないか。」

ここで読者諸君も白隠と共にこの会見についてよくよく考えて欲しいと思う。そしてかくも歴歴と正受老人の証示するところのものが何であるかを自分自身で発見して欲しいものである。

禅は、心を空却して謂わば純粋の虚無に到らしめるような否定とは全然類を異にしている。禅には自己肯定的な何物かがある。だがそれは自在であり絶対であり局限を知ることなく抽象の手にかかることをどこまでも拒むものである。禅は一箇の生き物である。生命のない巌石やむなしい空間の類ではない。この生き物に打ち当ることが、否、実生活の折に触れ縁に応じてこれを把得して行くこ

51

南泉（西暦七四八―八三五）が或る時法弟の百丈（西暦七二〇―八一四）にたずねられた、「貴僧には嘗て人に説いたことのない法があるか、どうか。」

泉曰く、「有る。」

丈はさらに突込んだ、「その法というのは一体何だ。」

泉曰く、「不是心、不是仏、不是物。」

丈曰く、「自分は善知識の柄ではない。説不説など頓と与かり知らぬのだ。」

泉曰く、「自分にはこういうより仕方がないのだ。貴僧なら何というか。」

丈曰く、「と言えば、もうちゃんと説いてしまったじゃないか。」

百丈は問う、

泉曰く、「それは受取れぬ。」

丈曰く、「やれ貴僧のためについ諄くしゃべり過ぎたようだ。」

これは絶対虚無を説くものの如くであるが、しかもなお否定を通じて顕われんとするものの消息が窺われる。なお続く問答について見られたい。

禅に関して何とか話が通じ得るためには、この論理的説述を許さぬ内的自覚の何物であるかが分っていなければならぬ。言葉はこの自覚の一境に対してインデックスであるに過ぎぬ。言葉を通じてその意味に参じ得るのだ。先ず第一に如何なる心境から禅匠たちがそのような行動に出ているかを知るように努むべきである。彼等は恣意のもよおすままにこうした荒唐無稽を行じ、また見様によっては馬鹿げ切った暇

とがあらゆる禅修行の目的であるのだ。

52

第三章　禅は虚無主義か

潰しを行じているのではない。彼等は深い個人的経験によって得た一定の堅固な基礎を置いているのである。彼等の一見狂気沙汰かとも思われる振舞のすべてが実は最も活き活きとした真理の脈絡一貫した証示（デモンストレーション）であるのだ。この真理から見るとき、全宇宙の運行すら蚊がとび扇が動く以上の意味をもたないのである。要は、これらのすべてを貫いてはたらく一箇の精神を看て取るにある。それは一箇絶対の肯定である。そこには虚無主義の片影もないのだ。

一僧が趙州に問うた、

「もし一物をも携えずにやってきたら貴僧は何と言われるか。」

州曰く、「そんなものは大地へ放り出してしまえ、とこうだ。」

僧は抗議する、「一物を携えずというているのに、何を放り出すというのだ。」

「それがいやなら引担いで帰るがいい。」

これが趙州の答であった。

趙州はこのようにして虚無主義的哲学のむなしさを白日のもとに曝け出したのである。禅の目標に達するためには、「一物をも持たぬ」という観念すら掃蕩しなければならぬ。仏は、仏、仏と固執することもなくなったとき、おのずと顕現する。すなわち仏のためにこそ仏を捨てなければならぬのだ。これこそ禅の真理を体得する唯一の途である。無とか絶対とかを口にしている限り禅を距（へだ）てること甚だ遠いばかりではなく、刻一刻禅が遠ざかりつつあるのである。

空（シューニャター）の足場さえ蹴放してしまわねばならぬ。救われる唯一の途は直に無底の深淵に身を躍らせることである。

53

そしてこれは全くたやすい業ではないのだ。

以下は圜悟（西暦一五六六―一六四二）の大胆に主張するところである。

「地上には嘗て如何なる仏も出生したことはない。また聖教として伝うべきものもない。初祖達磨は嘗て西来したことなく心印を伝えたなどということもない。このことの分らぬ徒輩のみが自身の外に真理を求めているのだ。しかも彼等の求めてやまぬその真理は、外ならぬ彼等自身の足下に踏みつけられているのである。これは千聖の智を尽しても得られるものではないのだ。にも拘わらず、我々はちゃんと見ている。しかもなお見てはいないのだ。ちゃんと聞いているのだ。それを語っている癖にまだやはり語っていないのだ。知っている癖にまだやはり知っていないのだ。試みに問おう、これは一体どうしたわけなのか。」

これはその外見どおり質問を提出したものだろうか。それとも実は一箇瞭瞭とした精神態度を肯定的に打ち出したものであろうか。

このように禅の否定は必ずしも論理的な意味をもつものではない。それと同じことが肯定について言えるのである。要するに、究竟の経験的事実は、構成的もしくは図式的な思惟法則に隷従すべきものでもなく、或はまた曖昧の失せた認識論の構造式に隷従すべきものでもないのだ。尤もそれは外見だけのことではあるが。従って禅がその肯定の対照法に隷従すべきものでもなく、或は肯定・否定の対照法に始終背理・非合理を駆使するのは紛れもない事実である。そが始終背理・非合理を駆使するのは紛れもない事実である。その当然の結果――誤解、曲解、屢々悪意を秘めた揶揄等――を免れ得ないのも無理はない。虚無主義を以て擬するのはそれらの中の只一つに過ぎない。

第三章　禅は虚無主義か

維摩が文殊に菩薩不二の法門の何であるかをたずねたとき文殊は答えた。

「自分の思うところでは、一切の存在を無言・無説・無示・無識にして見るとき理解せられるものである。これで自分の所見は申上げた。今度は高説を承りたい。」

維摩は促されながらも黙然として遂に一語をも発しなかった。唇を閉じるという神秘的な応答は、何か言いたいが言えぬという、禅もよく追いこまれる、そのような窮地に立った場合にそれを脱け出す唯一の途であるらしい。されば圜悟もこれを評して次のように言わねばならなかった。

「是というも肯定すべきものがあるわけではない。非というも否定すべきものがあるわけではない。是非既に去り、得失両ながら忘じて、浄裸裸赤灑灑（しゃくしゃ）なるところを見なければならぬ。試みに、汝の背後にあるものは何か、また面前にあるものは何かを語って見よ。一僧あって進み出て「面前は是れ仏殿三門、背後は是れ寝室方丈」と答えたとすれば、この僧は果して眼を具してみているかどうか。古来の諸聖と親しく相見したことを認めてやろう。」

沈黙では埒があかぬなら、我々も圜悟に倣って一言して見よう。曰く、

「上には天国の門ひらけ、下には劫火洞然たり。」

「是（イエス）」と「非（ノー）」の二元論に息づまることのない禅の真意がこれで明かになったかどうか。我他彼此（がたひし）の意識の最後の一すじでも残っている間は、何人も禅に徹底することはできない。幾多の古聖もまた我々と没交渉の人となるであろう。内なる財は永久に持ち腐れとなるであろう。

一僧が問うた。

「維摩経には、浄土を得んと欲せばその心を浄くすべし、とあるが心清浄とはどういうことですか。」

これに対して禅匠は次のように答えている。

「心が絶対に清浄であるとき心清浄を得るのだ。絶対に清浄であるとは浄不浄を超えるということである。おまえはどうしてこれを体得するかが知りたいだろう。それには心をあらゆる縁に触れて徹底的にむなしくすることだ。そうすれば浄が得られる。だが体得してもそれに念を生じてはならぬ。念を生ずるとき、もう不浄である。然しまた不浄となってもその念を生ずるな。そうすれば不浄に囚われることもないのだ。これが絶対清浄である。」

この絶対清浄は絶対肯定に外ならぬ。浄不浄を超えつつ、より高い綜合の立場に於て却って両者を統一するからである。此処にはもはや否定もなければ矛盾もない。禅の目ざすところは、かかる統一を日常の実生活に実現するにある。生活を一種の形而上学的訓練と見做すものではないのだ。すべての禅「問答」はこの光に照らして考うべきである。地口、言葉の遊戯、詭弁、そんなものは何一つないのだ。禅こそ何物にもまして真摯な関心事なのである。

この章を閉じるに当って、最も初期に属する一禅籍から次の例を引くこととしよう。

仏教哲学者であり特に唯識学者である道光というものが、一禅匠を訪ねて問うた。

「禅師は何の心を用いて道を修せられるか。」

曰く、「自分には心の用うべきものもなく、道の修すべきものもない。」

曰く、「それなら、どうして毎日衆を聚め人に勧めて学禅修道せしめられるのか。」

第三章　禅は虚無主義か

曰く、「自分には卓錐の地すらないのだから衆を聚めようがないのだから、人を勧めるにも聚めようがない。また自分には舌というものがないのだから、人を勧めるにも勧めようがない。」

哲学者は思わず叫んだ、「面と向ってよくもそんなでたらめが言えたものだ。」

曰く、「人を勧める舌さえ持たぬのにでたらめが言えるわけがない。」

道光はついに匙を投げた、「自分には禅師の考え方はさっぱり分らない。」

「自分にも自分のことが分らないのだ。」

禅匠はこう結んだ。

原　註

（1）　空 シューニャター の理説が実際上何を意味するかは拙著英文『禅論』第三巻、The Philosophy and Religion of the Prajñāpāramitā-sūtra, pp. 207-288.（「般若経の哲学と宗教」）の章に幾らか詳細に説明しておいた。

（2）　前掲（頁三八）石霜からの引文を見よ。それはことさらに空 アナイヒレーション 却の説を擁護するものの如く屢ミ誤解されている。サンスクリット原典、玄奘の漢訳より文献学的で、正確な英訳については、拙著英文『禅論』第三巻、The Significance of the Prajñāpāramitā-hridaya Sūtra in Zen Buddhism, pp. 190-206.（「般若波羅蜜多心経の禅宗に於ける意義」）参照。著者はそこでこの重要経典の意義について著者自身の解釈を下している。

（3）　これはヘラクレイトスの Enantiodromia すなわち対立の調整的機能に相当すると考えることができよう。

(4) 大珠慧海『頓悟要門論』所収、諸方門人参問語録、巻下、十三参照。

第四章　禅の没論理性

空手把鋤頭　歩行騎水牛
人従橋上過　橋流水不流

これは善慧大士（通称傅大士　西暦四九七—五六九）の有名な偈であって、簡潔にしてよく禅者の見方を示している。禅の真理を——それが可能なこととして——知性的に明かにしようと思う者は、先ずこの短詩の意味を理解しなければならぬ。この四行の詩以上に没論理的、没常識的なものはあり得ない。批評家なら禅を、不合理で混乱していて普通の考え方では頓と分らぬものだ、といいたいところである。然し禅は何等動ずることなく主張するだろう。いわゆる常識的な物の見方は何等窮極的なものではない、と。もし我々が真に生の源底に徹しようと思うならば、我々は用い慣れた推論式（シロジズム）を放棄し一箇の新見地に立って論理の専横と我々日常語法の一面性とを脱し得るところがなければならぬ。如何

第四章　禅の没論理性

に逆説と見えようとも、お構いなく禅は主張するのである。鋤は空手にして執らねばならぬ。脚下に流れるのは水ではなくて橋なのだ、と。

然し禅のやる非合理的な説き方はこれに止まるものではない。同じように人をまごつかせるような表現がまだまだいくらもあるのだ。禅は狂気もしくは愚昧の沙汰であって、何とも手の施し様がない、と断定する人もあろう。

実際、次のような主張に対して諸君は何というだろうか。

「李公が酒を飲んだら張公が酔うた。」
「三世諸仏の師は誰か。料理番の熊公だ。」
「昨夜木馬が嘶き石人が舞を舞うた。」
「見よ、海中から紅塵が立ち騰っている。大地には白浪滔滔として耳を聾するばかりだ。」

時として禅は次のような問を発する。

「ひどく雨が降っているが、どうしてこれを止めるか。」
「両手を拍てば声が出るが、両手ならぬ隻手の声を聞くのだ。」
「隻手の声が聞えたら、この自分にも聞かせて見よ。」
「見渡したところ山は高く聳え海は低きに充ちているのに、経には是法平等で高下あることなし、とある。これはどうだ。」

禅者は日常の分別を失ったのだろうか。それとも只管に神秘化に没頭しているのだろうか。これらの言葉には、我々を混乱させる以外に、内的な意義、啓発するところある意義はさらにないものだろうか。これらの暇潰し

61

とも非合理とも見える言葉を通じて禅が敢て我々に理解せしめようとしているのは何だろうか。その答は簡単である。禅は我々に、一箇の全然新しい見地を得来って生の神秘と自然の秘密とを洞見せよ、と迫るのである。これは禅が、普通の論理的な思惟の方法では人間最深の精神的要求に最後の満足を与え得るものではない、ということをはっきりと見極めたからである。

我々は普通「AはAである」という命題を絶対と考え、「Aは非Aである」、或は「AはBである」などという命題は考えられないものとしている。我々は嘗てこうした悟性の諸条件を突き破ることができなかった。それらは余りにも強く喰い込んでいた。ところがここに禅は、言葉は言葉であり、言葉だけのものだ、と宣言するのである。言葉が事実に対応しなくなるときこそ、言葉を去って事実に還るべき時である。論理が実際的価値をもつかぎり大いにこれを活用すべきであるが、もはや役に立たぬか或はその分限を踏み越えようとするときは躊躇なく「停れ！」を命じなければならぬ。意識の覚醒以来我々は存在の神秘を解き論理への渇望を医そうとして、これを「A」と「非A」との二元論、すなわち橋を橋と呼び、水を流れるものとし、塵は地上に立つものとする二元論に求めた。ところが期待は大いにはずれて我々は、精神の平和も、完全な幸福も、生と世界との徹底した理解をも遂に得ることはできなかったのである。より広大な実在の世界へ一歩を進める謂わば我々は途方に暮れたのであった。まさにこのとき、我々全存在の上に光明が訪れたのである。これが禅の出現である。何故ならば、今にして我々は結局「Aは非Aである」ことを悟り、また論理は一面的であること、いわゆる没論理性も究め来れば必ずしも没論理的ではないこと、を知ったからである。一見非合理的と見えるものも結局存在の実相に対応する独自の論理を有することを知ったからである。

第四章　禅の没論理性

「空手にして、看よ、鋤はわが手にあり」である。かくて初めて我々は完全に幸福となったのだ。何故ならば、奇しくもこの矛盾（コントラディクション）こそ、知性の黎明以来我々の始終たずねて止まなかったものだからである。「AはAである」という命題の意味は「Aは非Aである」意味が手に入って初めて分るのである。それ自身である、ということは、それ自身ではないということである——これこそ禅の論理であり、我々のあらゆる渇望を充たすに足るものである。

「花は紅ならず、柳緑ならず」。これは禅者の道い得て妙とするところである。我々は束縛せられて精神の自由を得ず、歴歴たる生の事実は見失われるより外はない。論理を最後のものと思っているかぎり、我々は実在の主である。言葉は我々に対するその支配を放棄した。然し今や我々は全面的転換の秘鑰を手に入れたのである。我々にはそうするだけの完全な権利があるのだ。鋤はいつでも鋤でなければならぬ道理はない。それだけではない。禅匠によれば、むしろ鋤は鋤ならずとするとき、名に縛りつけられるのを拒む物の実相がいよいよはっきりするのである。

この名と論理との専制の崩壊は同時に精神的解放である。何故ならば魂はもはやその本然に反して二分せられることがないからである。知性の上の自由を獲得することによって自らを剰りなく享有するのである。生死ももはや魂を苦しめない。何故ならばそのような二元性はどこにもないからである。我々は死をすら生きるのである。これまでは我々は物を矛盾・差別の相に於て見、その見方に相応した、すなわち、多少とも敵対的な態度を取ってきた。ところがこれが一回転して我々は世界が謂わば内から見られる見地に到達したのである。さればこそ「鉄樹花を開く」のであり、「雨降りしぶく中にあって少しも濡れることがない」のである。かくて魂は一箇完全なものとなり、祝福を以て充たされるのである。

63

禅は直ちに事実を扱うものであって、その論理の上、言葉の上の、先入観念に規定された、いびつな表現と関係するところはないのである。単刀直入は禅の神髄であり、従ってその潑剌として自在なところ、他の追随を許さぬところである。基督教は心情の単純について多くを教え他の宗教も同様であるが、それは必ずしも純朴であること、シモンの如く初心であることを意味するものではない。禅にあっては、それは知性的穿鑿に煩わされないこと、とかく巧妙で詭弁にみちた哲学的思惟に足をさらわれないこと、を意味する。さらにいえば、事実を事実として認め、言葉を言葉として知り余事に亘らないこと、を意味する。禅は屢々心を曇りなき明鏡に喩える。従って禅によれば、単純であるということはこの鏡をつねに明浄にし、現われるものは何であろうと無心に映るという風にして置くことである。そこから、鋤は鋤であって同時に鋤でないことを認める、ということが出てくる。鋤を鋤と認めるだけでは常識底である。それと同時に鋤は鋤ではないということが肯われない限り禅はない。常識底は平板で無気力であるが禅の見地はつねに独創的で刺戟に富む。禅の挙揚されるところ、すべてに精彩が加わり創造の作用があらわれる。

禅は、我々は余りにも言葉や論理の奴隷になっていると考える。このように足枷を嵌められている限り我々は悲惨であり数知れぬ苦しみを嘗めなければならぬ。然しもし真に知るに値するもの、すなわち我々の精神的幸福を打ち開くに足るものを見出したいと思うならば、全力を傾けて即今限りあらゆる条件から自在を得るよう努力しなければならぬ。全世界を一眸におさめ、生の秘義をその内から捉えるような新見地が得られないものか、否か、を突きとめなければならぬ。こうした考えが人を駆って「無名」の深淵に身を躍らせ、世界創造の業をいとなむそのままの精神を直接に把握せしめたのである。ここには論理もなければ哲学もない。事実を撓めて人為の尺度に合致さ

第四章　禅の没論理性

せるということもない。知性的解剖に附して人間性を殺してかかるということもない。一箇の精神が他の精神に対すること譬えば両鏡相対するごとくである。両者映発するところ微塵の介在をもゆるすものではないのだ。禅は諸君の眼の前にある鋤を把り、それを突きつけて臆面もなく言い放つのである。「自分は鋤を持っているが持っていない」。神を説くこともなく霊魂を説くこともない。無限者を語らず死後の生を談ずることもない。見栄えもせぬ一梃の鋤、身近に見受けるごく有りふれた一事物がこういう風に扱われると、人生遭遇底の全秘密をあますところなく開示するのである。そしてそれ以上に求めるところは何もないのだ。何故ならば禅は今や存在の実相に通ずる新しい途を豁開したからである。石垣の隙間に咲く一輪の花が理解されるとき、全宇宙とその内外のすべてが理解されるのである。禅にあってはこの鋤こそすべての謎を解く秘鑰なのだ。このやり方はまた何と新鮮で生気に充ちていることだろう――盤根錯節する哲学の諸問題と取り組む禅のこのやり方は。

有名な中世基督教の一教父は嘗て次のように叫んでいる。「おお今は亡きアリストテレスよ。おんみは異端者のために弁証の術を、組み立てては壊す術を、すべてを論じて何物をも完成することのない術を発見した」と。正しく空騒ぎである。すべての時代を通じて哲学者たちがいわゆる科学と知識の問題について論理の鋭さと分析の巧みを尽した挙句、互に撞着し合う有様を見るがよい。同じ教父がかかる無益の論議を永久に止めようとして次のような爆弾を此等砂上建築者の真只中へ大胆に投じたのも宜なるかなである。曰く、「不可能なるが故に信ずるのだ」「不合理なるが故に確実なのだ」（'Credo quia absurdum est.'）。或はさらに論理的に、（'Certum est quia impossibile est.'）。これは無条件に禅を確認するものではないか。

65

或る老師は自分の杖を衆僧の面前に放り出していった。

「どうだ、これが見えるか。見えるなら一体何だ。杖だというのか。それならお前たちは只の凡くらだ。禅など頭から分っていない。だが杖などというものは見えない、というなら、自分は現にこうして杖を持っているではないか。どうしてこの厳たる事実を否定するのだ。」

第三の眼を打ち開いて存在の秘義を洞見しない限り、古賢と相談ずることはできぬ。それではこの杖を見て杖を見ない第三眼とは何であろうか。この没論理的な物の見方を何処に向って体得せよというのであろうか。

禅はいう、

「仏陀は四十九年間説法したのであるが、その長広舌は嘗て動いたことはないのだ。」

舌を動かさずして語ることができるだろうか。こういう背理がどうして出てくるのか。玄沙（げんしゃ）（西暦八三七—九〇八）の説明がその後を承けて現われる。

「諸方の知識と呼ばれる人々はいずれも接物利生を主張しているが、次の三種の病人に遭遇した場合何とするだろうか。盲を患う者は機に応じて杖や槌（つち）を活用したところでこれを見ることができぬ。唖を患う者は物をいわせようと思っても云わせることができぬ。聾を患う者は説法がいかに甚深微妙であっても聞くことができぬ。然しそれぞれに悩む此等の人々が接化から洩れるようなことがあるならば、仏教もついに霊験なしということになりはしないか。」

曰く、

この説明は一向説明しているようにも思われぬ。この点について仏眼の註釈はさらに啓発するところがあろう。

第四章　禅の没論理性

「お前たちはみんな二つの耳を持っているが、それで何を説いたというのだ。実際は何一つとして説きもせず聞きもせず見もしなかったのだ。またそれぞれ一つの舌を持っているが、それで何を説いたというのだ。実際は何一つとして説きもせず聞きもせず見もしなかったのだ。それではこうした色・声・香・味はどこからやってくるのか。」（いい換えるならば、この世界はどこからくるのか。）

なおもって不可解なら、さらに巨匠雲門（―西暦九四九）について見ることにしよう。

一僧が雲門を訪ねて上掲の玄沙の言葉について教示を乞うた。雲門は先ず、型のごとく挨拶せよ、と命じた。僧が拝伏して起ち上ったところを雲門は杖で突いた。僧は思わず数歩退いた。門曰く、

「お前は盲ではないな。」

今度は近く寄れと命じた。その通りにすると、門曰く、

「聾でもないな。」

最後に、今のが皆分ったかどうか、とたずねた。僧が、

「さっぱり分りません。」

というと、雲門は、

「というところを見れば啞でもないじゃないか。」

と結んだ。

こうした註釈やゼスチュアを以てしてもなお五里霧中の態であるならば、振り出しへ戻って例の偈を繰返すより外はない。

空手に鋤頭を把り、歩行して水牛に騎る。

さらに二言三言補って置こう。禅が何故に論理を攻撃するにかく急であるか、またこの書が何故に没論理性を真先に取り上げたのかといえば、それは大抵の人が、論理即ち生であり論理なくして生の意味はない、と思い込む程に論理がひろく生活の中へ滲み亘っているからである。人生の地図は論理によってはっきりと隅々までも描かれて居り、我々の仕事はといえば只それに従うことであり、窮極の意味をもつ思惟の法則を侵すなどとは思いもよらぬ。このような人生観を大抵の人が懐くようになったのである。しかも事実に於ては彼等はそのいわゆる侵すべからざるものを絶えず侵しつづけているのであるが、謂わば彼等は2に2を加えて3にして見たり5にして見たりしているのである。只彼等はこの事実を悟らずして自分らの生活は論理的に或は数学的に法則にかなっていると想像しているのだ。禅はこの顛倒の砦を襲って、我々は心理的に或は生物的に生きているのであって論理的に生きているのではないことを知らしめようとするのである。

論理には努力と労苦の跡が読まれる。論理は自意識的である。倫理も同様である。倫理は論理を人生の諸事実に適用したものである。倫理的な人は立派な奉仕の行を行ずる。然し彼等は始終意識してそれを行ずるのである。さらに何か将来の酬いを考えないとも限らぬ。だからその行為は客観的に或は社会的に善なるものであっても、その心はむしろ染汚して居り、なかなか清浄とはいわれないのである。毫末も努力や痛苦の感をのこすものであってはならぬ。禅によれば、生は空飛ぶ鳥のごとく水を行く魚のごとく生くべきである。作為の萌しが現われるとき、人はもはや運命づけられたのであり、もはや自由な存在ではないのだ。諸君は生くべきように生きていない。環境の圧制下に置かれて

第四章　禅の没論理性

いる。何か或る強制を感じている。諸君の独立性は失われている。ここに禅は諸君の生気を、諸君の本然の自由を、とり分け諸君の存在としての全一性を昧まさざらんとするものである。法則に縛られず自分自身の法則を作り出して行く——これこそ禅が我々に要望する生き方である。その没論理的もしくは超論理的な説述の存する所以である。

五祖法演（―西暦一一〇四）はその説教中に述べている。

「釈迦一代の経は五千四十八巻に及ぶという。その中には空を説くものもあり、有を説くものもあれば、漸を説くものもある。これは一箇の肯定ではないか。

ところが永嘉によれば「亦無人亦無仏、大千沙界海中漚、一切聖賢如電払」である。これは一箇の否定ではないか。

弟子たちよ。有り、といえばかの永嘉に反し、無しといえば釈迦に背く。もし彼をして我々と共にあらしめるならば、どうしてこのディレンマを脱することだろう。だが、我々の所在さえはっきり分っているならば、そのまま朝には釈迦に対面し夕には弥勒に挨拶する境涯である。もし分らぬというならばその秘要を教えてやろう。有というも必ずしも肯定ではない。無というも必ずしも否定ではない。さあ、東を望んで西山を見、南に面して北斗を指せ。」

原　註

（1）永嘉『証道歌』参照。

第五章　大肯定の禅

首山省念（西暦九二六─九九三）が或る時弟子たちに竹篦を拈じて言った、

「これを竹篦だと言えば肯定に堕する。竹篦でないといえば事実に反する。さあこれを何と言うか。」

すると一人の弟子が進み出てその竹篦を師から奪うが早いか二つにへし折って叫んだ、

「是は何か。」

抽象を事とし、高遠な問題を扱いつけている人々にとっては、これは全く取るに足らぬ事件と思われるかも知れぬ。一体彼等深遠博識の哲学者がこの何でもない竹の一片とどういう関係があるのか。それが竹篦と呼ばれようと、折られようと投げ出されようと、深い瞑想にふける学者に何の係わりがあろうか。ところが禅者にとっては首山の言葉は甚だ意味深長なのである。彼がこの問を持ち出した心境が真に会得されたら、既に禅の領分へ一歩を踏み入れたものということができる。首山のこの例に倣って竹篦を拈提し弟子たちに会心の答を要求した禅匠は数多いのである。

72

第五章　大肯定の禅

抽象的にいうならば、そしてその方が大抵の読者には向いていると思うが、問題は肯定と否定との論理的対立よりももう一つ高次の肯定に達するということにあるのだ。通常我々は敢て対立を超えようとはしないのであるが、それは正しく、できないものだ、と思いこんでいるからである。論理の威圧のために我々はその名が出ると尻ごみし、身慄いするようになっている。知性が目醒めて以来、論理的二元論の厳格極まる規律の下に働かされるようになった心は、その想像上の首枷（くびかせ）をどうしても取除こうとはしないのである。我々には自ら引被ったこの知性的制約を離脱するなどということは到底思いもよらなかったのだ。実際この「然り」（イエス）と「否」（ノー）との対立を突破しない限り真に自在な生を生きることは望むべくもないのである。また魂は絶えずこれを呼び求めて来たのであるが、否定と肯定とが対立のまま撞著することのない一箇高次の肯定に達することが結局そんなに難しいものではないということは、迂闊（うかつ）にも気がつかなかったのである。この高次の肯定がかの禅匠の拈ずる竹篦によって自分のものとなった、ということは正しく禅によるものである。

ここに突きつけられた竹篦がこの差別の世界に存在する数限りもない事物のどの一つであってもよいことは改めて断るまでもなかろう。この竹篦の中には、あらゆる可能な存在と我々のあらゆる可能な経験とが集中されているのである。これを——この見栄えもせぬ竹の一片を——知るとき、我々は真に徹底した仕方でそのすべてを知るのである。それがわが手に取るとき、そのままに全宇宙を手に取るのである。それについて語ることは爾余の一切にあてはまって行くのである。一点が手に入れば他の諸点も悉くこれに従うのである。華厳哲学の教えるように、「一」は「一切」を摂め「一切」は「一」に入る。「一」は「一切」であり、「一切」は「一」である。「一」は「一切」に徧（あまね）く、「一切」は「一」に含まれる。これは如何なる対象、如何なる存在についても同様である。だが此処

73

には汎神論もなければ同一性の哲学もないことに心しなければならぬ。何故ならば諸君の面前にかの竹箆の抂出されるとき、それは正しく竹箆であって、そこには全宇宙が摂入されているのでもなく、「一切」もなければ「一」もない。「竹箆だ」とか「竹箆がある」というてさえ、箭既に新羅を過ぐである。もはや禅はない。況んや華厳哲学をや、である。

禅の没論理性については前章に述べた。読者諸君は今や禅が、形式的であると否とに拘わらず、論理なるものに対立する理由を知るであろう。好んで没論理的に出るのが禅の目的ではない。論理との合致が窮極のものではないことを、また単なる知性的技巧を以てしては達することのできぬ或は超越的な道い方の厳存することを知らせるのが目的なのだ。「然り」イェスと「否」ノーとの知性的軌道は物事が註文通りに動いてくれる間はまことに好都合であるが、一旦人生窮極の問題が頭を抬げてくると、もはや知性では満足な解答ができない。「然り」と主張することによって我々自身を限定するのである。排除と限定とは結局同一物であって魂を殺すものである。「否」というときは否定するのであり、換言すれば排除するのである。排除や限定には自由もなければ統一もない。禅はこのことをよく知っている。さればこそ我々の内なる生の求めに応じて如何なる対立もない絶対境へ我々を導くのである。

とはいえ、我々は肯定に生きるものであって否定に生きるものではないことを記憶しなければならぬ。只この肯定は、否定を伴い、それによって条件づけられるものであってはならぬ。そのような肯定に従うとき、生はその創造的な独自性を失い、相対的であって、如何なる意味に於ても絶対的ではない。魂なき肉と骨とを動かして行くだけの機械的過程となり終るのである。自由であるためには、

第五章　大肯定の禅

生は一箇絶対の肯定とならなければならぬ。その自由なはたらきを妨げる、有りとあらゆる条件・制限・対立を超え出るところがなければならぬ。首山が竹箆を拈示したとき、その念とするところは弟子たちにこうした絶対の肯定を体得させるにあったのだ。人間存在の内奥より噴湧する答なら何であろうと十分には常に一箇絶対の肯定であるからだ。従って禅は単に知性の監禁からの脱出に尽きるものではない。単にそれだけでは、屢々只の放逸に終るものである。禅匠は、弟子たちから、その生れ持つ一切の足場、相対的な意味の足場とは異った足場、を与えるものではなく、手当り次第何でも役立り、正しく足場ならぬ足場を与えようと努めるのである。単にそれだけでは、言葉や論理と一緒にされるだろう。禅は虚無主義ではない。何故ならばこの竹箆は、或は何であっても構わぬが、言葉や論理と一緒に片附けてしまうことができぬものだからである。これは禅を学ぶ上に看過してはならぬところである。

これを二、三の実例について見ることにしよう。徳山（西暦七八〇―八六五）は上堂の際、いつも長い棒を揮（ふる）って、「道い得るも三十棒、道い得ざるも三十棒」と叫んだ。彼が弟子たちに語ったのは只これだけであった。宗教や道徳に関する長広舌もなく、抽象的な論議もなく、精細を誇る形而上学もない。あるものは、凡そ正反対の傍若無人な接得振りのみである。宗教を弱気や信心振りに結びつける人々には、禅匠は恐しく粗暴な人間とも思われるであろう。だが、事実が事実として直接に扱われる場合、ごつごつしているのが普通である。我々は事実と四つに組まねばならぬ。見ぬ振りをしても避けようとしても何の役にも立つものではない。雨と降る三十棒の下にこそ心眼を開くべきである。一箇絶対の肯定は生自らの噴火口より噴出するものでなければならぬ。

五祖山の法演（―西暦一一〇四）が或る時間うた、

「路で達道の人に逢うた場合、語を以て対することなく黙を以ても対しないとするなら何を以て対するか。」

この意は、自分のいう絶対の肯定をさとらしめるにある。「然り」と「否」との対立を脱するのみではなく、対立が対立のままで調和を現ずる如き積極的な道を発見する。これがこの問の狙いである。

一禅匠は嘗て炭火を指して弟子に言った、

「自分はこれを火と呼ぼう。お前はそう呼んではならぬ。さあ何と呼ぶか。」

趣意は全く同様である。師は弟子の心を論理の束縛から救おうとしているのである。論理の束縛こそは久しく人類の苦厄となって来たものである。

これを何か判じ物のように受取ってはならぬ。戯れの気分は微塵もないのだ。答えられなければ当然その結果を受けなければならぬ。諸君の自ら課する思惟の法則によって永遠に繋がれようとするか、或は無終の生を自ら背って完全な自由を得ようとするのであるか。諸君は躊躇を許されない。事実を捉えるか、然らずんば逃がすかである。それ以外の途はないのだ。禅の訓練は一般にディレンマに追いこむという方法をとる。そこから何とかして脱出しなければならぬ。それは、どうしても論理では駄目で、或る高次元の心作用によるの外はないのだ。

薬山（西暦七四五―八二八）は石頭（西暦七〇〇―七九〇）について初めて禅を学んだ。その時彼は問うた、

「三乗十二分教については略ぼ承知していますが、聞くところによれば南方には直指人心、見性成仏を説く教えがある由、これは未だ明にして居りませぬ。何卒御示教を乞う。」

石頭曰く、「こうだというても駄目、こうでないというても駄目だ。両方とも全然駄目ならどういうか。」

薬山は問の意味が分らぬので只茫然としていた。師は江西の馬大師ならこの男の心眼を開かせることができるか

第五章　大肯定の禅

も知れぬと思い、彼の許を訪ねるように奨めた。そこで薬山は新しい師匠の許に到り恭しく礼して同じ問を呈した。

馬祖が言うには、

「自分は眉を揚げたり目を瞬いたりすることもあるが、全然そうしないこともある。或る時の揚眉瞬目は真実に当っているし、或る時の揚眉瞬目は全然当っていない。どうだ、分るか。」

薬山は言下に契悟し師を礼拝した。

馬祖曰く、「何の道理が分ったというのか。」

曰く、「自分が石頭和尚のところにいた時は蚊が鉄牛に喰いついているようなものでした。」

唐朝の高官李翺（りこう）が南泉（西暦七四八―八三五）にたずねた、

「昔或る人が瓶の中に鵞鳥を飼っていた。それが段段大きくなって瓶から出せなくなってしまった。彼は瓶を壊したくなかったし、鵞鳥も傷けたくなかった。貴僧ならどうして鵞鳥を出されるか。」

師はだしぬけに呼んだ、

「大夫！」

李翺は思わず返事をした、

「そら出た。」

これが南泉の鵞鳥を救い出したやり方である。李翺は果してその大肯定を得たか、どうか。

香厳は言う。

「今誰かが千尺懸崖上の樹に上り、口に枝を啣えたまま宙ぶらりんになっている。足も樹にかかっていないし、手も枝を把えていない。そこへ不意に人が現われて祖師西来意（仏教の根本義）を問うたとする。さあ、もし答えたら立ちどころに喪身失命しなければならぬ。答えなければ問者を無視したことになる。どうしてこの窮境を脱するか。」

これは寓話の形になっているが、主旨は上述の諸例と同様である。肯定にせよ否定にせよ、一旦口を開いたら命はない。だが無為にじっとしていても同じことになる。そこらの石は沈黙している。窓外の花も沈黙している。そのいずれにも禅は分らぬ。沈黙と雄弁とが期せずして同じものとなり、否定と肯定とが統一されて絶対の一句となって打ち出される。そういう出方がどうしてもなければならぬのだ。ここにいたって初めて禅が分るのである。

では絶対肯定の一句とは何であるか。百丈（西暦七二〇—八一四）が大潙山の住持を決めようとして高弟二人を呼び、衆僧の前で各之一語を著けさせることにした。やがて百丈は浄瓶を取って地上に置いた。（ちなみに浄瓶というのは僧が通常身辺に所持する水瓶のことである。）曰く、

「これを浄瓶と呼んではならぬ。さあ何と呼ぶか。」

第一の高弟は答えた、

「木棪とも呼べますまい。」

師は肯わずかえりみて今一人の弟子を促した。彼は進み出て軽く浄瓶を倒したまま、何も言わずにさっさと出て行ってしまった。

彼は選ばれて一山の主となり、後、「千五百を擁する僧団の主」となった。この浄瓶趯倒が絶対の肯定であった

第五章　大肯定の禅

のだろうか。この動作を何度繰返したところで禅を理解したとはいえない。何事によらず禅は反覆や模倣を忌む。それは殺すからである。同じ理由からである。禅は決して説明に亘らない。唯肯定するだけである。生は事実である。如何なる説明も、必要でもなければ相応わしくもない。説明は弁護である。生きることに何の弁護が要ろうか。生きる、それで十分ではないか。肯定しようではないか。浄裸裸、赤灑灑のところにこそ禅があるのだ。

南泉（西暦七四八─八三五）のいた寺で、東西両堂の僧たちが一匹の猫の所有を争っていた。師はそれをつまみ上げ、争う僧たちの面前へ突きつけていった。

「お前たちが一言道い得たらこの猫を助けてやろうし、道い得なかったら斬って捨てるまでだ。」

誰も肯定の一語を下すことができなかったので、南泉はこの物議の種を一刀両断してしまった。後刻趙州が外出から帰ってきたので南泉は事の次第を告げ、お前ならどうして猫を助けるか、と問うた。趙州は即座に草履を脱して頭上に載せ、さっさと部屋を出てしまった。南泉はこれを見て、

「あの時うまくお前が居合せたら、猫は殺さずとも済んだであろうに。」

と歎息したという。

これは一体何を意味するのか。罪もない生物が何故犠牲に供せられたのか。生物を殺害した南泉は、宗教的どころか、血も涙もないということになるのか。趙州が草履を頭上に載せたことが喧嘩騒ぎとどういう関係があるのか。あのような突拍子もないことをやってのける趙州は実は馬鹿だったのか。さらに、「絶対否定」と「絶対肯定」の

二者は実際別別のものだろうか。この二人の登場人物、南泉と趙州には恐しく真剣な何物かがあるのである。これが分らない限り、禅は全く他愛もない道化芝居である。然し猫はたしかに徒らに殺されたのではない。蠢動含霊（しゅんどう）悉く成仏するものならば、この猫の成仏するこそ必定である。

この同じ趙州が一僧からたずねられたことがある。

「万法一に帰するものならば、その一は何処に帰するのか。」

これに対して彼は次のように答えている。

「自分が青州にいた時、一領の布衫（ふさん）を作ったが、なかなか重くて七斤ばかりあった。」

これは禅者の口から出た言葉の中で最ももてはやされているものの一つである。ここで誰しも問いたくなるだろう。

「これがいうところの絶対肯定なのか。布衫と万法帰一と一体どういう関係があるのか。」

ところで自分からも問いたいことがある。諸君は万物は神のうちに存在すると信じているが、その神のありかはどこなのか。それは趙州七斤の布衫にあるのか。神はそこにいる、と口に出していうとき、もう神はそんなところにいる筈がない。然し諸君は神はどこにもいないとはいうことができぬ。外ならぬ諸君の定義によって神は遍在者であるからだ。知性に縛られている間は、あるが儘の神に逢うことはできぬ。我々は神を随所に求めようとするが、知性は神の所在を定めたがるが限定できぬのが神の本性なのだ。ではどうここに知性の当面しなければならぬ大きいディレンマがある。それは知性にとって不可避のものである。趙州の布衫は我々のものではない。彼の解決法に盲従するわけには行かぬ。人々各自して活路を開けばよいのか。神はいつもその手をすり抜けて片影をも止めない。

第五章　大肯定の禅

の道を打ち開かねばならぬ。もし誰かが同じ問を持って諸君のところへやって来たら、諸君は何と答えるか。また我々は人生到るところでこの問題に出会しているのではないか。しかもそれは迅速にして最も実際的な解決を迫っているのではないか。

俱胝(ぐてい)和尚は、何か問われるところがあれば決まって只一指を堅てるばかりであった。ところがその常随の童子が彼の真似をして、人から師の教えについてたずねられるといつもその指を堅て見せた。これを耳にした和尚はある日童子を呼び入れ、刃物を以てその指を截り落してしまった。童子が恐愕と痛みに堪えかねて泣きわめきながら立ち去ろうとすると師匠に鋭く呼びとめられた。頭をめぐらすと、師匠は間髪を容れず一指を堅て見せた。童子は忽然としてその意味をさとったという。大肯定は精神にあって生きるものである。模倣は隷従である。文字に囚われてはならぬ。ではその精神とは何処にあるのか。精神をこそ摑むべきであり、それは諸君の日常経験に求めるがよかろう。そこには歴歴とした証拠が我々の必要を充してなお有り余っているのだ。

次のような物語が或る経典に出ている。

「町の東側に仏陀と日を同じうして生れた老女がいた。また両人とも生涯同じ地域に住んでいた。この老女は仏陀に会うことを好まず、仏陀が近辺へ来ることがあるとあちこち駈け廻って避けるのであった。ところが一日ばったりと出会ってどうしても避ける方法がなかったので、彼女は自分の顔を両手で掩い隠した。ところが、何と、仏陀はその十本の指の一つ一つの間からはっきりと現われたのである。試みに問うとしよう。「この老女は誰だろうか。」

絶対の肯定こそ仏陀である。そこから逃げ出すことはできない。何故ならばそれはどちらを向いても我々と面面

相対しているからだ。然しそうはいうものの倶胝の童子のように指の一本も失わない限り、我々はなかなかそれを認めようとはせぬのである。我々は「米俵の傍に坐して餓死する人間」、むしろ「川の真中でずぶ濡れになったまま渇き死ぬ人間」であるといえば、奇矯に響くかも知れぬが真実たるを失わぬ。一禅者はさらに一歩を進めてこう言っている。「我々は米そのもの、水そのものなのだ」。もしそうなら、餓えているも渇いているもないものである。本来何の欠けるところもないのだから。

曹山（西暦八四〇―九〇一）の許へ一僧が訪ね来って窮乏を訴え慈悲を乞うた。曹山は「貴僧！」と呼んだ。僧はすぐさま返事をした。曹山の曰く、

「貴僧はこれでなみなみ三杯も美禄を平らげたではないか。そのくせまだ唇をうるおしたことがないようなことを言う。」

どうやら我々もみなこのみじめにも富裕な僧の仲間であるらしい。申し分なく充たされている時には却ってその事実に気づかぬものである。

最後に禅録に出てくる数え切れぬ程の表現の中から、禅の絶対肯定を打ち出したものを今ひとつ掲げて置こう。

清平（西暦八四五―九一九）が翠微にたずねた、

「仏教の根本義（西来的的意）は何ですか。」

微曰く、「暫く待て。誰もいないときに教えてやろう。」

ややあって清平は再び乞うた、

「今ちょうど誰も居りません。どうかお示し下さい。」

第五章　大肯定の禅

翠微は禅牀を下りて彼を竹林に連れて行ったが一語も発しない。そこで今一度返答を求めると、翠微は竹を指して言った。
「この竹は何と丈が高いじゃないか。またあの竹は何と丈が低いじゃないか。」

原　註
（1）割竹を以て作り頭の部分を籐で巻く。長さ約一フィート半。シッペイと発音する。
（2）禅は他の仏教諸派に対してシナの南部諸地方から発生している。
（3）潙山（西暦七七一―八五三）の法弟。
（4）九世紀在世、天龍の弟子。
（5）『景徳伝燈録』第十五巻参照。

83

第六章　禅の日常性

一

上来知性的観点から禅を論じてきたのは、この観点から禅を把握することの不可能な所以を理解するためであった。実際禅をそのように哲学的に扱うということは当を得たものではない。禅は媒介を嫌う。知性的媒介とて同様である。禅は徹頭徹尾説明とは没交渉な訓練であり経験である。説明から得られるものは実物についての誤解と偏見ばかりである。説明は時間と労力とを費してしかも要領を得ない。禅が諸君に砂糖の甘さを知らせようと思うならば、直にその一塊を口中に含ませて一言の贅弁（ぜいべん）をも弄しないであろう。真逆といいたいところだが、指がなければ月を指すわけには行かぬが、指を月と間違えては大変である。禅者のよくいうように、我々は知らず識らず幾度となくこの過ちを冒しているのである。気がつかないばかりに好い気になっていられるのだ。禅についてものを書くとしても月を指すこと以上に出ることはできぬ。今述べたような事情であって見れば、著者に許される唯一の仕事はこの問題をこそ十分に究明すべきである。著者は如何にもしてこの月を指すということだからである。禅を形而上学的に取扱って行くとすれば、その分りにくいのに失望される向きもあるかも知れぬ。大抵の人々は通例、思弁や観

第六章　禅の日常性

想には深く馴染んでいないからである。自分は或る全く異った観点、恐らくは一層禅に相応わしい観点から入って行くことにしたい。

趙州が南泉に、「道とは何か」とたずねた。

南泉曰く、「平常心是道」。

これを言い換えるならば、ゆったりと落ちついた物に動じない諸君自身の存在、これこそ道であり禅の真理であろう。自分が禅はすぐれて実際的であるという意味も此処にあるのだ。禅は直に生に訴える。魂、神、その他何であろうと、日常の生の流れを停めるものには何等言及するところがないのだ。禅の趣意は生をその流れのままに認得するにある。禅には別に突飛なものも神秘なものもない。手を挙げる、机の向側の本を取る、窓外のボール投げをしている少年たちの声を聞く、近くの木立の向うを流れて行く雲を眺める――こうしたすべてに禅を行じ禅を生きているのである。言葉の上の議論や説明は無用である。その理由を知らぬままに――また明かにする必要もないのだが――太陽が昇れば地上は挙げて歓喜に躍り、誰の心も祝福を以て充たされる。ともかくも禅というものが考えられるとすれば、それは即今この場に於て把握すべきものである。

さればこそ菩提達摩は、「朕に対する者は誰ぞ」と問われて、「不識」と答えたのである。これは説明に窮したからでもなく、言葉の上の論議を避けたかったからでもない。自分はこうしているがままの自分である。この厳とした事実以外に自分が何であるかをも誰であるかをも知るところがないからである。理由は至極簡単であった。

南獄（西暦六七七―七四四）が六祖に参じた時、たずねられた、

「今こうしてやって来るのは何者だ。」

87

彼は答える術を知らなかった。爾来八年間この問題に没頭した挙句、ついに省覚して叫んだ、「説似一物即不中！」(こうだ、というときもう的を逸している。）

これは「不識」というのと同じである。

石頭は嘗てその弟子薬山（西暦七四五―八二八）にたずねた、

「お前はそこで何をしているのか。」

「何もしていません。」

「では只ぼんやりと坐っているのだな。」

「ぼんやり坐っている、といえばやっぱり何かをしていることではありませんか。」

「どこまでも何もしていないというのだな。ではその何もしない者は何だ。」

「千聖と雖も知るところはないでしょう。」

薬山の答は達摩の答と同じであった。

これは神秘化の意味に取られるかも知れないが、この答には何の不可知論も神秘主義もない。瞭瞭たる事実が瞭瞭たる言葉で述べられているだけである。もしそう思われないとするならば、それは読者諸君が、達摩や薬山をしてこの言葉を吐かしめた境地に達していないからである。

梁の武帝（在位五〇二―五四九）が傅大士（西暦四九七―五六九）に経典の講説を乞うた。傅大士は厳かに座に就いたが黙然として一語も発することなく、やがて座を起ってしまった。武帝曰く、「朕はおんみに講経を乞うたのである。何故一言も講説されないのか」。

第六章　禅の日常性

すると客臣の誌公が、「陛下、大士の講経はもう済んだのです」と説明を加えた。この無言の仏教哲学者の試みたのは、一体如何なる講説であったのか。後代一禅匠はこれを評して「直に得たり火星迸散するを」といい、その雄弁ぶりを歎じている。これが後世「維摩の一黙雷の如し」といわれるにいたったものである。『維摩経』の主人公たる維摩も不二法門を問われて同様の答を与えている。これが果して耳を聾するような力をもつものだろうか。もしそうなら自分も口を噤むとしようか、そうすれば全宇宙はその喧喧囂囂の騒ぎ諸共、一瞬にしてこの絶対の沈黙に吸い込まれてしまうだろう――とうっかり釣りこまれそうなところだが、猿真似では蛙を木の葉に変えることもできぬ。創造的な独自性のないところには禅はない。だからいわねばならぬ。「遅い、遅い、もう箭は弦を離れた」。

一僧が六祖慧能に問うた、
「黄梅（五祖弘忍）の衣鉢を継ぐ者は誰か。」
曰く、「仏法を会得した者だ。」
曰く、「あなたはどうなのか。」
曰く、「自分は継いでいない。」
僧はさらに問わざるを得なかった、「どうして継いでいないのか。」
「自分は仏法を会得していないからだ。」
これが慧能の答であった。

禅の真理とは何と難解でしかも何と容易であることか。難解というのは、理解しても理解にならないからである。

容易というのは、理解しないことがそのまま理解であるからだ。一禅匠は、釈迦も弥勒もこれを理解せず田夫野人が却ってこれを理解するのだ、とまでいい切っている。

ここに於て禅が、抽象・表現・文飾を嫌忌する理由が解ってくる。禅は、神・仏・魂・無限者・一者等の言葉に何等実質的な価値を認めない。此等は畢竟言葉や観念に過ぎず、従って禅の真実の理解に役立つものではないのだ。反対に屢ミ事実を味まし逆の作用を及ぼすものである。だから我々は不断に警戒を怠るわけには行かないのだ。一禅匠は語っている。「仏と一言いうてもその口をよく漱いでおけ」。或は、「自分の聞きたくない言葉がひとつある。それは仏だ」。或は、「仏のいるところはさっさと通り過ぎよ。仏のいないところにも止まっていてはならぬ」。禅者は何故そのように仏を目の敵にするのか。仏は彼等の教主ではないか。仏教最高の体現者ではないか。禅者に嫌われるような憎むべき或は汚らわしい存在である筈がない。彼等の好まないのは仏自身ではなく、その言葉について廻る習気なのだ。

「仏とは何か」という問に対して、禅匠の与える答はまことに多種多様である。それはまた何故だろうか。少くともその理由の一つと考えられるのは、外部からあてがわれた言葉・観念・願望等等がもたらす葛藤から我々を解放したいという彼等の念願である。若干の例を挙げるならば、

「土でこねて金を塗ったものだ。」
「優れた芸術家でも描くことはできぬ。」
「仏殿に安置してあるあれだ。」
「仏は仏ではない。」

第六章　禅の日常性

「お前は慧超だ。」
「乾屎橛(かんしけつ)(乾いた糞掻きべら)だ。」
「東山が水上を動いて行くではないか。」
「たわごとを言うな。」
「此処は四面みな山だ。」
「杖林山下の竹筋鞭。」
「麻三斤。」
「口は禍の門だ。」
「白浪が平地に起って天に漲(みなぎ)らんばかりだ。」
「三脚の驢馬が走って行くぞ。」
「脛を破って葦が生えてきた。」
「胸をはだけて赤はだしで行くのは誰だ。」

此等は手許にある二、三の禅録から目につくままに引いたものである。禅文献の全般に亙って系統的に悉しく調べて見たら、仏とは何か、というような簡単な問題についても一風変った答を夥(おびただ)しく集めることができるだろう。普通の考え方ではどうしても納得することができない。また他の或るものは全然見当がはずれている。こういう言葉を吐く禅匠たちは真面目であり、真に弟子たちの啓発を念としているということができるだろうか。然しここに肝腎とも要ともいうべきは、こうした奇矯

の言葉を吐く禅匠たちの境地に深く参到するという一事である。これさえできれば、此等のどの答も全く新しい光を浴びて現われ、驚くばかりに透明となるのである。

実際的で直ちに要点を捉えようとする禅は決して説明のために時間や言葉を浪費したりしない。その答は簡にして迫るものがある。禅には冗長なものがない。禅匠の言葉は巧まずして自然に発し、何の渋滞をも知らぬのである。銅羅を打てば振動が起る。気をつけていなければそれを捉えることはできぬ。一瞬にして永遠に的を失するのであある。禅はよく閃電光に喩えられるが如何にもその通りである。然しその速さが禅の本質だというのではない。その自然に発するところ、何の巧みもなく自由に発するところ、生命そのものの露現であるところ、独自の面目の動き出るところ——こういう点が如何にも禅に彷彿するのである。だから真に禅の核心を得ようと思うならば、外的な記号に鼻面を把られぬよう常に用心を怠ってはならぬ。「仏とは何か」の問に対する上掲の答を拠りどころとして禅を文字通りに、或は論理的に理解しようとすることの、如何に困難であり且つ途を誤っていることか。無論其等は答として与えられている限り仏の所在を求める指針であるに違いないが、月を指す指はどこまでも指であって、どうしても月自体に変ずるものではないことを忘れてはならぬのだ。知性がこっそりと忍び込んで指標を月そのものと決めてかかるところには常に危険がひそんでいる。

なお、上掲のような言葉の或るものを学問的、論理的な意味に解して、そこに何か汎神論的なものを見ようとする哲学者がある。例えば禅匠が「麻三斤」といい「乾屎橛」というとき汎神論的な立場にあることは明白だ、と主張するのである。換言すれば、禅匠たちは仏が万物の上に、すなわち麻にも木片にも水の流れにも聳え立つ山にも、或は美術作品にも、ひとしく顕現しているのだと考えている、ということになる。大乗仏教、殊に禅は、いくらか

第六章　禅の日常性

汎神論の精神を暗示しているように見えるかも知れないが、実はこの見方ほど禅から遠いものはないのだ。禅匠たちは初からこの危険を見抜いていた。だからこそ此等の一見全く筋の通らぬいい方を敢てしたのである。彼等の意図は、弟子や学人の心を、如何なる固定観念・先入観念或はいわゆる論理的解釈の圧迫からも離脱させるにあったのだ。洞山が、「如何なるか是れ仏」――序ながらこれは「神とは何か」と問うのと同じである――の問に対して「麻三斤」と答えた時、偶〻手にしていたらしいその麻が仏の顕現であるとか、智慧の眼を開けば仏は事事物物の上に親しく相見できるなどとは毛頭考えていなかった。この明明白白の日用底の言葉に形而上学的な意味は寸毫も含めなかったのである。彼の答は、「麻三斤」、只それだけである。この言葉は、泉が噴き溢れてくるように、陽を受けて蕾が花と開くように、彼の意識の内奥からおのずと迸り出たのだ。彼には何の準備観念も哲学もなかったのである。だから、「麻三斤」の意味をとらえようと思うならば、先ず洞山の意識の内奥に参ずべきであって、その口先について廻っていては駄目なのだ。別の時には全然別の答をするかも知れないし、その答は前の答と直接に撞著するものであるかも知れない。論理学者なら当然処置に窮するところである。彼等は言うかも知れぬ。この男は全く気が狂っている、と。然し禅者なら例えば次のように応ずるであろう。「雨群峯を洗って翠色を添う」と。彼等は自分の答が洞山の麻三斤とさながらに一致することをよく知っているのだ。

次の例は、恐らくいよいよ禅が汎神論の一形式ではないことをよく示すであろう。尤もこれは汎神論を、目に見える世界を直ちに神・心等の最高実在の顕現と考え、神はこの顕現の相を離れては存在し得ないとする哲学、と解した上のことであるが。実際禅はこんなところに止まっているものではないのだ。禅には哲学的論議で時間を潰している余裕はないのだ。とはいえ哲学も生命活動の一表現である以上、禅もむやみにこれを忌避するものではない。哲

学者が啓発を求めて訪れるならば禅匠はその独自の立場に於て快くこれを迎えるであろう。初期の禅匠たちは、単刀直入の接得を加えた臨済（一西暦八六七）や徳山（西暦七八〇—八六五）などに較べると、いわゆる哲学者に対しても態度が緩やかであり包容的であった。次に掲げるのは大珠慧海の、禅の原理を説いた、語録中の言葉である。この書は禅が漸く殷盛に赴いてその特色と精彩とをあらわし始めた八世紀乃至九世紀の頃編纂されたものである。

僧問、言語是心否。

師曰、言語是縁、不是心。

曰、離縁何者是心。

師曰、離言語無心。

曰、離言語既無心、若為是心。

師曰、心無形相、非離言語、非不離言語、心常湛然、応用自在。祖師云、若了心非心、始解心心法。

問、言葉は心であるか。

答、言葉は外的条件である。心ではない。

問、外的条件を離れて心を何処に求めるのか。

答、言葉を離れた心はない。

問、言葉を離れて心はないというなら、心とは何か。

答、心は形もなく相もない。言葉を離れているのでもなく言葉に著しているのでもない。心は常に湛然として、しかもそのはたらきは自在である。だから祖師も、「心が心ではないことを了得して初めて心とそのは

第六章　禅の日常性

大珠はさらに記している。

能生万法、喚作法性、亦名法身。馬鳴祖師云、所言法者、謂衆生心。若心生故、一切法生、若心無生、法無従生、亦無名字。迷人不知法身無象、応物現形、遂喚青青翠竹総是法身、鬱鬱黄華無非般若、黄華若是般若、般若即同無情、翠竹若是法身、法身即同草木。如人喫筍応総喫法身也。如此之言、寧堪歯録。

すべての存在を生み出すものを法性もしくは法身という。心が生ずるときすべての存在が生ずると。心が生じなかったら生ずるものはなく従ってその名もない。迷人は、法身が本来無象であって条件に応じて個個の形を現ずることを理解しない。そして青々たる翠竹が直ちに法身自体であり、鬱鬱たる黄華は直ちに般若そのものであると思いこんでいる。しかし黄華が般若なら般若は無情の一存在と同じくなり、翠竹が法身なら法身は一草木と同じくなる。だが、黄華はなくとも、法身は存在し般若も存在するのだ。さもなくば、筍（たけのこ）を食えば法身そのものを食うということになる。

このような見方は実際取り上げて論ずる価値がない。

二

曩（さき）に禅を没論理的なものとして或は高次の肯定として扱ったところはあるが甚だ捉えどころがない、という結論が出てくるかも知れぬ。またそれを咎めるわけにも行かぬ。従ってその寛（くつろ）いだ親しみのある近づきやすい方面をも示すべきところであ我々の日常生活とは没交渉で、惹きつけるところはあるが甚だ捉えどころがない、という結論が出てくるかも知れぬ。またそれを咎めるわけにも行かぬ。従ってその寛いだ親しみのある近づきやすい方面をも示すべきところであ

ろう。生はすべての依拠であり生を離れては何物も存在し得ない。如何なる哲学を以てしても力強い観念を以てしても、我々はあるがままの生を脱することはできぬ。星を仰ぐ人も、その足はやっぱり大地に著いているのだ。

それでは禅の親しみやすいところとはどんなところだろうかずねた、

趙州（西暦七七八―八九七）が或る時新参の僧にた

「今までにこちらへ来たことがあるか。」

「はい、あります。」

「お茶を一服やるがいい。」（喫茶去。）

やがて別の僧がやってくると趙州はまた同じ問を発した。今度の答は全く反対だった。ところが老師は全く前回と同じように告げた、

「お茶を一服やるがいい。」

後刻、院主（僧堂管理の僧）がたずねた、

「返答にはお構いなくお茶を一服といわれるのはどういう意味ですか。」

老師は叫んだ、「院主！」

直ちに応諾すると、「お茶を一服やるがいい。」

趙州は唐代の最も駿秀な禅匠の一人であって、シナ禅宗の発達は彼に負うところが多い。彼は八十になってもなお行脚していたという。ひとえに禅の修行を全うするためであった。彼は百二十歳の高齢で歿した。彼の遺した言

第六章　禅の日常性

言句は宛ら眩い珠玉のようである。「口唇皮上に光を放つ」といわれる所以である。叢林に入ったばかりの僧が彼を訪ねて禅について示教を求めた。州曰く、

「朝飯はすんだか。」

「はい、すみました。」

「では持鉢を洗うがよい。」

ここに僧は忽然と省悟するところがあった。

一日彼が庭を掃いていると一僧がやって来てたずねた、

「和尚、貴方は善知識でいらっしゃる。どうして塵が積るのであろうか。御教示を願いたい。」

「そら、またひとつ塵が飛んできた。」

「この清浄伽藍にも塵が積るのはどうしたわけでしょうか。」

また問う者があって、

「外からやってくるのだ。」

趙州の僧院には有名な石橋があって、あたりに聞えていた。偶ミ外来の一僧が問うた、

「趙州石橋の名はかねがね聞いているが、見たところ独木橋が一つあるきりで、何もそれらしいものはないじゃありませんか。」

州曰く、「独木橋は見えても石橋は見えぬらしいな。」

僧曰く、「ではその石橋はどこにありますか。」

「たった今お前が渡ったばかりじゃないか。」

これが趙州の機敏な答であった。また或る時同じ石橋を問われて次のように答えている。

「馬を渡し、人を渡し、生きとし生けるものを渡す。」

こうした問答には、身辺の自然・人事についての何でもない応待しか見られぬものだろうか。に資する精神的なものはないのだろうか。それでは禅は余りにも実際的で平凡なものになりはしないか。宗教的な魂の開眼論の高みから日常底へあまりにも呆気なく跳び降りるということになりはしないか。遮莫、それらはすべて諸君の見方によることだ。一本の線香が今この机の上でしずかに燃えている。これは取るに足らぬことだろうか。大地が震動して富士山が崩壊する。これは大事件だろうか。然り、空間的な見方にある限りその通りだ。だが、我々は本当に空間という囲いの中に閉じこめられて生きているのだろうか。禅は直ちに答えるだろう。「一本の線香の燃焼と共に三界悉く燃えているのだ。趙州一服の茶碗には人魚の群が自由自在に踊り廻っている」。時間空間を意識する限りは、禅は諸君から程遠く、休日にも落ちついた気分になれず、夜も安楽に眠れない、ということになる。

かくては諸君の一生涯は挙げて失敗である。

潙山と仰山との間に交された次の問答について見られたい。夏安居（げあんご）の終りに、仰山が潙山を訪ねると潙山は問うた、

「この夏中顔を見なかったようだが、下で何をしていたか。」
「少しばかり地面を耕して黍（きび）の植付を済ませました。」
「それでは夏中ぼんやりしていたわけではないな。」

第六章　禅の日常性

今度は仰山が潙山に問う番になった。曰く、
「老師はこの夏を如何お過しになりましたか。」
「一日一食、夜はぐっすり眠る、という風に過した。」
そこで仰山が附け加えた。
「それでは夏中ぼんやりしていたわけじゃありませんね。」

一儒者は、「道は邇きに在り、これを遠きに求む」としるしている。禅についても同じことがいえる。我々は、凡そ見付かりそうにもないところに、すなわち言語的表現や体系的精緻の上に、秘訣を求めるのであるが、禅の真理は却って日常生活の具体的なところにあるのだ。一僧がその師にたずねた、
「仏道を求めてこちらへ参ってから大分久しくなりますが、まだそれらしいものも承ったことがありません。何卒慈悲を垂れ給え。」
これに対して師の与えた答は次の如くである。
「弟子よ、お前は何を考えているのか。毎日、お前が挨拶すればいつも挨拶を返しているではないか。お前がお茶を淹れて呉れたら喜んで受けているではないか。それ以上に何を聞きたいというのか。これが禅なのか。これが禅の味到させようとする生の経験なのか。」一禅詩人は詠じている。
「何たる不思議、何たる奇蹟
　　水を運び、柴を搬ぶ。」

禅が没論理的であり非合理的であるというとき、気の弱い読者は怖気をふるって掛り合うまいと思われるかも知

れぬが、禅の実際面に当てたこの章は、知性面の扱いで生じたかも知れぬ厳しく取りつきにくい印象を和らげるのに役立つであろう。禅の真理がその実際面にあって非合理性にない限り、余り非合理性を強調するのはよくない。ここではさらに、禅が如何に単純常凡な事柄であるかを示し、同時に禅の日常に即した方面を強調するために、誰しも持ち得る最も素朴な人間経験に訴えた「事例」を挙げて見たいと思う。それらは概念的弁証や知性的分析に煩わされないという意味に於て正しく素朴なものである。何かちょっとした道具を取ってくれ、という。杖を挙げて見せる。只名を呼ぶ。こんなことは日々出会して深く気にもとめぬ最も単純な事件であるが、禅はまさしくそこにあるのだ、非合理に充ちているとばかり思われ、またいい得べくんば人間の理解し得る最も単純で直接で実際的で深い意味を宿した事例を若干追補するものである。以下はそのような単純で直接に実際的で深い意味を宿した事例を若干追補するものである。

石鞏（せっきょう）が得法の一友人に問うた、

「貴僧は虚空を捉えることができるか。」

「できる。」

「やって見ろ。」

彼は腕を伸ばして虚空を捉えて見せた。

「それでしまいか。結局何も捉えていないじゃないか。」

「では師兄（すひん）のやり方は。」

鞏（きょう）は直ちに友人の鼻孔を捉えて、ぐい、と引張った。友人は痛声を挙げて、

第六章　禅の日常性

「人の鼻を、何ということをするのだ。早く放してくれ。」

鞏曰く、「自分は直ちにこういう風に捉えるのだ。」

馬祖の弟子塩官は、一僧に本身毘盧舎那仏とは何かと問われて、手近にある浄瓶を取ってくるようにいいつけた。僧はそのとおりやってきてから再び本身盧舎那を問うた、

塩官曰く、「古仏はもう此処にはいない。」

一禅匠はこれに著語して、「古仏はずっと昔から此処にいるのだ。」と語っている。

此等の例が未だ完全に知性的葛藤を脱していないというなら、諸君は南陽忠国師（―西暦七七五）の場合をどう考えるだろうか。彼は、「おい、居ないか」と侍者を呼ぶ。侍者が「はい」と応諾する、また呼ぶ、という風に三回同じ喚応を繰返すのが毎日の例であった。

一日ついに国師は次のように語った。

「俺の方がお前に対していらざることをしたのであった。」（将謂吾孤負汝。却是汝孤負我。）

只その人の名を呼ぶ、まことに単純至極ではないか。忠国師の最後に洩らした言葉は、普通の論理的な見方からすれば頗る不可解とも見られようが、呼べば応えるという一事ほど日常的で実際的なものはない。真理はまさしく此処にある、と禅は明言するのだ。ここに我々は禅が如何に日常的なもの、身近なものであるかを知ることができ

るのである。そこには何の神秘もない。事実はすっかり開け放しである。自分が呼べば君が応える。一つの「やあ」がいま一つの「やあ」を期せずして呼び出す。そしてこの外に何があろうか。

良遂は麻谷（臨済の同時代人）の下で禅を学んでいた。或る時麻谷が、「良遂」と喚んだので、彼は直に「はい」と応じた。かくすること三回に及んで、師匠は大喝した。

「この間抜者、下れ。」

この一声に良遂は省覚し初めて禅の何たるかをさとったのである。その時彼は叫んだ。

「師よ、もはや良遂は欺かれませぬ。もし私が師の門を敲かなかったら、経論にすかされて空しく一生を過したことでしょう。」

後、良遂は仏教哲学の研究にかかりはてている仲間の僧たちに次のように語っている。

「君たちの知っていることは自分もよく知っている。だが自分の知っていることは君たちは全然知っていない。」

師が自分の名を喚んだというそのことの意義を認得しただけで、良遂がこのような言葉を吐き得た、ということは驚くべきことではないか。

これらの実例で、問題は幾分なりとも明瞭に分り易くなっただろうか。このような例は際限なく挙げることができるが、詮ずるところ、禅が何ら持って廻った面倒なものでもなく、また高度の抽象的、思弁的能力を要求するものでもないことは、以上引くところによって十分知られるであろう。禅の真理と力とは、正しくその単純性、直接性、極度の実際性にある。「お早う、如何です」「有難う、相変らず達者で」——ここに禅があるのだ。「何卒、お

第六章　禅の日常性

茶を一服」——ここにも禅はあり余るほどだ。仕事に励んでかなり腹の空いてきた雲水が、食事の合図を耳にするなり仕事をやめて食堂に現われる。老師はこれを見て心から微笑する。何故ならばこの僧はぎりぎり一杯のところまで禅を行じているからだ。これよりも自然なものはない。唯一つ忘れてはならぬのは、まさしくその全意義に対してはっきりと眼を開くということである。

然し此処にまた禅を学ぶ者が特に注意して避けねばならぬ危険な陥穽（かんせい）がある。これらは、その起原や価値の如何に拘わらず、人間の自然的傾向に従おうとするものである。禅は断じて自然主義（ナチュラリズム）や放縦主義（リバティニズム）と混同してはならぬ。人間の行為も、道徳的直観も宗教意識も持たぬ動物の行動との間には大きな距りがある。動物はその生活状態を改善するために、或は徳性を昂めるために工夫努力することを知らぬ。

石鞏が一日厨（くりや）で働いていると、師匠の馬祖がやってきて、何をしているか、とたずねた。

「牛の世話をしています。」

「どういう風にやっているか。」

「一度でも路から踏み出すようなことがあれば、すぐ鼻づらを把って引き戻します。」

「お前は飼い方をよく心得ているわい。」

これは自然主義ではない。或は有名な師匠が厨で仕事を行う努力がある。

「老師にも真理の修得に努力するということがありますか。」

「その通り。」

「それはどういう方法で。」

「腹が空いてくれば食べる。疲れたら眠る。」

「それは誰でもやっていることじゃありませんか。誰でも老師と同じ修行をしている、といっていいのですか。」

「それは駄目だ。」

「何故でしょうか。」

「彼等は食べながら食べないで余計なことに意を用い、徒(いたずら)に自分の心を労している。眠りながら眠らないで数知れぬ夢を見ている。これが自分と違うところだ。」

一歩譲って禅を自然主義の中に数えるとすれば、厳しい訓練に裏打ちされた自然主義ということになろう。禅が自然主義といえるのはこの意味に於てであって、放縦主義流に解してはならぬ。彼等は外から来る力に手足を縛られ、その前に全く無力である。放縦主義者は意志の自由をもたぬ。般若経典によく出てくる表現を藉(か)りるなら、禅は「住処」を持たぬのである。すなわち随処為主である。ものが固定したあたりかをもつとき、そこに束縛が生じて絶対性を失う。次の問答はこの間の消息を至極明瞭に伝えている。

一僧問う、「心の住処はどこですか。」

師曰く、「心は無所住のところに住する。」

「無所住とは何の意味ですか。」

「これという特定の対象に心が住しないとき無所住に住するというのだ。」

104

第六章　禅の日常性

「特定の対象に住しないとはどういう意味ですか。」
「善と悪、心と物、そういう二元論に住しないことだ。無所住のところこそ心の真の住処である。」

雪峯（西暦八二二—九〇八）は唐朝禅宗史上最も熱烈な求道者の一人である。彼はその長い禅修行の行脚を通じていつも柄杓を担いでいたという。彼は僧堂でも、最も人のいやがるそして最も難しい仕事つまり典座（炊事係）を引受けてやろうと心掛けていたのだ。柄杓はその象徴であった。

ついに徳山の法嗣となったとき、一僧来り問う、

「貴僧は徳山の許で何を得て、かくも悠悠自在の境涯に達せられたのですか。」
「自分は空手で出掛けて行って空手で帰ってきたのだ。」

これこそ無所住の教えを実地に説明するものではないか。

僧たちがその師百丈涅槃に禅の講説を乞うと、

「田圃へ行ってひと働きしてくるがよい。その後でやろう。」

という返事であった。いよいよその作業がすんで、一同が、約束どおりにやって貰いたい、と促したところ、彼は自分の両手を展いて見せただけで一語も発しなかった。これが彼の大説法だったのである。

105

原　註

（1）大珠慧海は馬祖の弟子であって、その『頓悟要門論』と名づける二部の著作は当時行われていた禅法の概要を示している。

（2）馬祖の弟子、前身は猟師であった。馬祖の接得に逢い、弓を捨てて出家した。

第七章　悟り——新見地の獲得

禅修行の目的は、ものの本質を洞見する新見地の獲得にある。もし諸君が二元論の規定に従って一にも二にも論理的な考え方をする習慣になっているなら、その状態を脱するがよい。そうすればいくらか禅の見地に近づいたということができよう。諸君と自分とは先ずまず同じ世界に住んでいるとして、この窓外の石、実は石と呼びならわしているものが、我々各人にとって果して同じものであり得るだろうか。諸君も一服の茶を啜り自分も一服の茶を啜る。動作は一見相等しいようであるが、我々各人の一服には心境的にどれ程か大きい距りがないとも限らぬ。或る人の一服には禅がないかも知れず、或る人の一服には禅が横溢しているかも知れぬ。その理由は外でもない。一人は論理の円周内を動きまわるが、一人はその外に立っているからである。いわゆる禅の新見地には実際は何の新しさもないのであるが、この「新しい」という言葉は禅の見方をいい表わすのに好都合だから使用したまでであって、禅の方からいえば一歩譲った表現なのだ。

この新見地の獲得を禅では悟りという。動詞にすれば悟るである。悟りのないところに禅はない。禅の生活はこ

第七章　悟り──新見地の獲得

の悟りから始まるからである。悟りは知性論理的理解に対して直覚的洞察と定義することができよう。定義はともあれ、悟りは二元論的な考え方に昧まされて今迄気がつかなかった新世界の開け来ることを意味する。以上記すところを念頭に置いて、次の問答を考えて頂きたい。それが実地に如何なるものであるかがはっきりすることと思う。

叢林に入って間もない一僧が、趙州に心要を問うた、

州曰く、「朝粥はすんだかどうか。」

僧曰く、「頂きました。」

趙州は直ちに応じて言った、

「それでは持鉢を洗ってくるがよい。」

この指示に僧は忽然と省悟するところがあった。

後に雲門はこの応答を評して次のように述べている。

「趙州のこの言葉には何か特別に指示するところがあったのかどうか。あったとすればそれは何だ。なかったとしたら僧の得た悟りとは何だ。」

さらに後、翠巖（中国五代の禅僧）は雲門の言葉を次のように反駁している。

「巨匠雲門もさっぱり解っていない。自分はそんな見方をしない。だからこんな評をするのだ。これは全然蛇に足を画き宦官に鬚を添えるようなものだ。何か悟りのようなものを得たというその雲水は地獄へ真逆様だ。」

趙州の持鉢を洗え、という言葉、僧の省悟、雲門の選言命題、翠巖の断案──これらは一体何を意味するものか。彼等は互に相手を貶しつけているのだろうか。それは只の空騒ぎに過ぎないものだろうか。自分の見るところ

では、それらはいずれも一つの道を指し示すものである。件の僧が何処へ行こうと、彼の悟りは決して無駄ではないのだ。

徳山は『金剛経』の権威であった。偶々禅宗なるものがあって不立文字・直指人心を説くことを聞いて龍潭（唐代の禅僧）の許に赴き教えを乞うた。一夜徳山が禅の秘要を求めて戸外に打坐していると、龍潭が問うた、

「何故入らないのか。」

「真暗ですから。」

師は紙燭をともし徳山に差し出した。彼がそれを受取ろうとした途端に龍潭はそれを吹き消してしまった。その時徳山の心は忽然と開けた。

百丈がその師馬祖に伴うて外出した時偶々野鴨の飛ぶのを見た。馬祖が問うた、

「あれは何だ。」

「野鴨です。」

「どこへ行くのか。」

「もうどこかへ行ってしまいましたよ。」

馬祖は突如として百丈の鼻頭を把り、ぐいと捻った。百丈は痛みの余り思わず、あ、あ、と声を出した。

「これでもいないというのか。初めからちゃんと此処にいるじゃないか。」

この一言に百丈は背に冷汗を流した。彼はまさしく悟ったのである。持鉢を洗い、紙燭を吹き消し、鼻頭を把る。

第七章　悟り──新見地の獲得

此等の間に何のつながりがあるのか。我々は雲門と共に言わねばならぬ。何もないなら、彼等がそろって禅の真理を悟ることができたのはどうしてか。もしあるなら、それらは内的にどうつながるか。この悟りというのは何か。これはどういう風に新しい見地であるか。

宋朝の偉大な禅匠大慧(2)の許に道謙なる僧があった。彼は多年禅を学んで未だその心要を得るところがなく、すっかり絶望していた。偶ミ彼は遠方の都まで使者にやられることになった。半年もかかる長途の旅行は、参学上の助けになるよりは妨げになることが思いやられた。ところが彼の同輩に宗元（南宋の禅僧）なるものがあって彼にいたく同情し、次のように語って力づけた。

「自分も一緒について行って微力ながらできる限り助けてやろう。旅をしながらでも工夫の続けられぬわけはない。」

或る夜道謙は、一生の大事の解決にどうか力を藉して欲しい、と泣く泣く訴えた。宗元曰く、

「途中代って弁ずべきことがあったら何でも代ってやろう。だがどうしても代ってやれないことが五つある。著衣・喫飯・屙屎・放尿・駝箇死屍路上行、これだけだ。」

道謙は、どうかそれを聞かせて欲しいと切願した。元曰く、

「これだけは、何としても君が弁じなければ駄目だ。」

求道の僧は言下に心開け、手の舞い足の踏むところを知らなかった。そこで元は、

「自分の仕事はこれで済んだようなものだ。これ以上同伴して行っても何の意味もない。自分は一先ず帰ろう。」

111

と別れを告げて、道謙を今度は独りで旅をさせた。半年の後、道謙は使命を果して寺へ帰った。偶々大慧は山を降りてくる途中だったが、道謙の顔を見るなりこういった。

「おお、今度はすっかり別物になって来たな。」

試みに問おう、友人の宗元があの極まり切った忠告を与えた時、道謙の心に閃き出たものは何であったか、と。

香厳（唐末の禅僧）は百丈の弟子であった。師が歿して後、兄弟子の潙山の許へ行った。潙山は彼にたずねた。

「自分はおんみが先師のもとで参究し、すぐれて聡明怜悧であることも聞いている。然しそういうものを頼りにして得た禅はどうしても知性的、分析的理解を出ることはできぬ。それは実は生死の根源をなすものだ。とはいうものの、おんみはもう禅の真理を体得しているかも知れぬ。父母未生以前のおんみ自身は何だ。試みに一句道うて見よ。」

香厳は答える術を知らず茫然と寮へ退いたが、思い直して先師の講録その他典籍をとり出して熱心に調べに掛った。然しこれぞと思う文句はついに見当らなかった。そこで彼は潙山の許に引返して幾度となく示教を乞うたが、潙山は次のように答えるばかりであった。

「実のところ、何もおんみに与えるようなものはないのだ。またそんな真似をすればおんみに嗤いものにされる日が来るだろう。何か話し得ることがあるとしても、それは自分のもので、決しておんみのものではないのだ。」

彼は落胆し潙山の不親切を怨んだ。ついに彼は意を決して、従来親しんできた、然し今は何ら安心を得る助けとはならぬ書物・覚え書の数々を悉く焼却してしまった。そして、余生はふっつりと世間との交渉を断ち、仏弟子の

第七章　悟り――新見地の獲得

「難解で教わることもできぬような仏法はもはや一生学ぶまい。暫く長行の粥飯僧となって心神を労することから遠ざかろう。」

これが当時の彼の心境であった。彼は潙山を辞して南陽忠国師の遺跡に草庵を結んだ。一日地面を掃いていると、その箒に触れた礫が飛んで竹に当った。不意に発する戛然の響きに彼はついに大悟することができたのである。彼の喜びはいい知れぬものがあった。潙山の提示した問も今は瞭瞭として一点の不明をも止めなかった。それはまさしく失った父母にめぐり遇う思いであった。のみならず潙山が示教を拒んだ理由も深く思い当るところがあった。もし潙山が不親切にも彼に何か教示するところがあったら、この経験を得る日はついにならなかったであろうことを、今や彼ははっきりと悟ったからである。

禅は、師匠が説明によってすべての弟子を悟らせるという風にはいかぬものだろうか。悟りとは全然知性的分析を許さぬものだろうか。その通り、それはどれだけ説明や論証を積み重ねても体得者以外には伝えることのできぬ経験である。もし分析によって全然これを知らぬ者にも剰すところなく明白に示すことができる、という意味で悟りが分析を許すものならば、その悟りはもはや悟りではない。概念となった悟りは死物である。そこにはもはや禅の経験はない。従って禅に於て訓育上為し得ることは、注意を目標に向けさせるように指示を与えること、或は道を示すこと、唯それだけである。目標に達し親しくそのものを手に取るということは当事者自らがやらねばならぬ。誰も代ってやるわけにはいかぬからだ。指示についていうならば、それは到るところにある。微かな音、何でもない言葉、ふと咲いている花、悟りへの心機の熟している時には、到るところで逢著するものだ。

何かに躓くというような些細な出来事が、心を悟りへと打ち開く条件もしくは機縁となるのである。一見とるに足らぬ出来事がその意義に於て凡そ均衡を絶した結果を生ずるのである。導火線の軽い接触が、大地をその底から揺り動かすような大爆発を誘うのである。それらは成熟の時機を待っているに過ぎない。何かの理由で心にその準備が整ってくると、鳥がとび、鈴が鳴る、只それだけの機縁で、諸君は忽然と本来の故郷へ帰るのである。悟りのあらゆる原因、あらゆる条件は心にある。抑この初から、何一つ隠されていたのは諸君だけだったのだ。このように禅には、説明すべきもの、教示すべきもの、事実に眼を閉じていたようなものは、何一つないのだ。諸君の見たいものはすべて常恒不断に諸君の眼前にあったのだ。諸君自身から生れてこない限り、如何なる知識も真に諸君のものではない。それは借りものの晴着に過ぎぬ。本来の面目を発見するのである。

宋代の儒者で、また詩人でもあり政治家でもあった黄山谷が晦堂（宋代の禅僧）のところへ禅の手ほどきを乞うてきた。晦堂曰く、

「貴官の親炙していられる経書には、禅の教えにそっくり符合するところがある。孔子がいうているではないか、『二三子以我為隠乎。吾無隠乎爾』と。貴官はこれをどう解されるか。」

山谷は何か言おうとしたが早くも晦堂は、

「不是、不是。」

と抑えてしまった。この儒者は心中大いに煩悶を覚えたが、何ともしようがなかった。堂曰く、時恰も木犀が満開で香気が四辺に馥郁としていた。その後二人が山中を歩いたことがあった。

第七章　悟り——新見地の獲得

「この香りが分るか。」
「分ります。」
「自分は何も隠してはいないのだ。」（吾無隠乎爾。）

この示唆に黄山谷は釈然として悟るところがあった。

以上の諸例で悟りが何であり、また如何にして開けてくるかを略ゞ示し得たかと思う。だが諸君はたずねるかも知れない。

「君の説明や指示を丹念に読んだが、さっぱり分らぬままだ。ともかくも悟りに何かの内容があるなら、それをはっきり記述できないものか。君の事例や説述は多分に試図的なもので、我々に分るのは風の向きだけだ。小舟が最後に落ち着くその港はどこにあるのだ。」

これに対して禅者は次のように答えるだろう。すなわち、内容の点になると悟りにも諸君の知性的理解に合うように記述し提示し証示し得るものは何もないのだ。何故ならば禅は観念とは没交渉であり、悟りは一種の内的知覚——個々の対象の知覚ではなく謂わば実在そのものの知覚であるからだ。悟りの最後に落ち着くところは自己（セルフ）にある。それは自己自身の裡に還帰するより外はないのだ。だから趙州は「喫茶去」と言い、南泉は「這鎌子（このかまは）、我用得最快（よくきれる）」と言う。自己はこういう風にはたらくのだ。それは、もし捉えられるものなら、そのはたらきの只中に捉えなければならぬ。

悟りは存在の根柢を衝くものであるところから、その獲得は一般に人生の転機を劃する。然しその獲得は徹底的にきっぱりしたものでなければならぬ。生ぬるい悟りというようなものがあればそれは悟らぬよりも悪い。次の例

臨済が黄檗の三十棒を素直に受けているときその有様は惨めなものであったが、一度悟りを得ると全く別人になってしまった。「黄檗の仏法多子なし」。これが彼の新生の第一声であった。やがて再び黄檗に会うた時、彼はその面上に一掌を与えてその恩顧に酬いた。何たる傲慢、何たる無礼、と誰しも思うであろう。ところが臨済の粗放にははっきり理由があったのだ。黄檗がこの挨拶の仕方に深く満足するところがあったのも尤もである。
徳山は一旦禅の真理に眼を開くや、直ちに『金剛経』の疏鈔の一切を取り出して焼き捨ててしまった。それらは嘗ては最も貴重なものであり、何処へ出るにも背に負うて身から離さなかった程であった。その時彼は次のように叫んでいる。

「諸この玄弁を窮むとも一毫を太虚に置くが如し。世の枢機を竭すとも一滴を巨壑(きょがく)に投ずるに似たり。」

例の野鴨子の問答のあった翌日、馬祖が陞堂(しょうどう)して衆僧の前で説法を始めようとすると、百丈はつと進み出て師の礼拝のために展べられてある坐具を捲いてしまった。普通坐具を捲けば説法が終ったという意味になる。馬祖は別に咎めもせずに壇を降りて方丈へ帰ってしまった。やがて百丈を呼んで、

「まだ口も開かぬさきに席を捲くとはどうしたことか。」

とたずねた。丈曰く、

「昨日は和尚に鼻をやられて随分いたみました。」

「昨日はどこをうろうろと迷っていたのだ。」

「今日は痛くも痒(かゆ)くもありません。」

第七章　悟り——新見地の獲得

この一言で馬祖は百丈の透過を認めたのである。

以上で悟りの獲得によって心中にどんな変化が生ずるかを示し得たかと思う。悟りを得るまでは何と僧たちの無力であったことか。彼等はさながら沙漠に途を失った旅人のようである。ところが悟りを得て後の彼等は絶対君主の如くである。彼等はもはや誰に対しても隷従しない。彼等は彼等自身の主人公である。

なお、説述の序でに、この悟りと名づける心的開発について、次の諸点を吟味し併せて所見を要約しておくのも徒事ではなかろう。

一、往往禅の修行は、瞑想によって自己暗示の状態を生み出すものだ、と考える人がある。これは上掲の様々な実例からも知られるように完全に正鵠を失している。悟りは、強度の思念集中によって一定の予期された意識状態を生み出すという風なものではないのだ。それは新見地の獲得である。意識の発生以来我々は一定の概念的、分析的な仕方で内外の諸条件に対応するようになった。禅の修行は、この基礎工事を一挙に顚覆してその旧い骨組フレームを全然新しい基礎の上に再建しようとするにある。従って相対的意識の産物たる形而上学的、象徴的な命題を瞑想するなどということが禅に於て何の役割をも演じないのは明白である。

二、悟りを獲得しなければ誰も禅の真理に参入することはできぬ。悟りとは、今迄は夢想だにもしなかった新しい真理が突如として意識に閃き出ることである。それは、知性的、論証的な作為をどこまでも積み重ねて行ってその挙句一時に起る一種の精神的大変動カタストロフィーである。集積が安定の限度に達すると全建築がついに地上へ倒壊する。その時に、見よ、新しい天が豁然とひらけわたるのである。氷点に達すると水はいつとはなく氷になる。液体はいつとはなく固体になって流動しなくなる。悟りは求道者がもはや自分の全存在を消耗し尽したと感じているとき予期

せずしてやってくるのだ。宗教的にいえばそれは新生である。知性的にいえば新見地の獲得である。世界は今や風光を一新したように思われる。そしてその新風光は仏教で無明と名づける二元論の醜悪さのすべてを包み隠してしまうかとも思われるばかりである。

三、悟りは禅の存在理由（レーゾン・デートル）である。

悟りなくして禅は禅ではない。従って訓練上・教説上のあらゆる方便は悟りに向って傾注されるのである。禅匠たちは、悟りがおのずと訪れる、すなわちあちこちからやってくるのを待つような、悠長なことはしていられなかった。禅の真理を求める弟子たちを何とかして助けようと思うその熱意から、より施設的に、やがてはどうしても悟りへ出なければならぬような境地へ追いこむために、あのどう見ても不可解な提示が案出されたのだ。大方の哲学的、宗教的指導者たちが行った知性的弁証や諄諄たる説得はすべて望む結果を得ることができず、弟子たちはそのためにいよいよ遠く迷い出て行ったのであった。これは、仏教がその高度に形而上学的な抽象的諸観念、複雑極まる瑜伽的修行の体系という風な印度的遺産のすべてを携えて初めてシナに入った時、特に甚しいものがあった。これらはより実際的なシナ人をして、釈迦の教えの中心をどう捉えべきかに迷わせたのであった。菩提達摩・六祖慧能・馬祖道一・石頭希遷その他のシナの禅匠たちはこの事実をちゃんと認めていた。かく見来るとき禅の宣言と発展とは自然の勢であった。彼等によって悟りは経典の知識や論釈の学的論究の上位に置かれ、禅そのものと一つに見られたのである。従って悟りなき禅は辛味のない胡椒のようなものである。しかしまた過剰（ツー・マッチ）の悟りともいうべきものもある。これは心して避けなければならぬ。

四、禅に於ける悟りをこのように強調してくるとき、禅が、印度に於てまたシナ仏教の他宗派に於て修行する禅那の体系とは別個のものだ、という事実が極めて重要なものとなってくる。一般に禅那といえば一定の思想内容に

第七章　悟り——新見地の獲得

向けられた瞑想もしくは凝心ということになっている。その思想内容となるものは、小乗仏教に於ては無常観であったが、大乗仏教に於てはより屢と空観に求められた。心が訓練されて、意識の痕跡をも止めない、無意識であるという感じさえも消失する完全な空白の状態を現出し得るまでになるとき、換言すればあらゆる形式の心的活動が意識面よりすっかり拭い去られて心は一点の雲もなく只青々とひろがる虚空のようになるとき、禅那が完成の域に達したといわれるのである。これはエクスタシーもしくはトランスと呼ぶことはできても禅ではあり得ない。

禅には悟りがなければならぬ。旧い知性作用の累積を一気に推倒して新生命の基礎を打ち樹てる底の全面的な心的隆起がなければならぬ。今まで夢想もしなかった視角から旧い事事物物を見渡す新しいセンスの覚醒がなければならぬ。禅那にはそうしたものは何一つない。何故ならばそれは心を鎮静に帰する訓練に過ぎないからだ。かような禅那にも疑もなくそれ自身の長所はある。しかし禅はこれと同一視してはならぬのだ。

五、悟りは、基督教神秘家の主張するように神を如実に観ることではない。禅はこれを当初から明瞭にし且つ主張して来た。禅は自分自身のはたらきを念念に転じてやることはないのだ。それは一創造主の支持に依属するものではない。この生を生きる理由を把握するところに禅は満足するのである。五祖山の法演（—西暦一一〇四）はよく自分の手を突き出して、これは誰の手なのか、とたずねた。我々がその理由を知るとき悟りがあり禅があるのだ。神秘主義の神が考えられるところには、どうしても特定の創造主の仕事場そのものを覗くことである。禅はこれを如実に且つ主張して来た。禅は自分自身のはたらきを念念に転じてやめることはないのだ。それは一創造主の支持に依属するものではない。この生を生きる理由を把握するところに禅は満足するのである。神秘主義の神が考えられるところには、どうしても特定の対象を把握するということがなければならぬ。神が把握されるとき、非神は排除される。おのずとはたらく限定の作用である。禅は絶対の自由を求める。神からさえ自由を求めるのだ。「無所住」とはまさにこのことである。

「仏というも既にその口を漱げ」も同じ意味である。禅は好んで病的に不敬虔であり無神論であろうとするのではなく、単なる名の不完全を認めるのである。であればこそ薬山（西暦七四五―八二八）は説法を求められたとき、一語も発することなく壇を降りて方丈へ帰ってしまったのである。百丈は二、三歩進み出て手を展いて見せただけだったが、実にこの間の消息をよく伝えているではないか。

六、悟りは、異常心理研究の好題目たる病態意識ではない。心的隆起などというと、禅は常人の避くべきもののように思う人があるかも知れぬ。甚しい謬見であるが、不幸にしてこれは先入観念に災された批評家の屢〻支持するところとなっている。趙州もいっているように禅は「平常心」である。扉が内へ開くか外へ開くかは全く蝶番のつけ方による。一瞬にして事態が転換し、禅は諸君のものとなる。諸君は旧のままに完全であり正常である。のみならず諸君はその間に全然新しい何物かを得ているのである。諸君の全精神活動は今や全然別個の基調に立ってはたらきつつある、ということになろう。それは、嘗て経験した何物にもまして、より満足な、より平和な、より喜びに充ちたものであろう。生の調べが一変するであろう。禅を得るということには何か活気を甦らせるものがある。春の花はより可憐に、渓流はより冷くより清冽になる。このような事態を招来する心境の転換を異常などと呼ぶことはできぬ。生がいよいよその味わいを深めそのひろがりが全宇宙を内に包むに到るとき、悟りには全く貴重で十分求めるに価する何物かがある、といわねばならぬ。

第七章　悟り――新見地の獲得

原　註
(1) この主題をより詳細に取扱ったものとしては拙著英文『禅論』第一巻、頁二二五―二五〇と、第二巻、頁四以下参照。
(2) 圜悟の弟子。西暦一一六三年歿。

第八章　公案

禅は東洋精神独自の所産であって、その独自性は、実際面に関する限り、心機を成熟せしめてついに悟りへ打って出させるその組織的な訓練法にある。禅の秘密はかくして開顕されるのである。仮に禅を神秘主義の中に数えるとしても、それは組織に於て、訓練に於て、また最後の到達点に於て、他のすべての神秘主義と全くその形態を異にするものである。かくいうとき自分の念頭にあるのは主として公案による訓練と坐禅とである。

坐禅、サンスクリットでいえば、禅那は結跏趺坐して沈思凝心することを意味する。この行法は印度に発生し東洋全土に普及したものである。それは幾世紀を通じて実践せられ、今日の禅修行者も厳格にこれを守っている。

この点に於て坐禅は東洋を通じての実践的精神訓練法であるが、公案と相結んで用いられるときは特別の相貌を呈し、禅ならでは見られぬものとなるのである。

然し坐禅もしくは禅那について詳説するのは本章の目的ではない。此処では、主として、現在極東で行われている禅の本質的なものをはっきり表示している公案について考察したいと思うのである。その当初仏教では禅那は、

第八章　公　案

三学、すなわち尸羅（戒）・禅那（定）・般若（慧）の一つとされていた。三学の趣意は、よき仏弟子は道徳的には仏陀の制戒を遵守しなければならぬ、また放恣な情念を統御する方法に通暁しなければならぬ、最後に深遠な仏教形而上学のあらゆる複雑な論理を知悉し得る知性的能力を具えなければならぬ、というにある。此等の資格のいずれを欠いても真の仏弟子ということはできなかったのである。然し時とともに分化を生じ仏教徒の中にもそれらのいずれか一つを特別に強調するものが現われてきた。或る者は戒律の遵守を他のいずれよりも重しとし、或る者は禅那の修行者になり、さらに或る者は仏教の教説に含まれている精緻な知性的構造の研究に専心したのである。禅者も禅那の修行者だと考える人があるかも知れないが、禅に於ては禅那はもう原の意味を失っている。禅は、この特殊な印度的精神訓練法の実践にあたって自家独特の目的を有するに到ったのである。

天台宗の開祖智者大師の『釈禅波羅蜜次第法門』に引用されている大乗経典によれば、禅那は、敬虔な仏教徒の通願である四弘誓願を成就するために行ぜられるのである。

　　禅為利智蔵　　功徳之福田　　禅如清浄水　　能洗諸欲塵
　　得金剛三昧　　摧砕結使山　　禅為金剛鎧　　能遮煩悩箭
　　得六神通力　　能度無量人　　畳塵蔽天日　　大雨能淹之
　　　　　　　　　　　　　　　　覚観風動之　　禅定能滅之
　　　　　　　　　　　　　　　　雖未得無為　　涅槃分已得

禅那、すなわち dhyāna は語根 dhī（知覚する、反省する、心を集中する）から来ているが、この dhī は語原的に dhṛ（持つ、保つ、支持する）と何かつながりがあるかも知れぬ。このように禅那は思念を集中して定められた通路から逸脱させないこと、すなわち心を或る単一な思念の対象に集中することを意味している。従って禅或は禅那を実修する場合、外界にかかわる事柄は細密に隅々にいたるまで統制しなければならぬ。これは心を、動いてやまぬ情念や官能の作用から漸次脱却するに最も有利な状態へ導き入れるためである。例えば飲食はその度を保つよ

125

うにしなければならぬ。睡眠を貪ってはならぬ。体軀はゆったりと無理のないように、しかし背筋は真直に立てるようにしなければならぬ、という風である。呼吸の調節に関しては、周知の通り、印度人は非の打ちどころのない芸術家である。次に、禅那修行者の坐する場所の選択も同様に慎重な考慮を要する問題である。市場とか工場とか事務所とかは避ける方がよい、とせられているのは蓋し当然であろう。身心の制御に関する規則や指示はまだまだ沢山あって、智者大師の禅那波羅蜜に関する著述には詳細に取扱われている。

この簡単な禅那の説明によっても明かであるように、禅者の行う坐禅は仏教徒一般の行うものと同一物ではない。禅那もしくは坐禅は、禅に於ては公案の解決に達する手段として用いられる。禅は禅那そのものを目的としているのではない。公案の参究を離れては坐禅は第二義的な意味を有するに過ぎない。それは疑もなく禅を体解するための必須条件である。たとい公案が解けても、坐禅に於て徹底的な修行を積まなければ、その深い精神的真理を究尽することはできないであろう。公案と坐禅とは禅そのものの二人の侍女である。前者は目であり後者は足である。

シナ仏教初期に於ては先ず哲学的な論議が熱心な仏教学徒の注意を引いて、『華厳』・『法華』・『般若』・『涅槃』等の経典は早くシナ語に翻訳された。此等の聖典に含まれている深い形而上学的思想は他の何物にもましてシナの学者たちの関心を捉えた。シナの仏教徒たちに聖典の思想的研究への大きな刺戟が与えられたのは、恐らく主としてあの卓絶した鳩摩羅什のお蔭である。次に来るのは仏教の実修的研究である。禅の初祖菩提達摩が六世紀にシナへやってきたとき、彼は幾分猜疑の目を以て一種の異端者と見做された。六祖慧能がその微賤と韜晦から身を現わして、自分こそ禅の正統を嗣ぐものであると名告ったときも、他の禅那修行者の注意を惹くことはほとんどなかったのである。初期シナ仏教の伝記的述作に見られるかぎり、またその時代までに翻訳せられた禅那関係の経典から

第八章　公案

推測されるかぎり、禅那もしくは坐禅は主として小乗的様式に従って修せられていたのである。今我々の考えるような禅が事実上成立したのは慧能以後一、二世紀のことであって、爾後急速に発展し、他の仏教諸宗を顔色なからしめるに到ったのである。今日シナには禅宗に所属しない仏教の僧院は見当らない。そしてその多くは臨済宗に属するものである。かく他宗を圧倒した理由のひとつは、公案を究明し、かくて悟りに到達するための手段として坐禅を修した、ということに見出すことができる。

公案は字義上「公府の案牘」、すなわち「権威ある法令の如きもの」を意味し、唐朝末期に到って用いられるようになった言葉である。現在では、昔の禅匠の逸話、禅匠と僧たちとの問答、禅匠の提示或は質問等を指すようになっている。そしてそれらはすべて禅の真理に眼を開くための手段として用いられるのである。無論当初には現在考えられているような公案はなかった。それは後代の禅匠たちの黙しがたい老婆心から案出された一種の人為的手段であって、禅匠たちはこれによって比較的天分に恵まれぬ弟子たちの心に強いて禅意識を開発せしめようとしたのである。

　心は自然に任せておいてもひとりでに成長してそれ自身の目的を達するかも知れないが、人間は必ずしもこれを待っていることはできぬ。そこで善いにつけ悪いにつけて手出しをするということになる。人間はどうしても悠長に構えていられないのだ。手を出す機会さえあればきっとそれをやる。干渉も時には助けとなるが、断じてそうはない場合もある。それは通例二様に作用する。人間の干渉によって失うよりも得る方が多い場合、我々はこれを歓迎して改良或は進歩などというが、それが反対の結果になると退歩と称する。文明は人間的であり人為的である。従ってそれに満足できないで自然へ還りたがる人がどうしてもあるものだ。いわゆる近代的進歩が何等無条件の幸

福を意味するものではない、というのはその通りである。然し大体に於て、少くとも物質的な生活面に於ては、この頃は以前よりもはげしくは唱えられぬのである。

同様に、純粋で自然で基本的な禅の中へ公案という組織を持ちこむということは改悪であり同時に改良であった。然し一旦成立するとその組織を廃するわけにはなかなか行かぬらしい。自分自身よりも天分に恵まれず、そのために恐らく開悟の機会を得ずに終るであろうところの薄倖の後輩たちのことを心にかけるのは、禅匠の立場として人情の自然であった。彼は何とかして、自分が嘗て禅の参究によって得たあの微妙不思議な理解を分ちたいと思ったのだ。彼の母性的本能が彼を駆って弟子たちの心を未だ知らぬ霊妙な悟りを開かせるために、さらにいうならば強いて開かせるための方法に想い到らしめたのである。もし弟子たち自身の蒙昧なやり方に任せておいたならば、稀有の幸運にでも恵まれないかぎり、その悟りは決して彼等に開けることはないであろうと思われたのだ。禅匠たちは公案という風な仕組みが人為であり贅物であることはよく承知していた。蓋し、禅が、人間自身の内的なはたらきから出るものでなければ、当然そうあるべきように純粋でもあり得ないし、創造的な活力をゆたかに持つこともできない。然し純粋なものが極めて得難く、得ることは稀である場合、類似のものでも結構とすべきであろう。さらに、そのまま放って置けば純粋な禅は恐らく人間の経験知からその跡を絶つであろう、という状態にあったのである。類似物必ずしも単に糊塗的なものとは限らない。その中に全く真実で可能性に充ちた何物かをやどしているかも知れぬ。然りとすれば、これを採用し、思う存分活用して悪い筈があろうか。公案と坐禅という組織も、適切に利用するならば、正しく心を打ち開いて禅の真理に面せしめるのである。

128

第八章　公案

その初め禅匠は謂わば独学の士であった。彼は学校教育を受けることもなく、専門の学校へ行って一定の課目を履修するということもなかった。只、その精神を揺り動かす止むにやまれぬものがあって、諸方を遊歴してその欲する知識を求めざるを得なかった。彼は独力で自己を完成したのである。無論彼にも教師はあったが、その教師は今日の学徒が助力を与えられるよ以上に手を藉しすぎるあの仕方――学徒が実地に必要としている以上に、また学徒にとって真に有益であるり以上に手を藉しすぎるあの仕方――で弟子に助力を与えはしなかった。これこそ唐時代の禅宗初期に於て禅があのように能動的に強力ならしめ、遥かに旺盛な気力を与えたのである。宋朝に入って公案方式が流行するに及んで禅の全盛時代はほとんど過ぎ去り、次第に没落衰退の徴をあらわしたのである。

ここで後世の学人に与えられた最初の公案の一つを示すこととしよう。六祖が明上座に、禅とは何か、とたずねられて次のように答えた。「不思善不思悪。正与麼時。那箇是明上座。本来面目」。（この「面目」を見せよ。禅の秘義はそれからだ。或はこういってもよい。アブラハムの生れる以前の君は誰なのか。もし諸君がこの人（パーソネージ）に親しく相逢うたことがあるなら、諸君が何であり神が何であるかをも一層よく知っている筈である。明上座はここでこの本来人（オリジナル・マン）、形而上学的にいえば、彼自身の内なる自己と握手することを教えられたのである。）

この問が発せられたとき、明上座は既に心的にその真理を洞見するだけの準備ができていた。問いかける、ということは単に表面上のことであって、その実は聴き手の心を打ち開こうとする状態にあることを看破していたのである。六祖は明上座の心境が今にも禅の真理に向って触発しようとする一箇の肯定であったのだ。彼の心は熟していた。ちょっと揺ぶっただけでもう地に落ちる果実を思わせる熱心に暗中摸索を続けて来たのだ。この僧は長らく

ほどに熟していたのだ。彼の心は導き手の最後の一触を待つ許りであったのだ。「本来の面目」の要請は、どうしても必要な最後の仕上げであった。かくて明の心は直下に開けて真理を把握したのである。ところで、「本来の面目」についての問という形をとったこの言葉が、禅の修行に明ほどの苦労をしていない初心者に向って与えられた場合にはどうか。それは通常学人をして彼が今まで極まりきった事実、或は論理的に不可能なこととして受入れてきた事柄が必ずしもそうではないという事実、また従前の物の見方が必ずしも正確ではなく、安心立命に何の寄与をもするものでないという事実に気付かせようという意図をもつものと解せられるであろう。これが分れば学人はこの言葉に専ら心を止めて、何であれその真理を得ようと努力する、という風に向いてこないでもなかろう。強いて学人にこの探求的態度をとらせる、というのが公案の狙いである。かくして学人は、謂わば飛び降りる以外にもはや途のない心的断崖の絶端に達するまでこの探求的態度を推し進めなければならなくなる。この、生への最後の手懸りを放棄するということによって、初めて学人は六祖の要求する「その本来の面目」の全露現を見るにいたるのである。以上によって、公案が、今日、その初期と全く同様のものに当っていないことが分るであろう。彼の努力はこの公案の最後に於て最後の仕上げを施されたのである。近来は公案は始動機として用いられている。今日のように禅修行の最初のものの絶頂点に当ってくる代りに、六祖慧能の問はスターター初めて提示されたとき、それは謂わば明上座の心に作用し来った一切のものの絶頂点に当っていた。彼の努力はこの公案の最後に於て最後の仕上げを施されたのである。近来は公案は始動機として用いられている。今日のように禅修行の最初のものに作用してくる代りに、六祖慧能の問は競技の最後にやって来たのだ。初動に於て多少機械的であることを免れないが、この運動はやがて禅意識の成熟にその初動を与えるものとなっている。公案は謂わば酵母として作用するのである。諸条件がすべて熟するとき、おのずと心開けて悟りの開花を見るのである。このように公案を、心自身の秘密に心を打ち開くための機インストルメント具として用いるということは近

第八章　公案

　白隠はよく片手をつき出して弟子たちに、隻手(せきしゅ)の声を聞け、と要求した。通常音響は両手を拍った時にのみ聞かれるものであって、その限り片手だけからはどんな響も聞える筈がない。ところが白隠は、いわゆる科学的、もしくは論理的な基礎の上に組み立てられた我々の日常経験の根柢を撃とうとしたのである。この根柢的覆滅は、禅経験の基礎の上に新しいものの秩序を打ち樹てる上にどうしてもなくてはならぬものである。さればこそ白隠も弟子たちにこの一見甚しく不自然な非論理的な要求を持ちかけたのである。前の公案は「面目(ザ・フェイス)」に関するもの、すなわち何か見らるべきものであるのに対して、後の方は「声(ザ・サウンド)」に関するもの、すなわち聴覚に訴えるものとなっている。然しその主旨は同じであって、両方とも無尽の宝を秘めた心の密室を開き放とうとするものである。見るとか聞くとかの感官の作用は公案の本質的な意味に何ら影響するものではない。禅匠もいうているように公案は門を敲(たた)くための一片の瓦子、月を指す一本の指に過ぎぬ。意識作用の二元論を綜合もしくは超越——どちらの表現をとるにもせよ——することだけが主眼なのだ。心が隻手の声を聞き得るまでに自由でない限り、自らに反して限定され分割されているのである。創造の秘密を開く鍵をとらえる代りに、心はものの相対性の中に、従ってその皮相性の中に昏昏と埋没しているのである。心がその枷(かせ)を脱しない限り、満ち足りた思いを以て全世界を見得る時期は決してやってくるものではない。隻手の声は当然にして天界に達し地獄に届くのである。それは正しく、個人本来の面目が創造の全領域を時劫のその涯まで見渡し見通すものであるのと同様である。白隠と六祖とは相携えて同じプラットフォームに立っているのだ。

　別の例をとるならば、趙州が祖師西来意(そしせいらいい)(仏教の根本原理の問として通っている)についてたずねられた時「庭(てい)

前の柏樹子」と答えた。

「それでは境(オブジェクティヴ・シンボル)を以て示すということになります。」

「いや、境を以て示してはいない。」

「ではもう一度、仏教の根本原理とは何ですか。」

「庭前の柏樹子。」

趙州の答は依然として同様であった。

これもまた公案として初心者に与えられるものである。

抽象的にいって、此等の公案は常識的な立場からしても全然無意味であるということはできぬ。それらについて推論しようと思えば恐らくその余地は十分あるだろう。例えば白隠の隻手を宇宙或は絶対者の象徴とし、趙州の柏樹子を最高原理の具体的示現とし、これによって仏教の汎神論的傾向を認め得るとするが如きはそれである。然し公案をそのように知性的に理解するのは禅ではない。またこのような形而上学的象徴主義は此処には全然存在しないのである。禅は禅として存在すべき理由を自身に有するものではないのだ。「柏樹子」は永遠に柏樹子であって、汎神論その他のイズムとは全く没交渉である。趙州は最も広い、最も通俗的な意味に於ても哲学者ではなかった。彼はどこまでも禅匠であった。彼の唇頭を衝いて出るものはすべて直に彼の霊的経験(スピリチュアル・イクスピーリエンス)に発する言葉であったのだ。だから、実際、禅には主観と客観、思惟と世界というような二元的対立は存在しないのであるが、如上の主観主義(サブジェクティヴィズム)を離れては、柏樹子も全くその意義を失うのである。もしそれが知性的、概念的

この事実を見失ってはならぬ。さもなければ禅の全構造はばらばらになってしまう。

第八章　公案

説述であるとすれば、我々がそこに含まれている諸観念の論理的聯関を通してその意味の理解に努めようと、ついに難問を解決したと信じようと随意であるが、禅匠たちはその場合ですら禅を去ること三千里、と断言するであろうし、趙州の霊は我々のついに取り払い得なかった帳(スクリーン)の彼方から我々を嘲笑するのであろう。公案は論理的分析のいたり得ぬ心の奥所に於て密密に工夫するのが本旨である。心が熟して、趙州のそれと相諧和するにいたれば柏樹子の意味はおのずと明かになり、もはや問うまでもなく問題の了畢を確信するであろう。

覚鉄觜(かくてつし)と呼ぶ趙州の一弟子は、師匠の死後、趙州が本当に、柏樹子、と答えたかどうか、と質された時、即座に「師匠はそんなことは言わなかった」と明言した。これは全然事実に反している。何故ならば、趙州がそう言ったことは当時周知の事柄であり、覚鉄觜に質した当人も実は承知の上であったのだ。彼の質問はこの趙州の弟子が柏樹子の話についてどれだけの見所を持っているかを試すためであった。そこでなお追及して、「だがこれは誰でも認めていることだ。貴僧ひとり否認するのはどうした訳か」。ところが鉄觜はなおも次のようにべもない否定に対してどれだけ知性的便法を講じて見ても、紛れもない事実そのものと何とか折合をつけることは到底できないのである。このように禅は、柏樹子の話を大乗的汎神論を彷彿する表現のように解する批評家に対しては飽くまで無慈悲である。

以上見来ったように、公案は一般に合理化へのありとあらゆる通路を断ち切るものである。二、三回も師家の前

へ自分の所見を提出すると――これを専門語では参禅というが――諸君は何とも手の下しようがなくなること、必定である。この窮地こそ正しく禅を学ぶ上の真の出発点である。誰しもこの経験なくして禅に入ることはできぬ、この点に達すれば公案はその目的とする所を半ば成就したといってよかろう。

便宜ないい方をすれば――そして一般の読者にはそういう風に禅を表示する方が親しみがあろうと思うが――我々の心には相対的な構造をもつ意識の領域を超えたところに横たわる未知の奥深い世界がある。それを「下意識的」（サブコンシアス）といっても「超意識的」（スプラコンシアス）といっても正確ではない。「超えて」（ビヨンド）という言葉はその漠然たる所在を示すのに極く都合がいいというそれだけの理由で、用いたまでである。ところが実際上我々の意識には「超えて」（ビヨンド）もなければ「下部に」（アンダーニーズ）もなければ「上部に」（アッポン）もなく、いわゆる「未知の領域」（テラ・インコグニタ）は我々普通の物のいい方に対する禅の譲歩である。心は不可分の一全体であって分割を許さないものである。何故ならば我々の知っている意識のどの領域も、一般に概念のぼろ屑が詰っているからである。それらのぼろ屑を脱することが禅経験の成熟に絶対に必要なのであるが、そのために禅の心理学者は時として、我々の心には何か近づきがたい領域があるように示唆するのである。事実上我々の日常意識を離れてそのような領域はないのであるが、一般に理解により便であるためにそういういい方をするまでである。公案がすべての邪魔物を打ち摧いて最後の真理を了得するとき、我々は結局「心の秘密の奥所」などというもの、或は始終神秘的に思われた禅の真理などというものすら、全然存在しないことを悟るのである。

公案は謎でもなければ当意即妙の応酬でもない。それは極く明確な目的、すなわち疑情を呼び起し極限まで推し進める、という目的を有するものである。論理的な根拠によって立つ論述はその合理性を通じて近づくことができ

134

第八章　公案

る。そこに逢着するどんな疑問も困難も、観念の自然の流れを辿ることによっておのずと解決するものである。すべての川は大海に注ぐにきまっている。だが公案は、途上に立ちはだかって、通過しようと焦る如何なる知性的努力をも圧倒し去ろうとする鉄壁である。趙州が「庭前の柏樹子」という、白隠がその片手を突き出すとき、これにとりつく論理的な方途というものはさらにないのである。思想の進展が突然中断されたように感じられる。諸君は躊躇し疑惑し動揺するが、全然通過を許さぬように見えるこの壁をどう打ち破ってよいかは分らぬ。これが極点に達すると、諸君の全人格、内奥の意志、最も深い性情ともいうべきものは、今や全状況に結末をつけるという退っ引きならぬ一途に追いこまれて、もはや自己（ノー・セルフ）を思わず非己を思わず、かれを思わずこれを思わず、遅疑なく逡巡せずして従来嘗て知らぬ心の領域を打開するのである。知性的にはこれは論理の二元論の限界超越であるが、同時に新生であり、物のあるがままの作用に観入するを得しめる内的感能の覚醒である。公案の意味はここに初めて明瞭になる。氷がつめたく凍結することは誰しも知っているが、それと同様に明明白白となるのである。眼は見、耳は聞く、それはその通りであるが、より高次の知覚である、全一全体としての心である。或は心の奥の心であるといってよい。禅の修行は、正しく単なる知性の作用以上に出る何物かがあるという不動の確信を懐かしめる点にその価値を有している。

一旦公案の壁が突き破られ、知性的障礙（がい）が取り払われると、謂わば諸君は、自身の日常的、相対的意識へ還帰するのである。片方の手はいま一方の手と拍ち合さない限り音を発することはない。柏樹子は庭前にすっくと立っている。人々は悉く眼横鼻直（がんのうびじょく）である。禅は今や何物にも況して平常的なものである。以前には遥かの遠方にあると思

っていた田地が実は我々の明けても暮れても踏み歩いているこの田地であるということが、今にしてようやく分っていたのだ。悟りから出てくるとき、眼前には、多種多様の事物あり観念あり、兼ねてその論理性をも具えた親しい世界がある。我々はそれらを「すべて善し」と肯定するのである。

未だ公案の組織の現われない時代には、禅はより自然であり恐らくはより純粋であった。しかしその精神に参じ得るものは少数の選ばれたるものに過ぎなかった。諸君がその時代に生きていたとして、荒々しく肩を摑まれたらどうするだろうか。乾屎橛と呼ばれたら何と解するだろうか。通りにしてその報酬に打たれたらどうするだろうか。諸君に、禅の涯底を究めようとする鋼鉄のような決心があり、通りにしてその報酬に打たれたらどうするだろうか。諸君に、禅の涯底を究めようとする鋼鉄のような決心があり、多年工夫の後首尾よく禅を体得するかも知れない。然しかかる例は今日の時代では稀有のことに属する。我々はあらゆる種類の仕事に心を奪われているため、なかなか独力で禅への迷路にも似た通路へ踏み込めるものではない。唐朝初期の頃は、人々の心はより単純であり、信篤く、知性的偏執を詰込まれてはいなかった。然しこのような状態は物の性質上いつまでも続くものではない。禅の活力を維持するためには、禅をより近づき易くその程度にまで通俗化し得るような仕組みを案出する必要があった。公案による訓練は、若き世代のため、来らんとする者のために、どうしても確立されなければならなかったのだ。禅はその性質上真宗や基督教と同じ意味での民衆的宗教とはなり得ないのであるが、それが、やはり、幾世紀もの間その伝統を守り続けてきたという事実は、主として公案の組織によるものと思われる。それ程までに、浄土教的な念仏修行が滲みこんでいる。禅の純粋な形では存続せず、相承の系譜も絶たれている。そしてこの事実が、坐禅の修行とが依然としてその正統的代表者を擁しているのはひとり日本に於てのみである。

第八章　公案

相俟って公案に参ずるという組織に基づいている、と信ずべき理由は多多存している。この組織が著しく人工的であり深刻な危険を蔵していることは疑わないが、その受け渡しが適切である場合、禅の命脈はそれを通じて伝わるのである。真に有能な師匠の下で正しくこれを追究する者に対して、禅経験は可能であり、悟りは必ず開けるであろう。

かくして我々はこの禅経験が一定の修行の過程を透過することによって得られるものであることを知るのである。すなわち公案訓練は、はっきりした目的を念頭に置いて明確に打ち樹てた一つの組織であるのだ。禅は、神秘経験が得られる幸運を、その偶然に来り訪れるのに委ねて為すところのない神秘主義の諸形式とはその趣を異にするものである。従って公案の組織化こそ禅の特色を鮮かに示すものである。禅を、忘我（トランス）への沈降、単なる凝心への没溺、黙照的訓練への没頭から救うものはこれである。禅は生きるそのはたらきに於て生を把握しようとする。生の流れを停めてこれを観ようというのは禅の仕事ではない。不断に公案が念頭にあるということは、心をつねに一杯にしておくこと、すなわち十分に働かせておくことである。悟りはこのはたらきの只中に得られるものであって、まま想像されるようにそれを抑圧することによって得られるものではない。禅が、通常理解され行われている「瞑想」と如何に相違するものであるかは、公案の性質について以上述べ来ったところによって一層はっきりしたことと思う。

この禅の組織化はシナでは五代すなわち十世紀に始まっているが、その完成は徳川時代の白隠の天才に負うている。公案の弊もさることながら、日本の禅を全滅より救ったものは公案であったのだ。今日シナの禅は如何なる帰趣を辿りつつあるだろうか。我々の関知する限り、それは先ず名目だけのものである。また今日の日本に於ける曹洞宗

137

の禅修行の一般的傾向について見るならば、そのやり方に幾多の長所の存することは否定できぬ。それは十分心して学ばねばならぬ。然し禅を生きる、という点に関しては公案組織を依用する臨済宗に恐らくより活発なものがあろう。

あるいはいうかも知れぬ。「禅が事実君の主張する程に知性の視圏を超えるものであるなら、そこには如何なる組織もあってはならぬ。また実際如何なる組織もあり得ない。何故ならば、組織の概念そのものが知性的だからである。一貫した立場に立とうというなら、禅は過程とか組織とか訓練などという臭味を一切払拭した一箇単純絶対の経験に止まらねばならぬ」。理論的には、というよりも窮極的には、全くその通りである。さればこそ禅を「直下」に主張するに当っては、公案もなければ、迂遠な説示もないのだ。唯一本の杖、唯一本の扇子、唯一語、それでよいのだ。「それは杖だ」とか「音が聞えた」とか「拳が見える」とかいうてさえ、もう禅は影も形もない。それは電光の閃きにも似たものである。禅には一念の思いを容れる空間や時間さえもないのである。前にも断っておいたように、こういう書物を書くというのも実際は譲歩であり、弁護であり、妥協であるのだ。況んや禅の全面的組織化に於てをやである。

外部の人々にとってはこの「組織化」も組織とは思われぬであろう。何故ならばそれは矛盾に充ちて居り、また禅匠たちの間でさえも数々の相違があって、全く去就に迷わせるからである。一人が主張するところを他の一人はにべもなく否定するか、さもなくば辛辣な批評を下すという有様に、門外者はこの何時果てるとも思われぬ絶望的な葛藤の解釈に苦しむのである。然し、禅は実際上その表面から考うべきではないのだ。組織とか合理性とか、一

第八章　公案

貫性とか、矛盾とか、相違とか、そういう言葉は禅の表面にこそ相当するものである。禅を理解するには、無縫の金襴を一度すっかり裏返しにして裏側から吟味しなければならぬ。それでこそ縦糸・横糸の交錯を一目に見てとることができるのである。この裏返して見るということが禅には必要なのである。

禅匠によって公案の扱い方が如何に違うかを見るために一例を挙げることとしよう。唐朝の偉大な禅匠であった汾陽は次のように語っている。

「この拄杖（しゅじょう）が何であるかが分るものがあったら、その人間の禅の修行は終ったようなものだ。」

これはいかにも単純な公案のようである。通常禅匠は一本の長い杖を持っている。今日ではその宗教的権威の標幟の一種となっているが、昔は実地の行脚に携えたものであって、山を登るにも川を渡るにも用いられたものである。そういう最も手近なものの一つであったので、禅匠は何かというとこれを弟子たちの前へ突き出してその説法を活かしたのである。それが屢々僧たちの間では大議論の種となったものだ。さていま一人の禅匠、泐潭澄（ろくたんちょう）は、あからさまに汾陽の意見に反対して次のように断言している。

「その拄杖が何であるかが分るようなものがいたら、その男は地獄に入ること箭（や）のごとくであろう。」

これが本当なら、禅を学ぼうと思い立つものはいないだろう。澄の真意は一体どこにあるのだろう。彼は急進的ではなく、いかにも合理的で無邪気で三人目の禅匠破庵は、やはりこの拄杖について一言を吐いている。曰く、

「その拄杖の何であるかが分る者がいたら、すぐ傍の壁へ立てかけさせたらいいじゃないか。」

此等の師匠たちは、皆、同じ事実を主張し同じ真理を指しているのだろうか。それとも彼等は言葉の上のみなら

睡龍は或る日壇に上りその拄杖を示してこう言った、
「自分はこの三十年間此処で過して来たが、それというのも全くこの杖のお蔭である。」
すると一僧が進み出て問うた、
「どんなお蔭ですか。」
「この杖をついて川も渡ったし山も越えた、全くこの杖がなかったらどうすることもできはしない。」
後に招慶という別の禅匠がこの話を聞いて言った、
「自分ならそうは言わなかったろう。」
すかさず一僧がたずねた、
「ではどう言われますか。」
すると招慶は拄杖を取って地面に降りさっさとどこかへ出て行った。
破庵はこの二人について次のように見ている。
「睡龍の杖は仲々佳い。だが惜しいことには龍頭蛇尾であった。そこを招慶がとらえたのだ。然しその結果もやはり面白くなかった。彼のやり方は虎を画いて斑点を附するようなものである。どんなお蔭かとたずねられた時、何故彼はその杖を取って衆僧の前へ放り出さなかったのか。そうすれば本物の龍となり虎となって雲を呼び風を起したであろうに。」
これは一体どうしたことなのだ、結局は空騒ぎではないか、と言いたいところである。近代の禅が一つの体系で

140

第八章　公案

あるというなら、それはどういう体系なのか、それは一見いかにも混沌としているではないか、また禅匠たちの見方は矛盾・撞著も甚しいではないか、と反問したいところである。然し禅の観点からすれば、これらの混乱のすべてを貫くひとつの流れがあるのだ。そしてどの禅匠も、他の禅匠を最も力強い仕方で支持しているのだ。外見上の背反は何等真実の保証を妨げるものではない。このように、論理的な仕方に於てではなく如何にも禅らしい仕方に於て互に補足し合うところに、公案の生命と真理とがあるのである。かくも豊富な効果を生み出すということ、死せる説述の到底能くすることではない。白隠の「隻手」、趙州の「柏樹子」、六祖の「本来の面目」は、いずれも髄の髄まで生気が充実している。一度その核心に触れるとき、全宇宙は、我々が論理や分析で埋葬したその墓場から動き出してくるであろう。

禅修行者に課せられる公案についてなお進んで知りたいと思う人々のために、さらに二、三の例を挙げることとする。仰山が潙山から鏡を受けたときのことである。彼はそれを衆僧の前へ持ち出して言った。

「此処に潙山から届けられた鏡がある。これは潙山のものだろうか、自分のものだろうか。もし自分のものであるというなら、どうして潙山から送ってきたのか。また潙山のものであるというのはどうしたわけか。能く一句を道い得るものがあれば鏡はこのままにしておく。もしなければ粉々に打ち砕いてしまうが、どうだ。」

彼はこれを三度繰返したがついに応ずる者がなかったので、鏡は毀されてしまった。

洞山が雲門を訪ねて教えを求めた時、雲門は問うた。

「何処から来たか。」

「査度からです。」

「この夏は何処で過したか。」

「湖南の報慈で。」

「いつそこを発ったか。」

「八月の二十五日に発ちました。」

雲門は突如として叫んだ。

「三十棒を喰わすべきところだが、まあ勘弁してやろう。」

夕刻洞山は再び雲門の室にやって来て、三十棒を受けなければならぬような落度はどこにあるのか、とたずねた。

雲門曰く、「飯袋子！ お前はそんな調子で江西・湖南とうろつき歩くつもりか。」

潙山が微睡しているところへ仰山が入って来た。人が来た気配に潙山は身を転じて壁の方を向いた。

仰山曰く、「和尚は弟子である私にどうしてそういう他人行儀をなさるのですか。」

仰山が部屋から出て行こうとすると、師はこれを呼び戻して言った。

すると師は睡から醒めたように身を動かした。仰山が部屋から出て行こうと思うと盥に水を満し、手拭を添えて持ってきた。その水で師匠は顔を洗った。ところ

「お前、ひとつ当てて見ないか。」

「今夢を見たところだ。話して聞かそうか。」

仰山が耳を澄まして待っていると、潙山が言った。

仰山は部屋を出て行ったと思うと盥に水を満し、手拭を添えて持ってきた。その水で師匠は顔を洗った。ところ

第八章　公案

が彼がまだ自分の席に帰らないうちに、いま一人の弟子香厳が入って来た。

師曰く、「我々は今神通を行じていたところだ。——それは並々の通力ではないのだ。——自分は今迄下にいて貴方がたのおやりになったことはよく承知して居ります。」

香厳曰く、「ではそれを話して見よ。」

香厳は、つと起って一杯の茶を持ってきた。「両人とも仲々よく分っている。潙山は両人を評して次のように語っている。その智慧と神通は舎利弗や目連以上である。」

石霜が歿した時、弟子たちは当然首座の僧が跡を継ぐものと考えた。ところが故石霜の侍者であった九峯（唐末五代の禅僧）が言った。

「お待ちなさい。ひとつたずねたいことがある。師の後継者はこの問に答え得る人でなければならぬ。先師はつねにこういわれた。『古廟裏の香炉の如くし去れ、冷湫湫地にし去れ、一条の白練の如くし去れ、口辺に醭（かび）を生ぜしめよ』。これをどう解するか。」

首座曰く、「一色辺の事（絶対に空じ去った境涯）を示すものである。」

九峯曰く、「果して貴僧には先師の真意が全然分っていない。」

首座曰く、「それでは香に火を点じてくれ。もし自分が先師の真意を得ていないなら、香煙の尽きるまでに空却の境地（トランス）に入ることはできないだろう。」

纔に香煙の起った頃には首座はもう無意識の状態に入り、もはや二度と覚醒しなかった。逝ける友の背を撫でながら九峯は言った。

143

「空却（トランス）の状態に入るという点ではおんみは立派な範を示した。しかし残念なことには先師の真意は夢に見ることさえもできなかった。」

この例は、禅が空無に没し去るとは全然別物であることを雄弁に物語っている。

公案の数は千七百といい伝えられているがこれは甚だ大まかな数え方である。実効に関する限り、禅の窮極的真理に心眼を開くには、精精十則以内、もしくは五則以内、乃至唯一則でも事足りるであろう。徹底した悟りは、禅の窮極性に対する不撓の信念によって裏づけられた最も自己犠牲的な傾倒によってのみ達せられるものである。それは臨済系修行者の普通にやるような、単に公案の階梯を一歩一歩登って行くというやり方では達し得られるものではない。公案の数は実際上大悟と何の関係もない。どうしても欠くことのできないのは信念であり人格的努力である。それなくしては禅は泡沫に過ぎなくなる。禅を思弁や抽象と見る人はその秘奥を得ることはできないであろう。それは最高の意志力を通じてのみ測り得るものである。幾百の公案があろうと、或は宇宙に充満する事事物物にも似て数え尽すことのできぬ公案があろうと、我々にとってはどうでもよいことである。事物の活きてはたらくところを看取して遺憾のない洞察力を得ることこそ緊要事である。これさえできれば、公案はひとりでに片が附くというものである。

公案方式の危険が潜んでいるのは此処である。動もすれば、内的生命の開発という禅の真実の目的を忘れて、公案が禅修行のすべてであるような気になる。この陥穽に落ちた人の数は多く、その結果は禅の腐敗と衰運となって現われている。大慧がその師圜悟の編纂した公案一百則を焼き棄てたのもこの弊を知り過ぎる程知っていたからである。この一百則は雪竇（せっちょう）禅師が禅文献中より精要をすぐってその一一に頌古を附したものである。大慧は真の禅

第八章　公案

者であった。その師圜悟が此等の抜萃に垂示・評唱・著語を附したとき、彼は師の意図を察知した。また、此等がやがて禅の自殺的武器となるであろうことをも見抜いた。さればこそこれを悉く火の中へ投じたのである。

然しこの書は焼け残って依然我々の手中にあり、いわゆる宗門第一の書となっている。それは今以て禅学上の疑点解決のために参照される標準的テキストであり権威である。この書は日本では『碧巖集』の名で知られている。

然し門外の人々にとっては封印された書物である。第一にその漢文は古典的な語彙・語法に従うものではなく、語勢は如何にも壮であるが唐宋時代の俗語が到る処に駆使されている。そしてその俗語は今日禅の文献以外に跡づけることのできないものである。第二にその文体はこの種述作に特有のものであり、その思想と表現とは、そこに普通の仏教的語彙或は少くとも穏かな古典的様式を期待する読者を狼狽させる程である。此等の文学上の難点に加えて、この『碧巖』には当然禅が横溢している。然し公案が禅者によって如何に扱われるかを知りたい人はやはりこの書を参看した方がよい。

この外にも幾分『碧巖』の様式に倣って公案を扱った典籍がいくつかある。『從容録』・『無門関』・『槐安国語』等がそれである。また実際、語録として知られている種類の多い禅籍や禅匠たちの伝記は、いずれも公案を禅独特の仕方で扱っている。知名の禅匠のほとんど誰もがその語録を遺している。そういう語録がいわゆる禅文学の大部分を形造っているのである。仏教の哲学的研究が各種の詳細複雑な註疏・釈義・科文に富んでいるのに対して、禅の提供するところはこれと著しい対照をなす寸鉄的な言葉、警句的な暗示、辛辣な評唱である。『碧巖集』もしくは『從容録』はその特色はその詩への傾斜である。公案は詩的に鑑識され或は批評されている。禅文学の今一つの好箇の一例である。前者は上記雪竇の手に成るものであり、後者は宏智（南宋の禅僧）が別種の公案の集録に同

じく詩文的評唱を附したものである。禅が最も意を得た表現を哲学よりもむしろ詩に見出すのは当然である。何故ならば禅は知性よりも一層感性に親しいからである。その詩的偏倚は自然避けがたいものである。

原註
(1) この主題をより詳細に取扱ったものとしては拙著英文『禅論』第二巻参照。
(2) 般若は我々の霊的生の深さを尽す最高の直観力であり、当然単なる知性をはるかに超えるものである。それ以上のことは、拙著英文『禅論』第三巻、般若波羅蜜の章について見られたい。
(3) 衆生無辺誓願度　煩悩無尽誓願断　法門無量誓願学　仏道無上誓願成。
(4) 日本に於ける坐禅の修行に関しては、拙著英文『禅論』第二巻、頁二八四―二八七参照。
(5) 今日のシナ仏教は、大抵の僧院が禅宗に属すると称しているにも拘わらず、禅と念仏との奇異な混合である。そこでは『般若心経』と並んで『阿弥陀経』が読誦されている。
(6) 此等はいずれも参禅の手始めに与えられる公案である。

第九章

禅堂と雲水の生活

禅堂は禅がその僧たちを教育する道場である。それがどういう仕組みになっているかを見れば禅の実践的、訓練的な方面はあらまし分るというものである。それは独自(ユニーク)であって日本禅宗の主要な寺院は大抵これを備えている。
　禅堂に於ける雲水の生活を見るとき、我々は印度に於ける僧伽(サンガ)の生活を憶わしめられるのである。
　この方式(システム)は一千年以上も昔、シナの禅匠百丈によって創設されたものである。彼は自身の生活の指導原理とした有名な格言を残している。「一日不作(いちじつなさざれば)、一日不食(いちじつくらわず)」、すなわち、働かざれば食わず、ということである。高齢の師匠にはその好んでやる野外の作務(ワーク)は無理である、と思った忠実な弟子たちは、幾度諫めても聴き入れようとしないので、彼の農具をすっかり隠してしまった。すると百丈は「一日不作、一日不食」とて食事を摂ろうとしなかった。どの禅堂に於ても作務、特に普通賤しい労働とされているような仕事が雲水の生活の重要な要素となっているのである。従って、掃き・拭き・炊事・薪拾い・耕作、遠近村落への托鉢等、その中には手仕事が随分多い。然しどんな仕事も彼等の威厳を傷つけるものとは考えられていない。そして彼等の間には濃(こま)やかな同胞としての感情が

第九章　禅堂と雲水の生活

行亘っている。彼等は手足を労する作業の神聖を信じている。その作業が如何に困難であろうと賤められているものであろうと、彼等は決して厭がることをせず、それぞれ分を尽して忙しく立ち働くのである。彼等は、たとえば印度に於て見られるような一部の僧侶や托鉢修道者のように怠け者ではないのだ。

心理学的に見てこれは素晴らしいことである。何故ならば筋肉を働かすということは瞑想の習慣から来る心の沈滞に対する最善の療法であるからである。禅は甚だこの思わしくない結果を生じ勝ちなのだ。大抵の宗教的隠遁者に附きものの困厄(トラブル)は、心と身の調和を欠くということである。彼等の体は常に心から引き離されている。彼等は、別別に体があり心がある、と想像し、この分離が単に観念的なものであることを忘れている。禅修行の目的はこの基本的な分別を払い去るにあるため、それはいずれか一方の観念を強く印象づけるような修行を避けるよう絶えず注意しているのである。悟りはまさしく、我々の分別的観念の掃蕩(そうとう)し去られた境涯に達するにある。尤もこれは決して空無の状態ではないのである。寂静主義的な瞑想から屢々生ずる心の沈滞が悟りの成熟に何の助けにもならないことはかくして明かであり、禅修行上一段の進境を希望する人々は、当然、それが心的活動の謂わば流動性をついには全く停止させてしまうようなことがないように、常にこの点に警戒すべきである。これは、少くとも、禅者が単なる禅那の修行に反対する理由の一つである。常に忙しい体は心をも常に忙しく、従って、新鮮に、健全に、そして慧敏にするであろう。

倫理(モラル)の点からいえば、体力を惜しみなく行使する作業は何によらず考え方の健全さを証立てるものである。これは禅に於ては特に真実である。実地の生活に力強く有効に反映しないような抽象的観念は何の価値もないものとせられる。確信は経験をとおして得らるべきものであって、抽象によって得らるべきものではない。倫理的主張は

149

何処にあっても知性的判断に優越するものでなければならぬ。怠惰な瞑想は我々の仕事ではない、というのが禅者の主張である。すなわち真理は個人の生ける経験に依拠しなければならぬ。勿論彼等はいわゆる「反芻」には終始反対し、静坐の間になした省察を行為に移して、その妥当性を活きて現実の上に検証するのである。もし禅宗寺院が作務の間に得られた教訓を同化しようと思うならば坐禅を修しなければならぬ。何にもあれ作務の間に得られた教訓を同化しようと思うならば坐禅を修しなければならぬ。何にもあれ坐禅の修行は単なる催眠的、忘我誘導(トランス)的方式の線まで堕落し、シナ・日本の禅匠たちが蓄積し来った財宝の一切は何の価値もない老廃物のように捨て去られたであろう、というのが私の強い確信である。

いわゆる禅堂は、その大きさは収容する雲水の数によって異っているが、一棟の長方形の建物である。例えば鎌倉の円覚寺に取れば約35×65呎(フィート)であって三、四十名の雲水を収容する。一人の雲水に割当てられる面積は畳一枚であって、そこで彼は坐禅し瞑想し就寝もするのである。夜具は夏冬に拘わらず約5×6呎の蒲団一枚を越えることはできぬ。定った枕などというものはなく、各自の所持品を臨時に枕に仕立てて間に合わせるのである。その所持品もほとんど無いにひとしい。袈裟と衣と二、三冊の書物、剃刀、持鉢一組がその全部で、彼等はこれを3×10×3½呎(インチ)位の一閑張(いっかんばり)の函に納めておくのである。これを袈裟文庫という。旅行の際はこの文庫を幅の広い紐で首に掛けて前へ下げる。こうして所持品全部がその持主と共に移動するのである。

「一衣一鉢、樹下石上」などというと印度の遊行僧の生活が彷彿と浮び出るが、これに較べるならば、今日の雲水は仲々多くをあてがわれているといわねばならぬ。とはいうものの、その需要品は最低限度まで押し約められたものであって、雲水の生活を手本にすれば誰でも単純な、恐らくはこの上なく単純な生活を営み得ること必定である。仏教では、所有欲は人間を苦しめ

150

第九章　禅堂と雲水の生活

最悪の煩悩の一つとされている。事実世間であのように多くの悲惨事を惹起するところのものは、人類一切を貫く所有への衝動である。権力を欲する許りに強者は常に弱者を制圧し、富が欲しい許りに富者と貧者とは常に仇敵の剣を交える。この獲得し所有したいという衝動が根こそぎにされない限り、国際間の戦争は暴威を逞しうし、社会不安は増大するばかりである。一体社会は、歴史始って以来いやという程見せつけられてきたような基礎とは全く異った基礎の上に再組織することができないものだろうか。我々は、個人的もしくは国家的強大を唯一の目的として富を蓄積し勢力を累積することを止められぬものだろうか。人間生活が非合理に終始するのに絶望した仏教徒たちは今一方の極端に走り、自然にかなった何ら邪心のない生の享受をすら捨離してしまった。それはともかくとして、雲水の所有を一箇の小函に納めしめるという禅の理念は、それだけではあまり有効ではないにしても、現今の社会秩序に対する無言の抗議であるのだ。

印度では比丘は決して午後には食事を摂らない。一日一食を度としている。その朝食は欧米流の朝食ではないのだ。雲水も夕食を摂らぬことになっているのであるが、気候からくる必要は無視しがたく、実際はそれに相当する一食をしたためている。然し気休めまでにこれを「薬石」と呼んでいる。早朝まだ暗いうちにしたためる朝食は粥と漬物である。主な食事は午前十時頃で、米（或は麦飯）と味噌汁と漬物とである。午後四時には昼飯の残りを喫することになっていて特にそのための調理をしない。親切な檀家から招待を受けたり、非時のお斎（とき）でも供せられない限り、彼等の食事は年が年中この通りである。清貧と単純とが彼等の規範である。

然し禁欲が禅僧の生活理想だ、などと結論してはならぬ。禅の第一義は禁欲にもなければ他のいかなる倫理的

方式(システム)にもない。もし禅が抑圧もしくは離脱の建前を擁護するように見えるとしても、それは単に表面上のことに過ぎぬ。というのは禅は仏教の一分枝として多少は印度教的禁欲的修行の習気を受け伝えているからである。然し禅堂生活の中心観念は、与えられるものを只浪費することなく真に活用することにあるのだ。これはまた我々自身の肉体も例外なく、事実、知性・想像力その他一切の心的能力は、我々を囲繞する自然的事物と共に、個人的恣意・欲望の満足のためにのみ与えられているのであって、個人的恣意・欲望の満足のためにのみ与えられているのではない。そのような恣意・欲望は他人の主張する利益や権利と衝突しこれを侵害すること必定である。雲水の生活の単純と清貧との基調をなす思想にはこうした考えが含まれているのである。

食事の時刻には雲板が鳴らされる。雲水たちは各自に一組の持鉢を携え列を作って禅堂を出、食堂に入る。然し直日(じきじつ)が鈴を鳴らすまでは著席しない。各自の携帯する持鉢は木製或は紙製の漆器であって、成り鳥の巣のように重なり合って納まるようになっている。『般若心経』を誦し「五観」(食事に関する省察五箇条)を唱すると、供給(くきゅう)(給仕役の僧)が飯と味噌汁を配る。いよいよ箸をとる段になると彼等はその素晴しい食事にとりかかる前に、幽界の鬼神諸霊の冥福を祈って各〻自分の鉢内から七粒ばかりの飯粒を供える。これを生(さ)飯(ば)という。食事中は静粛が一堂を支配する。持鉢は音をたてぬように扱われ、一語も発せられず、況して会話などは一切行われない。頼みたいことがあれば手の操作で合図をする。食事は彼等にとって厳粛な行事である。二杯目の飯を所望する場合は合掌した両手を前方へ出す。供給はそれを認めると飯櫃をもってその僧の前方頃合のところに坐る。所望の僧は椀をとり上げ自分の手でその底を軽く拭う。ほこりが附著していて供給の手を汚したりするこ

第九章　禅堂と雲水の生活

とのないように、飯を盛って貰う間は件の僧は合掌したままである。それで十分という場合には両の掌を静に擦り合せてその意を伝える。

あてがわれた食物は「残物の端切れをも集めて」すっかり頂戴するというのが雲水たちの規則になっている。それが彼等の宗教なのだ。三杯目か四杯目をすませると食事は終りになる。直日は柝木（ひょうしぎ）を叩き、供給は湯を運んでくる。僧たちは各こその一番大きな椀にそれを充して他の食器をその中で綺麗に洗い、その所持する布巾で拭う。次に木製の桶が搬ばれて汚れ物を受けて廻る。僧は各自旧のごとくその椀を組み合せて布で包む。食卓は元通りすっかり取り片附けられて、例の供養の飯粒のみが残る。もう一度柝木が鳴ると僧たちは再び入って来た時と同様に列を作って静粛に且つ整然と食堂を出て行く。

雲水の勤勉は人のよく知るところである。堂内の修行に当てられていない日は、普通朝食がすむとすぐに——夏なら五時半頃、冬なら六時半頃——境内に出たり禅堂附属の農園を耕したりしているのが見受けられる。やがて僧たちは幾組かに分れて近傍の村へ托鉢に出かける。彼等は寺院の内外を常にきちんと清掃し整頓しておく。「禅寺へ行ったようだ」といえば掃除が申分なく行届いていることを意味する程である。禅堂には普通檀家というものが附いていて、禅堂から定期的にその家を訪ね、米や野菜の提供を受けるのである。このような場合彼等は屢々数哩（マイル）の遠方まで出かけて行く。彼等が貰った南瓜や甘薯や大根を荷車に積んで田舎道を曳いて帰る風景は屢々見受けられるところである。彼等はまた時々薪や焚きつけを集めに山へ出かける。彼等は農業についても一通りを心得ている。彼等は自給自足して行かねばならぬので、農夫にもなれば熟練工にもなりまた慣れない労働者にもなる。彼

等は専門家の指導の下に禅堂その他の建物を建てることも珍しくない。彼等は普通の労働者と同様に、恐らくはそれ以上に真剣に働く。彼等の労働は決していい加減なものではない。真剣に働くことがその宗教だからである。

僧たちは自治的な一集団をなしている。彼等自身の中には炊事係もあれば監督もあり、支配人（マネジャー）、寺男（セックストン）、儀式を司る係りもある。禅堂の老師もしくは師家は集団の中心ではあるが、直接に監督に当ることなくこれを久参の僧たちに委ねている。その人格は多年の修行を通じて十分見届けられている。このように禅の諸原則を論ずるとき、その深遠微妙の「形而上学」に驚歎し、禅僧たちとは深刻な、色青ざめた、項垂れた、世間を忘れ果てた人々に違いない、と想像する人があっても不思議ではない。然しその実生活に於て彼等は下廻りの仕事を何でもやる極めて有り触れた人間なのである。彼等は快活で諧謔を弄する者もあり、何かというと互に助け合う。百丈の精神がここにはっきり現われているもののすべきことではないと思われている労働をも彼等は蔑視しない。普通に低級で教養あるものゝすべきことではないと思われている労働をも彼等は蔑視しない。僧たちの諸能力はこのようにして円満な発達を遂げるのである。彼等は形式的な、すなわち文学上の教育を受けない。そういう教育は大抵書物や抽象的教示によって得られるところのものである。彼等の修得するところは実際的で実効を有する。何故ならば禅堂生活の基本原理は「なすことによって学ぶ」（ラーニング・バイ・ドゥイング）にあるからだ。彼等は軟教育を蔑視し、病気上りの人間のためにこしらえた流動食同様に見做している。牝獅子は仔を産んで三日経つと断崖から突き落して、その仔が再び自分のところまで攀じ登ってくるかどうかを試すといわれている。このテストに合格できないものはその場限り見棄てられるという訳である。その真偽はともあれ、自分の弟子たちを屢ミ外見上不親切の限りをつくして扱う禅匠の狙いはこれによく似ている。

雲水たちは、衣は身を暖めるに足らず、食も飢を凌ぐに

第九章　禅堂と雲水の生活

足らず、睡眠も十分に摂れないことが珍しくない上に、有り余る肉体上・精神上の労働がある。此等の外部的などうしてもやらねばならぬ仕事と、内に燃える熱望とは相俟って禅僧の性格に作用し、屢々飽参者と呼ばれる典型的な人間性を生み出すのである。今日なお臨済系各禅堂で行われているこの独特な教育方式は在俗者の間では余り知られていないが、それでも此頃は禅堂生活をできるだけよく知ろうと望む傾向が見受けられる。しかし近代商業主義と機械化の無慈悲な荒波は全東洋を席捲して隅々に及び、静かな退隠の余地はほとんど残されていない有様である。この禅の孤島さえも遠からず卑しい物質主義の波濤下に没し去るかも知れぬ。僧たち自身すらそのかみの禅匠たちの精神を謬り始めている。この禅堂教育に改良すべきものがあることは否定できぬが、禅の命脈を将来長く存続させようと思う限り、その生活と労働に対するすぐれて宗教的な敬虔な精神は是非とも保存しなければならぬ。

理の上からいえば、禅は宇宙を包み込んで差別の法則に支配されないものである。しかしこれは全く足を踏み込らしやすい地盤であって、なかなか直立して歩くことができぬ。一部の中世神秘家のように禅修行者も時として放逸の徒と化し、あらゆる自制を失うことがある。歴史はその証人であり、心理学はかかる堕落の過程を容易に説明することができる。一禅匠は嘗て語っている。「意は毘盧頂顗(ねい)を踏み、行は三尺の童子を拝す」。禅堂の生活は細密に規定されて居り、その一々がこの精神に則って励行されるのである。これによって禅はかの一部中世神秘家の水準に堕ちることを免れたのである。禅の教育に於て禅堂生活が重きをなす所以である。

唐朝の丹霞が首都慧林寺に泊った時、偶々非常な寒さであった。彼は寺に安置してあった木仏の一体を持って

155

て薪の代りに燃やして暖を採った。院主はこれを見て大いに怒り詰問した。
「どうして貴僧はわが院の木仏を焼くなどという大それたことをするのか。」
ところが丹霞は杖で灰を掻きまぜて何かを探す真似をしながら言った。
「自分はこの灰から仏舎利を集めようと思っているのだ。」
「木仏からどうして舎利を集めようというのか。」
「舎利さえもないようなものなら残りの二体も焼いてしまおうか。」

その後院主は丹霞のこの冒瀆と見える行為を責めたがために眉毛が脱落してしまったが、丹霞は何の仏罰をも被らなかったという。

史実であるかどうかは疑わしいが、この話は有名であり、どの禅匠も冒瀆漢丹霞の見識を異口同音に認めている。一僧がその師に丹霞の仏像を焼いた趣意をたずねた時、師は答えた、
「寒ければ火の燃えている炉辺へ行くのは当り前だ。」
「では丹霞は行けなかったのでしょうか、どうですか。」
「お互に、暑ければ川のほとりの藪蔭へ出かけて行くじゃないか。」

純粋に禅的な立場から見た丹霞の真価はともかくとして、このような行為が甚だ冒瀆的であり、敬虔な仏教徒として避けるべきであると見做されることは疑を容れない。未だ禅の理解に徹しない者はどんな行き過ぎを、さらにどんな悪事を仕出かさないとも限らない――しかも禅の名に於て。こうした理由から、心の驕りが影をひそめ、謙譲の杯が最後の一雫まで飲み乾されるように、禅堂の規律は厳重を極めているのである。

第九章　禅堂と雲水の生活

明朝の雲棲袾宏が『緇門崇行録』を執筆していると、独りよがりの僧がやって来て問うた、
「禅には何ひとつ崇むべきも不崇むべきもないのに、そのような書物を書いて何になりますか。」
袾宏は答えた、「五蘊はとめどなく縺れ合い、四大は甚だ強盛であるのに、どうして悪がないなどというのか。」
僧はなおも主張した、「四大は畢竟空であり、五蘊も何ら実在とすべきものではありません。」
袾宏はその面上に一掌を与えていった、「学得底なら腐る程ある。お前も未だ本物ではなさそうだ。もう一度何とか言って見ろ。」
然し僧は何も言わず怒気を満面にあらわして出て行こうとした。禅匠は微笑を湛えていった、
「そこだ。何故お前は自分の面上の汚れを拭おうとしないのか。」
禅の修行に於ては一切を照破する洞察力が深い謙下の意識、柔軟の心情と相携えて動かねばならぬのである。

禅堂生活には僧たちの心的訓練のために特別に設けられた時期があって、その期間中僧たちは絶対に必要な場合の外は作務を一切止めることになっている。この期間は接心と称せられている。それは「夏安居」並に「雪安居」（もしくは「冬安居」）の二季に一週間を限りとして数回行われる。一般に夏安居は四月に始まり八月に終る。冬安居の方は十月から二月までである。接心とは「心を摂めて昏沈散乱させないこと」を意味する。接心中は僧は禅堂内に禁足され、朝は不断よりも早く起きて、夜は不断よりも遅くまで坐禅を続ける。また接心間は毎日「講座」もしくは「提唱」が行われる。用本は『碧巌集』・『臨済録』・『無門関』・『虚堂録』・『槐安国語』等のいずれかである。

『碧巌集』は前にも述べたように公案一百則をすぐってこれに頌古・垂示・評唱・著語を附したものである。『臨済録』は臨済宗の開祖の説法問答等の集録である。『無門関』も公案四十八則を集めたものであって、禅独特の評と頌とが附せられているが『碧巌』よりも遥かに簡単である。『虚堂録』は宋朝の虚堂禅師の語録・説法・詩偈等から成っている。彼は大応国師の師匠であって、その禅の系統は今なお日本に栄えているものの一つである。『槐安国語』は白隠が大燈国師の『龍宝開山国師語録』に著語し評唱したものである。普通の読者にとっては此等の書は痴を以て痴を説く（obscurum per obscurius）の類であろう。一通り講義を聞き終えても、禅の真理に眼が開けていない限り、僧もまた依然五里霧中である。この不可解は、その書が難解であるからではなく、聴き手の心が依然として相対意識の堅い殻に被われているところからくる。

接心の期間中は講座の外にいわゆる参禅がある。参禅とは師家に謁して自分の見解を呈し、その検閲を受けることである。大接心以外の場合は参禅は大体日に二回行われるが、この特別の「精神集中」すなわち接心の期間中は僧は日に四、五回は入室しなければならぬ。この師家との相見は公開的に行われるのではない。僧は単身師家の室内に赴かねばならぬ。そこで相見は作法正しく厳粛に行われる。僧は閾を跨ぐ前に一回毎に床の上に跪いて三拝の礼をする。愈々叉手して室内に入り師家に近づくと坐って今一度拝伏する。この作法が済むと、もう世間的な配慮は用いられない。禅の見地から必要とあらば打ち合いの演ぜられることもある。真摯率直に禅の真理を打ち出すというのが唯一の関心事であって、それ以外の事は単に従属的な注意を惹くに過ぎない。この呈示が終ると僧は入って来た時と同様の鄭重な作法で室を退出する。この接見は師家にとってもなかなか骨の折れる仕事である。何故ならば三十名からの者が一まわり参禅を了するには一時間半以上を要し、その間極めて厳格な注意を持ち続けねばな

第九章　禅堂と雲水の生活

らぬからである。

禅の理解に関する限り師家には絶対の信任が置かれているが、その力量を疑うだけの理由があると確信するならば、僧は参禅の際個人的にこれを解決することができる。このように見解の呈示は僧にとっても師家にとっても決して悠長な遊び事ではない。それは実際極めて真剣な事柄であり、その故に禅の修行は偉大な倫理的価値（モラル）を有するのである。これを例証するために、日本に於ける近代臨済禅の創始者白隠の生涯から一事件を取って考察するとしよう。

或る夏の夕方、白隠がその老師を訪ねると彼は縁側に涼んでいた。そこで見解を呈すると荒々しく「妄想情解！」と罵られた。白隠が声を張り上げて同じく「妄想情解！」と叫ぶと師匠はいきなり彼を捕えて瞋拳を雨ふらすこと二、三十、ついに地面へ突き落してしまった。偶々長雨の後であったので白隠は泥水の中へ顛倒した。やがてようやく気力を持ち直し縁側まで辿りついて拝礼すると師匠は声高く叫んだ。曰く、「此守蔵窮鬼子！」
また或る日、白隠は師匠が自分の見解の深さを十分認識していないのだと思い、何とかしてこの点を決著しようと考えた。愈々その時が来た。白隠は師の室に入ると今度こそは寸土をも許すまいと固く決心して秘術を尽して渡り合った。が、師匠の勢はすさまじく到頭白隠を捕えて打ち据えた挙句、縁側から突き落した。彼は今度は幾呎もある石垣の下に墜落し、ほとんど気息尽きて暫くは起き上ることもできなかった。師匠はこれを見下して快げに打ち笑った。これを聞いて我に還った白隠はようやく師匠の所まで這い上って行った。曰く、「此守蔵窮鬼子！」師匠はなおも仮借せず再び例の烙印を押し当てた。
白隠はついに自暴自棄の状態に陥り、この老師の膝下を永久に離れ去ろうと思うに到った。ところが一日村内を

托鉢しているうちに偶然起った一事件が、思いがけなく彼の眼を禅の真理に向って打ち開いたのである。それは従来全く与かり知らぬものであった。彼は踊躍歓喜の尽きる所を知らずすぐに師の許に馳せ帰った。師は彼が門内に入るか入らぬかに夙くもその身の上に何事かが起ったことを察知し、麾くようにしてこう言った。

「今日は何かいい事があったようだな、すぐに入るがよい。さあ、さあ。」

すぐに入室して所見を呈すると師匠は始めて会心の笑を浮べて深く首肯し、彼の苦修精励をねぎらうようにして言った。

「今日お前は大事を了した。ついに大事を了したのだ。」

この事あって以来、老師はふっつりと彼の悪口を言わなくなった。

現代日本禅の父祖はこうした修行を経なければならなかったのである。老師は何と苛酷であったことか。然しその弟子が数々の悪辣な取扱いを受けた挙句ついに大事を了畢したとき何と慈愛深かったことか。事実禅には微温的なものはない。微温的なものなら禅ではないのだ。禅は各人をして真理を底に徹して洞見せしめようとするものであり、その真理は各人が知性的な或はその他の粉飾の一切を脱ぎ捨てて本来の赤裸々な自己に還らない限り決して把握されるものではないのだ。正受の瞋拳は白隠の妄想と不誠実とを剥ぎ取ったのである。事実我々はすべて内奥の自己に還っているのである。さればこそ師匠は、弟子たちにこの内奥の自己に達せしめ、禅の真正の見解を得しめるために、屢〻一見冷酷とも見える、少くとも温情的どころではない方法に訴えたのである。

白隠を石垣の下へ突き落した師匠正受

第九章　禅堂と雲水の生活

禅堂生活には学校教育に見られるような定った卒業の時期はない。中には二十年禅堂にいても卒業しないものもあるが、普通の能力を具え倦まず撓まず努力するならば十年を出でずして数々の禅の教えの微細に通ずることができるであろう。然し禅の諸原理を念念刻刻に行じて行くということ、すなわち、全く禅の精神一枚になるということとは別の問題である。そのためには一生涯を以てしてもなお足りないであろう。釈迦も弥勒もまだ修行の最中であるといわれる所以である。

真に資格ある師家となるには禅の真理を単に理解しただけでは十分ではない。いわゆる「聖胎長養」（しょうたいちょうよう）の期間を通過しなければならぬ。この言葉はもと道教から出たものに相違ないが、今日禅で用いられるその意味は、概して、悟りに相応した生活を送る、ということである。有能な師匠の下で修行すればやがては禅の秘要を悟得することもできるであろう。然し悟得したといってもそれはなお知性的――この言葉をできるだけ高い意味に用いても――な性格を脱するものではない。僧の生活は内外共にこの悟得と完全に一致するようにならなければならぬ。そのためには今一段の自己訓練を必要とする。何故ならば彼が禅堂で得たところのものは結局方向の指示に過ぎないからである。然し彼はもはや禅堂に止まることを強制されない。反対にその知性的悟得は世間との現実的接触によって試練を受けなければならぬのである。この「長養」（マチュアリング）には定められた規則はない。折に触れ縁に応じて各人自らの判断によって行かねばならぬ。或は市中に出でて積極的に世事万般に携わるものもあろうし、或は山中にかくれて孤独の隠者となるものもあろう。彼が初めて山を出て印宗法師の講経の座を辞してから十五年間山中に止まり猟師と生活を共にしたといわれている。六祖は五祖の膝下に現われた時、世間は全く彼を知らなかった。忠国師は南陽に四十年を過して一度も都へ出なかった。然しその高名は遠近に聞え、

皇帝の懇請ついに黙しがたいものがあってその草庵を出たのである。潙山は数年を無人の山中に過し、橡や栗を食とし猿や鹿を相手としていた。然し彼は追々人の知るところとなり、ついに無人の山中に大僧院が建てられ僧千五百人を擁するに到ったのである。京都妙心寺の開祖関山は、初め美濃に隠遁して村人のために日傭人夫をしていた。一日不図したことから彼の素姓が分り、宮廷から一山を開基するように懲遇されるまでは、誰も彼を知る者はなかったのである。

白隠も初めは駿河在の見るかげもない一寺院の住持であった。それが彼の唯一の財産であったのだ。次の記述を読むとき、その荒廃の程も思いやられるのである。

「屋根らしい屋根もなく、夜になると星の光が射しこむ。床らしい床もない。本堂で何かが行われるとき、雨でも降ろうものなら傘をさし下駄を履かねばならなかった。寺の什物なども一切債権者の手中にあった。僧として常住使用するものすら抵当に入っていた。」

禅の歴史を繙けば、隠遁の或る期間を経て世に現われた巨匠の例は豊富に見出される。要は禁欲主義の実行にあるのではなく、如何にも適切に名づけられているように「長養」にあるのだ。数々の蛇や蝮が入口に待ち構えている。徹底的に踏み殺しておかなければまたしても頭を擡げてくるであろう。悟得に於て打ち樹てられた道徳的教養の全構築が一日にして崩壊しないとも限らぬ。無礙募りは禅者にとっても一つの陥穽である。これに対しては不断の戒心を必要とする。

或る点に於て禅堂で行われている教育が時代後れであることは疑いないが、生活の単純化、制欲、片時も無為に

第九章　禅堂と雲水の生活

過さないやり方、独立心、いわゆる「陰徳」等の指導原理はどの国へ持って行ってもまたどの時代に於いても健全なものである。陰徳の観念に到っては特にそうである。そしてこの観念こそ禅修行の紛れもない一特色であるのだ。それは天与の資源を周囲の世界をも浪費しないことを意味する。逢著する一切の事柄を道徳的にも経済的にも十分に活用すること、自分自身をも周囲の世界をも最も深い味得と敬虔の心持を以て扱うこと、思わずに善を行ずることを意味するものである。子どもが溺れようとしていることを思わずに善を行ずることを意味するものである。子どもが溺れようとしていることを。振り向こうともしない。もはやその事は念頭にも止めない。雲が去れば空はもとの如く青くもとの如く広い。禅はこれを「無功用行」(anābhogacaryā)と呼び、雪を搬んで井を埋めようとする痴聖人の行為に喩えている。

イエスはいっている、「なんじ施しをなすとき、右の手の為すことを左の手に知らしむ勿れ。かくするはその施しの隠れんがためなり」。これは仏教の陰徳である。しかしその説述が「さらば隠れたるに鑑みたまう爾の父はあらわに報いたまうべし」にさしかかるとき、我々は仏教と基督教との間の深い亀裂を見るのである。神であろうと悪魔であろうと、我々の行為を見とおしその報いを与えるような存在が念頭にある限り、「あなたはやはり自分たちの仲間ではない」と禅はいうであろう。かかる思念から生れた行為はどうしても「跡」を残し「影」を残すものである。もし何かの霊があって諸君の行為を見守る、と仮定するや否や、その霊は間髪を容れず諸君を捕え、諸君をして一一その行為を説明させようとするであろう。禅はそういうものを持とうとはしないのである。天衣は無縫にして一一そうとはしないのである。天衣は無縫にして一内側にも外側にも縫目がない。それは完全な一枚布であって誰もどこから仕事を始めてあるのか、またどうして織ってあるかを見分けることができないという。

同様に禅に於ては、善を行じたあとでも自惚や自己讚美の蹤跡は微

163

塵も残してはならぬのである。況んや報酬を思うに於てをや、である。よしそれが神から賜わるものであろうとも。

シナの哲学者列子はこの心境をさながらに写し出している。

横心之所念。横口之所言。亦不知我之是非利害歟。亦不知彼之是非利害歟。若人之為我友。我友。内外進矣。而後眼如耳。耳如鼻。鼻如口。無不同也。心凝形釈。骨肉都融。不覚形之所倚。足之所履。随風東西。猶木葉幹殻。意不如風乗我邪。我乗風乎。（列子、黄帝）

心の念うところをほしいままにし、口のいうところをほしいままにした。心は念念に集中し、形は釈然としてゆたかになり、骨肉はすべて融けやわらぎ、身は倚りつつ倚るところを知らず、足は履みつつ履むところを知らなかった。風に従って東西すること一ひらの落葉のごとく、一体自分が風に乗っているのか、風が自分に乗っているのかを知らなかった。

独逸神秘家たちはこの種の徳を「清貧」と称した。タウラーの定義によれば「死という最後の旅には一切を忘れてしまう丁度そのように、誰かに恩義を施してあるかどうか、などということがすっかり念頭になくなってしまうとき、絶対の清貧はおんみのものとなっているのである」。基督教に於ては、神の中に生き動きまた在ることを得るのだというが、神を意識する点に於て強きに過ぎるように思われる。禅は神の意識という最後の痕跡をも、できるかぎり抹消しようとする。禅匠が有仏の処は急いで過ぎ去れ、無仏の処にも足をとめてはいけない、と忠告す

第九章　禅堂と雲水の生活

のもこの意である。禅堂に於ける雲水の修行は、理に於ても行に於てもこの「無功用行」の原理を基礎としている。

これが詩的に表現されると次のようになる。

竹影掃階塵不動　　月穿潭底水無痕。
（ちくえいかいをはらってちりごかず）　（つきたんていをうがってみずにあとなし）

畢竟ずるところ、禅は何といっても個人的経験の事柄である。徹底して経験的なものがあるとすればそれは禅である。如何に書物を読破しても教説に通じても瞑想に心を凝らしても、禅匠になることはできぬ。生それ自らをその流れの只中に捉えなければならぬ。これを停めて吟味し分析しようとするのは、これを殺して空しく冷えた屍体を抱こうとするにひとしい。さればこそ禅堂の何一つを取って見ても、その訓練課程のどの細目を取って見ても、この主旨がはっきり浮出るように仕組まれている。極東仏教の歴史を通じて、禅宗が日本・シナの他の諸宗の間にあって維持し来った独特の地歩は疑もなく禅堂の制度に負うものである。

原註

（1）これについては拙著英文 *The Training of the Zen Buddhist Monk*（《禅僧の修行》）が全面的に取扱っている。なおこの書には鎌倉の佐藤禅忠師の豊富な挿画が附せられている。その他拙著英文『禅論』第一巻、頁二九九以降参照。

（2）「詩篇」第百二十八篇対照。「そはなんじおのが手の勤労を食らうべければなり。なんじはさいわいを得また安きにおるべし」。

165

（3）舎利（sarīra）の語義は「体」であるが、仏教に於ては火葬後に残る無機物の堆積、すなわち遺骨を意味する。仏教徒は、かかる堆積物の価値は、生前の聖者性と対応するものとしている。

巨霊のひびき
―― 改訳『禅学への道』のあとがき ――

第二次大戦も間近に迫った一日、鈴木大拙先生はその頃はまだ洛北の小山大野町に住み、週二回大谷大学に出講していられた。私は講義が終わるとお宅まで送っていくことにしていた。というよりはその暫くの時間――歩いて五分そこそこの道のりだった――を、いろいろと教示を乞う得がたい機会にしていたというのが正直なところであった。先生は拙ない問いにも一々力をこめて懇切に答えて下さった。時には道傍に立ち止まって、ステッキで地面に線を引いたり、円を描いたりしながら……。その二年ほど前に夫人を失い、さらにその一年後、講座の後事を嘱した横川氏を失い、先生の身辺にはおのずと寂寥の気があった。そうした先生に、少しでも後進に教えを与えておきたいという心願のようなものがひしひしと感じられた。そのようにして先生に同行した或る日、途中でどこかの開店披露を触れまわるチンドン屋の一行に行き会った。先生は立ち止まって、じっと彼らに眺め入る気配である。賑やかな囃し子と鳴り物につれて一しきり踊り終えると彼らは立ち去った。先生は私の方を向いてこういった。いかにも感に堪えた面持ちである。「あれだ、とにかく一生ああやって、思うざま踊り抜いて行ったら、よほど面白かろうじゃないか」。

原始的生のリズムへの共鳴とひびくかも知れぬ。それもあろう。しかしそれだけではない。先生はその中にお

ずと絶対肯定の動きを見、そのひびきを聞いているのである。耳を聾するあの無畏無碍の「蟬の声」を聞いているのである。チンドン屋自身はいうかも知れぬ。「滅相もない。こちらはこれで食っているのだ。つらいことも情ないことも辛抱してやっているのだ」。まさしく生きるということは懸命である。やむにやまれぬ煩悩の火の手は念々刻々にあがる。われわれは右往し左往する。にもかかわらず、はたらくものはその中から任運にはたらき出、ひびくものはその中からなおざりにひびき出る。ここに目覚めきたるとき、上がる火の手をそのままに絶対肯定の世界がひらける。

先生には、この絶対肯定のひびきはもっとも親しいものであった。それは先生の著述に、談話に、いや大拙その人に常にひびいている。ことに思い出されるのは、それより三年前の東西哲学者会議における先生の公開講演の結びのことばである。「ここで思い出すのは太鼓のひびきである。祭などで聞くあのドン・ドン・ドコ・ドンのひびきである。日に日に新しい生の搏動を伝え得て妙ではないか。ドン・ドコ・ドンに何故はない。ドン・ドコ・ドンがその意味なのだ。海の向うからやってきて私のしゃべったことは畢竟何かと問われるなら、これまたドン・ドコ・ドンだと答えよう」。

鈴木先生は絶対肯定の思想について次のように述べている。「生の最深奥から迸り出るもの、それが絶対肯定だ」。多くの人々はこれを非現実的、非実際的として斥け峻拒するであろう。しかし先生は絶対肯定のイメージをレンブラントやピカソのような独創的、天才的な芸術家を透視するような仕方で獲得したのではないだろうか。改めていうまでもなく大拙の思想は深い内的体験に基礎づけられている。それは、その謙虚な行文の間から錐が囊を脱するようにあらわれて人を打つのである。しかし大拙を最もめざましく特色づけているのは、むしろその頴

脱した択法眼すなわち批評的精神である。それは体験そのもののもつ意味を蔽い昧ますことなく、物に触れて積極的に打ち出して行くはたらきである。大拙は機宜に応じて東西宗教思想の諸形式と対決しつつ仏教的体験・禅的体験の真姿を積極的に闡明しようとする。そこに幾多の不羈にして創意ある見解が生れる。他者の特色ある学説が逆に大拙の創見を呼び醒ましていることも一再ではない。海外の思想に昧い仏教学者にまま見受けられる放漫な不見識（例えば禅と汎神論との同一視のごとき）は見たくても見られない。一面、大拙の仏教学者としての堅実克明な基礎的研究と該博な宗教学的教養はそれらの見所を重厚に裏打ちしているのである。

いま一つ先生の英文著作を引き立てている要素がある。それは在米十数年に亘る操觚者としての経験から磨き出された見事なオーサーシップである。欧米人のセンスと思惟方式とは先生に於ては申分なく身についている。むしろ血肉化されているといった方がよい。暢達したその英文は「巧み」よりも「自然さ」を感じさせる。読者は他国人の著作に有り勝ちなぎこちなさと晦渋さとを意識することなく極くアット・ホームに而も深い信頼の裡にその思想発展の糸を辿ることができるであろう。またそうしたセンスはイラストレーションや装幀や活字の組み方にまで行き亘ってすこしの隙をも感ぜしめないのである。何となく内輪の気楽さと寛やかさのただよう邦文の著作と自ら趣を異にするところである。昭和二年、英文『禅論』第一巻が公刊されるや、その新たに開拓した研究領域と独自の叡智的な研究方法とによって内外の学界並に思想界に甚大な反響を呼び起し、期せずして著者の世界的仏教思想家としての地位を不動ならしめたのも何ら不思議ではない。

ここに訳出した『禅学への道』（"An Introduction to Zen Buddhism," 1934）は、著者の序文にもあるように英文『禅論』三巻の後を承け海外読者の要望に応えて簡捷な禅への入門書として編述されたものである。専門に亘

る精細な論述は差し控えられている。然しこれはすこしも本書の価値を減殺するものではない。上叙の諸特色はよく選択された素材の上に遺憾なく発揮され、禅の相貌・形姿を簡潔に力づよく描き出しているのである。本書が欧米諸国民の間に一層広く読まれその啓蒙的使命を十二分に果したのも洵(まこと)に当然と云わなければならぬ。

このように本書は、直接には欧米の読者を対象としているのであるが、上叙の諸特色は国内の我々に対しても同様に深くタッチするものを有しているのである。西洋的な感じ方・考え方に親しい人々にとっては尚更であろう。この意味に於て本書は著者の数ある著作中禅の入門書としてユニークな地位を占めるものということができる。

平成十五年九月

訳者 坂本 弘

坂本　弘（さかもとひろし）
大正2年京都生まれ。大谷大学文学研究科修了の後、昭和16年哲学研究室助手。29年同大教授。文学部長などを経て54年退職。同大名誉教授。専攻は宗教学。鈴木大拙の同大教授時代の教え子でもある。

禅学への道

二〇〇三年十月二十日　発行

著　者　鈴木大拙

訳　者　坂本弘

企画協力　㈶松ヶ岡文庫

装　丁　山本ミノ

発行者　宮島正洋

発行所　株式会社アートデイズ
〒160−0008　東京都新宿区三栄町17　四谷和田ビル
電　話　（〇三）三三五三―二一九八
FAX　（〇三）三三五三―五八八七
http://www.artdays.co.jp

印刷所　中央精版印刷株式会社

乱丁・落丁本はお取替えいたします。

禅者のことば

―― CD版 鈴木大拙講演選集(全6巻) ――

「世界の禅者」鈴木大拙が生涯をかけて論究した禅思想から浄土思想までを、東西にわたる広い視野と深い宗教的体験に基づいて縦横に語り尽くす!――90歳近くまで欧米中心に活動を続けてきた大拙が最晩年の6年間(1960年～66年)に日本で行った講演を集めた貴重な音の記録。

第1巻 東洋の母なる思想　56分　　　　　　（昭和35年5月）
第2巻 禅の考え方―頌寿記念講演　65分　　（昭和35年10月）
第3巻 念仏とは何か　40分　　　　　　　　（昭和39年5月）
第4巻 キリスト教と仏教　55分　　　　　　（昭和39年11月）
第5巻 妙好人　40分　　　　　　　　　　　（昭和40年3月）
第6巻 対談＝鈴木大拙・金子大栄
　　　　「浄土信仰をめぐって」　55分　（昭和41年6月）

　解　説　　上田閑照（京都大学名誉教授）
　協　力　　（財）松ヶ岡文庫
　販売価格　15,000円（ＣＤ6枚＋解説書48ページ）
　発行・発売　アートデイズ（11月上旬刊行予定）

〔お申込みは直接小社まで〕
(株)アートデイズ
〒160-0008 東京都新宿区三栄町17 四谷和田ビル3F
FAX 03-3353-5887　TEL 0120-08-2298
http://www.artdays.co.jp

生誕800年記念出版

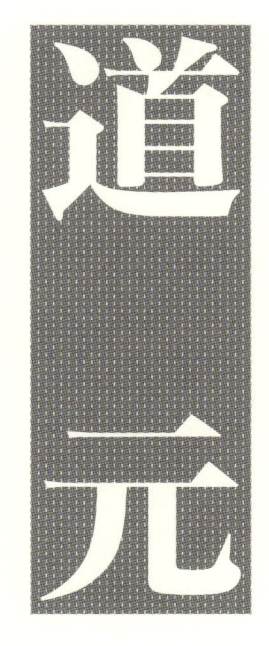

道元

仏道をならふといふは、自己をならふなり。
自己をならふといふは、自己をわするるなり。

全国書店にて
好評発売中!!

松原泰道・著

貴族に生まれながら、あらゆる名利を捨て、厳しく自己を探究し続けた禅思想の創造者道元。その言葉の数々は八百年の時を越えて人々を惹きつけ、生きる勇気と救いとを与えてくれる——道元の奥深い教えを松原師が平易にひもといた長編評伝。

本書で紹介される道元の言葉（一部）

生より死にうつるとこころうるは、これあやまり也／愛語よく廻天の力あるを学すべきなり／犯禁（かいてん）（戒律破り）は一時の非なり。愛名（ほっきん）（名利）は一生の累（るい）（誤まち）なり／自己をならふといふは、自己をわするるなり／師の正邪に随ひて悟りの偽と真とあり／学道の人は、只（ただ）、明日を期（ご）することなかれ／縦ひ曲木と雖も、もし好手に遇はば妙功忽ち現ず……他
（たと）（くせぎ）（いえど）
（たちま）

発行　アートデイズ　　　本体1,800円

〔注〕について
本書英文編集にあたって、著者による〔原注〕とは別に、翻訳家千葉隆章氏の協力を得て新たに〔編集部注〕を作成し、付記しました。

west, like a leaf of the tree detached from its stem ; I was unconscious whether I was riding on the wind, or the wind riding on me."

This kind of virtue is called by the German mystics "poverty" ; and Tauler's definition is, "Absolute poverty is thine when thou canst not remember whether anybody has owed thee or been indebted to thee for anything ; just as all things will be forgotten by thee in the last journey of death."

In Christianity we seem to be too conscious of God, though we say that in him we live and move and have our being. Zen wants to have this last trace of God-consciousness, if possible, obliterated.[1] That is why Zen masters advise us not to linger where the Buddha is, and to pass quickly away where he is not. All the training of the monk in the Zendo, in practice as well as in theory, is based on this principle of "meritless deed".[2] Poetically this idea is expressed as follows :

> The bamboo-shadows move over the stone steps
> as if to sweep them, but no dust is stirred ;
> The moon is reflected deep in the pool, but the
> water shows no trace of its penetration.

Taking it all in all, Zen is emphatically a matter of personal experience ; if anything can be called radically empirical,[3] it is Zen. No amount of reading, no amount of teaching, no amount of contemplation will ever make one a Zen master. Life itself must be grasped in the midst of its flow ; to stop it for examination and analysis is to kill it, leaving its cold corpse to be embraced. Therefore, everything in the Meditation Hall and every detail of its disciplinary curriculum is so arranged as to bring this idea into the most efficient prominence. The unique position maintained by the Zen sect among the other Buddhist sects in Japan and China throughout the history of Buddhism in the Far East is no doubt due to the institution known as the Meditation Hall, or Zendo.

---

(1) obliterate(d)　抹消する。　(2) "meritless deed"　「無功用行」。意識的な努力を必要としない行い。　(3) radically empirical　徹底して経験的な。

IX THE MEDITATION HALL AND THE MONK'S LIFE

I walk away, I never look backward, and nothing more is thought of it. A cloud passes and the sky is as blue as ever and as broad. Zen calls it "a deed without merit" (*anabhogacarya*), and compares it to a man's work who tries to fill up a well with snow.

Jesus said, "When thou doest alms,[1] let not thy left hand know what thy right hand doeth; that thine alms may be in secret." This is the "secret virtue" of Buddhism. But when the account goes on to say that "Thy Father who seeth in secret shall recompense thee", we see a deep cleavage between Buddhism and Christianity. As long as there is any thought of anybody, be he God or devil, knowing of our doings and making recompense, Zen would say, "You are not yet one of us." Deeds that are the product of such thought leave "traces" and "shadows". If a spirit is tracing your doings, he will in no time get hold of you and make you account for what you have done; Zen will have none of it. The perfect garment shows no seams, inside and outside; it is one complete piece and nobody can tell where the work began, or how it was woven. In Zen, therefore, no traces of self-conceit[2] or self-glorification[3] are to be left behind even after the doing of good, much less the thought of recompense, even by God.

Resshi[4] (Lieh-tzu), the Chinese philosopher, describes this frame of mind in a most graphic manner:

> "I allowed my mind without restraint to think of what it pleased, and my mouth to talk about whatever it pleased; I then forgot whether 'this and not-this' was mine or others', whether the gain or loss was mine or others'; nor did I know whether Lao-shang-shih[5] was my teacher and Pa-kao[6] was my friend. In and out, I was thoroughly transformed; and then it was that the eye became like the ear, and the ear like the nose, and the nose like the mouth; and there was nothing that was not identified. As the mind became concentrated, the form dissolved, the bones and flesh all thawed away; I did not know upon what my frame was supported, or where my feet were treading; I just moved along with the wind, east or

---

(1) alms　施し。　(2) self-conceit　自惚。　(3) self-glorification　自己讚美。　(4) Resshi　列子。道家。老子の後に活躍した。　(5) Lao-shng-shih　老商子。　(6) Pa-kao　伯高子。

Court insisted on his founding a monastery in the Capital.

In the beginning of his career Hakuin was the keeper of a deserted temple in Suruga, which was his sole heritage in the world. We can picture to ourselves the extent of its dilapidation[1] when we read this account: "There were no roofs properly speaking, and the stars shone through at night, nor were there any decent floors. It was necessary to have a rain-hat and to wear high *getas* if it rained when anything was going on in the main part of the temple. All the property attached to the temple was in the hands of creditors, and the priestly belongings were mortgaged to the trades-people...."

The history of Zen gives many such examples of great masters who emerged into the world after a period of retirement. The idea is[2] not the practice of asceticism, but is the "maturing", as has been properly designated, of one's moral character. Many serpents and adders[3] are waiting at the porch, and if one fails to trample them down effectively they raise their heads again, and the whole edifice of moral culture built up in vision may collapse even in a day. Antinomianism[4] is also a pitfall[5] for the followers of Zen, against which constant vigil is needed.

In some respects, no doubt, this kind of monastic education that prevails in the Zendo is behind the times; but its guiding principles, such as the simplification of life, restraint of desires, not wasting a moment idly, self-independence, and what they call "secret virtue",[6] are sound for all lands and in all ages. Especially is this true of the concept of "secret virtue", which is a very characteristic feature of Zen discipline. It means not to waste natural resources; it means to make full use, economic and moral, of everything that comes your way; it means to treat yourself and the world in the most appreciative and reverential frame of mind. It particularly means practising goodness without any thought of recognition by others. A child is drowning; I get into the water, and the child is saved. That is all there is to be done in the case; what is done is done.

(1) its dilapidation　その荒廃。　(2) the idea is　要は…。　(3) adders　蝮（まむし）。　(4) antinomianism　無礙（むげ）募り。道徳律廃棄論。　(5) a pitfall　一つの陥穽。　(6) "secret virtue"　「陰徳」。人に知られぬように行なう善行。

IX   THE MEDITATION HALL AND THE MONK'S LIFE

To become a perfectly qualified master, a mere understanding of the truth of Zen is not sufficient. He must go through a period which is known as "the long maturing of the sacred womb".[1] The term must have come originally from Taoism[2]; but in Zen nowadays it means, broadly speaking, living a life harmonious with the understanding. Under the direction of a competent master a monk may finally attain[3] to a thorough knowledge of all the mysteries of Zen, but it will be more or less intellectual though in the highest possible sense. The monk's life, in and out, must grow in perfect unison with this attainment. To do this a further self-training is necessary, for what he has gained in the Zendo is after all only the pointing of the finger in the direction where his utmost efforts must further be put forth. But it is no longer imperative for him to remain in the Zendo; on the contrary, his intellectual attainments must be put on trial by coming into actual contact with the world. There are no prescribed rules for this "maturing". Each must act under his own discretion[4] as he meets with the accidental circumstances of life. He may retire into the mountains and live as a solitary hermit, or he may come out into the market and be an active participant in all the affairs of the world. The Sixth Patriarch is said to have lived among the mountaineers for fifteen years after he had left the Fifth Patriarch. He was quite unknown in the world when he first returned to hear a lecture by Inshu[5] (Yin-tsung). Chu (Chung), the national teacher,[6] spent forty years in Nang-yang and never showed himself out in the city. But his holy life became known far and near, and at the earnest request of the Emperor he finally left his hut. Yisan[7] (Kuei-shan) spent several years in the wilderness, living on nuts and befriending monkeys and deer. He was found out, however, and great monasteries were built about his anchorage, and he became the master of one thousand and five hundred monks. Kwanzan,[8] the founder of the great Myoshinji in Kyoto, lived at first a retired life in Mino Province, working for the villagers as a day labourer. Nobody recognized him until one day an accident disclosed his identity and the

---

(1) "the long maturing of the sacred womb" 「聖胎長養」。仏としての素質を守り育てること。 (2) Taoism 道教。 (3) attain 悟得する。 (4) under his own discretion 自らの判断によって。 (5) Inshu 印宗法師。 (6) Chu (Chung), the national teacher 南陽忠国師 (p.80の注参照)。 (7) Yisan 潙山 (p.117の注参照)。 (8) Kwanzan 関山。

hitherto been completely hidden from him. His joy knew no bounds and he came back to the master in a most exalted state of mind. Before he could enter the front gate, the master recognized that something had happened to him and beckoned to him saying: "What good news have you brought home today? Come right in, be quick, quick!" Hakuin then told him all about what he had gone through during the day. The master tenderly stroked him on the back and said, "You have it now; you have it at last!" After this the master never called him names.

Such was the training the father of modern Japanese Zen had to go through. How terribly hard his old master, Shoju,[1] was when he pushed Hakuin over the stone wall! But how motherly he was when his disciple, after so much ill-treatment, finally came out triumphantly! Indeed, there is nothing lukewarm[2] in Zen; if it is lukewarm, it is not Zen. It expects one to penetrate into the very depths of truth, and the truth can never be grasped until, stripped of all trumperies,[3] intellectual or otherwise, one returns to one's own native nakedness. Each slap dealt by Shoju stripped Hakuin of his illusions and insincerities.[4] In fact, we are all living under many casings of illusions and insincerities which really have nothing to do with our inmost Self. To reach this inmost Self, therefore, whereby the disciple gains real knowledge of Zen, the master often resorts to methods seemingly inhuman; indeed, far from being kindhearted to say the least.

In the life of the Zendo there is no fixed period of graduation as in public education. With some, graduation may not take place after twenty years of living there, but with ordinary abilities and a good amount of perseverance and indefatigability a monk is able to probe[5] within a space of ten years into every intricacy of the teachings of Zen. To practise the principles of Zen, however, in every moment of life—that is, to become fully saturated in the spirit of Zen[6]—is another matter. One life may be too short for it; for it is said that even Sakyamuni and Maitreya[7] themselves are yet in the midst of self-training.

(1) Shoju 正受老人。 (2) lukewarm 微温的な。 (3) trumperies 粉飾。 (4) illusions and insincerities 妄想と不誠実。 (5) probe into …に通じる。 (6) to become fully saturated in the spirit of Zen まったく禅の精神一枚になる。 (7) Maitreya 弥勒。

IX THE MEDITATION HALL AND THE MONK'S LIFE

will occupy more than an hour and a half of most exacting attention.

Absolute confidence is placed in the master so far as his understanding of Zen goes, but if the monk thinks he has sufficient reason for doubting the master's ability he may settle it with him personally at the time of *sanzen*. This presentation of views, therefore, is no idle play for either master or monk. It is, indeed, a most serious affair, and because it is so this discipline of Zen has great moral value. To illustrate this let us consider an incident from the life of Hakuin, the founder of modern Rinzai Zen in Japan.

One summer evening when Hakuin came to present his view to his old master, who was cooling himself on the veranda, the master rudely said, "Stuff and nonsense!" Hakuin repeated loudly, "Stuff and nonsense!" Thereupon the master seized him, boxed his ear, and finally pushed him off the veranda. As it had been raining, poor Hakuin found himself rolling in mud and water. When he recovered himself he returned to the veranda and bowed to the master, who retorted, "O you denizen[1] of the dark cavern!"

Another day, thinking that the master failed to really appreciate the depths of his knowledge of Zen, Hakuin desired to have a settlement with him anyhow. When the time came Hakuin entered the master's room and exhausted all his ingenuity[2] in contest with him, making up his mind this time not to give up an inch of ground. The master was furious, and finally taking hold of Hakuin gave him several slaps and pushed him off the porch. He fell several feet to the foot of a stone wall, where he remained for a while almost senseless. The master looked down at him and laughed heartily; this brought Hakuin back to consciousness, and when he came back to the master he was all in perspiration. The master, however, did not release him yet but stigmatized[3] him as before, "O you denizen of the dark cavern!"

Hakuin grew desperate and thought of leaving the old master altogether, when one day as he was going about begging in the village a certain accident suddenly opened his eye to the truth of Zen, which had

---

(1) denizen　窮鬼子（ごくつぶし）。　(2) exhausted all his ingenuity　秘術を尽して。　(3) stigmatized　烙印を押し当てた。

also a collection of *koans*, forty-eight in number, with comments peculiar to Zen, and much simpler than the *Hekigan*. The *Kidoroku* contains the sayings, sermons, poems, and other works by Kido (Hsu-t'ang) of the Sung dynasty. He was the teacher of Dai-o Kokushi,[1] whose line of Zen transmission is the one still flourishing in Japan. The *Kwaian-kokugo* is the compilation by Hakuin of Daito Kokushi's sermons and critical commentary verses on some of the old masters. To an ordinary reader these books are a sort of *obscurum per obscurius*.[2] After listening to a series of lectures, the monk may be left in the same lurch[3] as ever unless he has opened an eye to the truth of Zen. This inscrutability[4] is not necessarily caused by the abstruse nature[5] of the books, but because the listener's mind is still encrusted[6] with the hard shell of relative consciousness.

During the *sesshin*, besides the lectures, the monks have what is known as "*sanzen*". To do *sanzen* is to go to the master and present their views[7] on the *koan* they have for the master's critical examination. In the days when a great *sesshin* is not going on, *sanzen* will probably take place twice a day, but during the special time of "thought collection"—which is the meaning of *sesshin*—the monk has to see the master four or five times a day. This seeing the master does not take place openly; the monk is required to go individually to the master's room, where the interview takes place in a most formal and solemn manner. When the monk is about to cross the threshold, he makes three bows, each time prostrating himself on the floor; he now enters the room keeping his hands palm to palm in front of his chest, and when he comes near the master he kneels down and makes still another prostration. This ceremony over, no further worldly considerations[8] are entertained; if necessary from the Zen point of view, even blows may be exchanged. To make manifest the truth of Zen with all sincerity of heart is the sole consideration; everything else receives only subordinate attention. The presentation over, the monk retires from the room with the same elaborate ceremony with which he entered. This exercise may be very trying[9] on the master, for one *sanzen* for thirty monks

(1) Dai-o Kokushi　大燈国師。(2) obscurum per obscurius　痴を以って痴を説く。(3) left in the same lurch　五里霧中である。(4) inscrutability　不可解。(5) the abstruse nature　難解。(6) encrusted　被われている。(7) present their views　見解を呈し。(8) worldly considerations　世間的な配慮。(9) trying　骨の折れる。

IX THE MEDITATION HALL AND THE MONK'S LIFE

the atom of a thing to be called laudable[1] or not-laudable?"

Shuko answered, "The five aggregates[2] (*skandha*) are entangling, and the four elements[3] (*mahabhuta*) grow rampant, and how can you say there are no evils?"

The monk still insisted, "The four elements are ultimately all empty and the five aggregates have no reality whatever."

Shuko, giving him a slap in the face, said, "So many are mere learned ones; you are not the real thing yet; give me another answer."

But the monk made no answer and started to go away filled with angry feelings.

"There," said the master smilingly, "why don't you wipe the dirt off your own face?"

In the study of Zen, the power of an all-illuminating insight must go hand in hand with a deep sense of humility and meekness of heart.[4]

There is a period in the monastic life which is exclusively set apart for the mental discipline of the monks, when they are not hampered by any manual labour except such as is absolutely necessary. This period is known as *sesshin*.[5] It takes place a few times, each time lasting a week, in the season known as the "summer sojourn" (*ge-ango*), and again in the one known as the "winter sojourn" (*setsu-ango*). Generally speaking, the summer sojourn begins in April and ends in August, while the winter one begins in October and ends in February. *Sesshin* means "collecting or concentrating the mind". While these *sesshins* last, the monks are confined in the Zendo, get up earlier than usual and sit further into the night. There is a "lecture" (*Koza* or *teisho*) every day during the *sesshin*. The textbook used may be any one of the Zen books such as *The Hekiganshu, The Rinzairoku, The Mumonkwan, The Kidoroku*,[6] *The Kwaian-kokugo*, etc. The *Rinzairoku* is a collection of sermons or sayings of the founder of the Rinzai Zen sect. *The Hekiganshu*, as mentioned before, is a collection of one hundred *koans* annotated, expounded, and appreciated. *The Mumonkwan* is

---

(1) laudable 賞賛に値する。崇とすべき。 (2) the five aggregates 五蘊。仏教で、肉体と精神を五つに分けたもの。 (3) the four elements 四大。物質を作りあげる地、水、火、風の四元素のこと。 (4) meekness of heart 柔軟の心情。 (5) sesshin 接心。 (6) *The Kidoroku* 『虚堂録』。虚堂禅師が残した語録。

"I am gathering the holy *sariras*[1](1) from the burnt ashes."

"How," said the keeper, "can you get *sariras* from a wooden Buddha?"

Tanka retorted, "If there are no *sariras* to be found in it, may I have the remaining two Buddhas for my fire?"

The shrine-keeper later lost both his eyebrows for remonstrating[(2)] against this apparent impiety[(3)] of Tanka, while the Buddha's wrath[(4)] never fell on the latter.

Though I am doubtful of its historic accuracy, this story is notable and all Zen masters agree as to the spiritual attainments of this Buddha-desecrating[(5)] Tanka. When a monk once asked his master about Tanka's idea of burning a statue of Buddha, the master replied:

"When cold we sit around the hearth with fire burning."

"When hot we go to the bamboo-grove by the stream."

"Was he then at fault or not?"

Whatever the merit of Tanka from a purely Zen point of view, there is no doubt that such deeds of Tanka are to be regarded as highly sacrilegious[(6)] and to be avoided by all pious Buddhists. Those who have not yet gained a thorough understanding of Zen may go to all lengths of committing every manner of excess and even crime—this in the name of Zen; and for this reason the regulations of the monastery are very rigid that pride of heart may depart and the cup of humility[(7)] be drunk to the dregs.[(8)]

When Shuko[(9)] (Chu-hung) of the Ming dynasty was writing a book on the ten laudable deeds of a monk, one of those self-assertive[(10)] fellows came to him, saying:

"What is the use of writing such a book when in Zen there is not even

---

1 *Sarira* (*shari* in J. and *she-li* in C.) literally means the "body", but in Buddhism it is a kind of mineral deposit found in the human body after cremation. The value of such deposits is understood by the Buddhists to correspond to the saintliness of life.

(1) the holy sariras 仏舎利。釈迦の遺骨。 (2) remonstrating 責めた。 (3) impiety 冒瀆。 (4) Buddha's wrath 仏罰。 (5) desecrating 冒瀆漢。 (6) sacrilegious 冒瀆的であり。 (7) humility 謙譲。 (8) drunk to the dregs 最後の一雫まで飲み乾される。 (9) Shuko 雲棲袾宏。明代の禅僧。 (10) self-assertive 独りよがりの。

IX THE MEDITATION HALL AND THE MONK'S LIFE

although there is at present the tendency for the latter to get as much information as possible of the life in the Zen monastery. But the merciless tide of modern commercialism and mechanization is rolling all over the East, so that almost no corners are left for a quiet retreat, and before long even this solitary island of Zen may be buried under the waves of sordid materialism.[1] Even the monks themselves are beginning to misunderstand the spirit of the early masters. Though we cannot deny the fact that there are some things in this monastic education which may be improved, its highly religious and reverential[2] spirit toward life and work must be preserved if Zen is to live at all for many years to come.

Theoretically, Zen envelops the whole universe and is not bound by the rule of antithesis.[3] But this is a very slippery ground and there are many who fail to walk upright; and when they tumble the fall is quite disastrous. Like some of the medieval mystics,[4] Zen students sometimes turn into libertines, losing all control of themselves; history is a witness of such, and psychology can readily explain the process of such degeneration. A Zen master once said: "Let a man's ideal rise as high as the crown of Vairochana (highest divinity), but let his life be so full of humility as to be prostrate even at the feet of a baby." The life in a Zen monastery is minutely[5] regulated and all the details are enforced in strict obedience to the above spirit. This is what has saved Zen from sinking to the level of some of the medieval mystics, and it is why the Zendo plays so great a part in the teaching of Zen.

When Tanka[6] (Tan-hsia) of the T'ang dynasty stopped at Yerinji in the Capital, it was severely cold; so taking down one of the Buddha images enshrined[7] there, he made a fire of it and warmed himself. The keeper of the shrine, seeing this, was greatly incensed[8] and exclaimed:

"How dare you burn my wooden image of the Buddha?"

Tanka began to search in the ashes as if he were looking for something, and said:

---

(1) sordid materialism 卑しい物質主義。 (2) reverential 敬虔な。 (3) antithesis 差別。 (4) the medieval mystics 中世神秘家。 (5) minutely 細密に。 (6) Tanka 丹霞天然。唐代の禅僧。 (7) enshrined 安置してあった。 (8) was incensed 怒って。

The monks are a self-governing body[1]; they have their own cooks, proctors, managers, sextons, masters of ceremony, etc. Though the master or teacher of a Zendo is its soul, he is not directly concerned with its government, which is left to the senior members[2] of the community, whose character has been tested through many years of discipline. When the principles of Zen are discussed, one may well marvel at their deep and subtle "metaphysics" and imagine what a serious, pale-faced, head-drooping, and world-forgetting group of people these monks must be; but in their actual life they are very common mortals engaged in menial work. They are cheerful, crack jokes, are ready to help one another, and despise no work which is usually considered low and unworthy of a cultured person. The spirit of Hyakujo is ever manifest here. The faculties of the monks thus receive an all-round development. They receive no formal or literary education, which is gained mostly from books and abstract instructions; but what they do gain is practical and efficient, for the basic principle of the Zendo life is "learning by doing". They disdain soft education and look upon it as a predigested food[3] meant for convalescents. When a lioness gives birth to her cubs it is proverbially believed that after three days she pushes them over a precipice to see if they can climb back to her. Those that fail to meet this test are no longer cared about. Whether this is true or not, something like it is aimed at by the Zen master, who will often treat his monks with every manner of seeming unkindness. The monks often have not enough clothes for comfort, not enough food to satisfy hunger, not enough time to sleep, and, to cap these, they have plenty of work, both menial and spiritual. These outer necessities and inner aspirations, working together upon the character of the monk, often end in producing a fine specimen of humanity called a full-fledged Zen master.[4] This unique system of education, which is still going on in every Rinzai Zendo, is not very well known among the laity,[5]

(1) a self-governing body　自治的な一集団。　(2) the senior members　古参の僧たち。
(3) a predigested food　流動食。　(4) a full-fledged Zen master　飽参者。悟りを得て参師の必要のなくなった禅僧。　(5) the laity　在俗者。

IX THE MEDITATION HALL AND THE MONK'S LIFE

folded[1]; the rubbing of his palms against each other shows that the waiter has put enough rice or soup in his bowl.

The rule is that each monk should eat up all that is served him, "gathering up the fragments that remain"; for that is their religion. After a third or fourth helping of rice, the meal comes to an end. The leader claps the wooden blocks and the waiters bring hot water; each monk fills his largest bowl with it and in it all the other bowls are neatly washed and wiped with the tiny napkin which is carried by him. Then a wooden pail goes round to receive the slop; each monk gathers up his dishes and wraps them up once more; the tables are now empty as before except for the grains of rice that had been offered at the beginning of the meal to the invisible beings. The wooden blocks are clapped again and the monks leave the room in the same quiet and orderly procession as they entered.

The industry[2] of the monks is proverbial. When the day is not set for study at home, they are generally seen soon after breakfast, about half past five in summer and half past six in winter, out in the monastery grounds or tilling the farm attached to the Zendo. Later, certain groups of them go into the neighbouring villages to beg for rice. They keep the monastery, inside and outside, in perfect order. When we say, "This is like a Zen temple," it means that the place is kept in the neatest possible order. Commonly attached to a Zendo are some patrons whose homes are visited regularly for a supply of rice or vegetables. When begging they will often go out miles away; they may often be seen along a country road pulling a cart loaded with pumpkins or potatoes or daikons. They sometimes go to the woods to gather fuel and kindling[3]. They know something[4] of agriculture, too. As they have to support themselves[5] they are at once farmers, skilled workmen, and unskilled labourers; they often build their own Zendo and other buildings under the direction of an expert. Their labour is not at all perfunctory; they work just as hard as ordinary labourers, perhaps harder, because to work so is their religion.

(1) keep his hands folded　合掌したまま。 (2) industry　勤勉。 (3) kindling　焚きつけ。 (4) know something　一通り心得ている。 (5) support themselves　自給自足して。

the best possible use of things as they are given us, which is also the spirit of Buddhism everywhere. In truth, the intellect, the imagination, and all the other mental faculties as well as the physical objects[1] that surround us, our own bodies not being excepted, are given for the unfolding and enhancing of the highest powers possessed by us, and not merely for the gratification of individual whims[2] and desires, which are sure to conflict with and injure the interests and rights to be asserted by others. These are some of the inner ideas underlying the simplicity and poverty of the monk's life.

At meal-time a gong[3] is struck and the monks come out of the Zendo in procession carrying their own set of bowls to the dining-room, but do not sit until the leader[4] rings a bell. The bowls which each brings are made of wood or paper and are well lacquered; they are usually four or five in number and fit into one another like a nest. The sutra (*Hridaya Sutra*)[5] and the "five meditations"[6] are recited, and then the monks who are serving as waiters serve the soup and rice. They are now ready to take up their chopsticks, but before they actually partake of their sumptuous[7] dinner, they think of those departed spirits and other beings[8] who are living in this and other worlds, and each taking out about seven grains of rice from his portion offers them to the unseen.[9] While eating perfect quietude prevails; the dishes are handled noiselessly, no word is uttered, no conversation goes on, and all their desires are indicated by folding and rubbing their hands. Eating is a serious affair[10] with them. When another bowl of rice is wanted, the monk holds out his folding hands, the waiter notices it and sits with the rice receptacle[11] before the hungry one; the latter takes up his bowl, lightly passes his hand around the bottom to wipe off whatever dirt may have attached itself and be likely to soil[12] the hand of the waiter. While the bowl is being filled, the eater keeps his hands

(1) the physical objects　自然的事物。　(2) whims　恣意。　(3) a gong　雲板。食事を知らせる青銅の楽器。　(4) the leader　直日（じきじつ）。その日の当直。　(5) the sutra (*Hridaya Sutra*)　『般若心経』。　(6) "five meditations"　五観。法華経の説く五種の観法で、真観、清浄観、広大智慧観、悲観、慈観をいう。　(7) sumptuous　素晴しい。　(8) those departed spirits and other beings　幽の鬼神諸霊。　(9) the unseen　目に見えぬものたち（幽界の鬼神諸霊）。　(10) a serious affair　厳粛な行事。　(11) the rice receptacle　おひつ。　(12) soil　汚す。

IX THE MEDITATION HALL AND THE MONK'S LIFE

unless this impulse to get and to hold is completely uprooted. Cannot society be reorganized upon an entirely different basis from what we have been used to see from the beginning of history? Cannot we ever hope to stop the massing of wealth[1] and the accumulation of power merely from the desire for individual or national aggrandizement[2]? Despairing of the utter irrationality of human affairs, Buddhist monks have gone to the other extreme and cut themselves off even from reasonable and perfectly innocent enjoyments of life. However, the Zen ideal[3] of putting a monk's belongings into a tiny box is his mute protest, though so far ineffective, against the present order of society.

In India the Bhikshu[4] never eats in the afternoon; he properly eats only once a day; for his breakfast, in the American or English sense, is no breakfast. The Zen monk is supposed to have no evening meal, but the climatic necessity being impossible to ignore, he has a meal after a fashion,[5] but to ease his conscience he calls it "medicinal food".[6] The breakfast, which is taken very early in the morning while still dark, consists of rice gruel[7] and pickled vegetables. The principal meal is at about ten in the morning and consists of rice (or rice mixed with barley), vegetable soup, and pickles. In the afternoon, at four, they have what was left from dinner, and no special cooking is done. Unless invited out or given an extra treatment at home by some generous patron, their meals are as described above, year in, year out.[8] Poverty and simplicity is their rule.

We ought not, however, to conclude that asceticism[9] is an ideal of life for Zen monks; for as far as the ultimate significance[10] of Zen is concerned, it is neither asceticism nor any other ethical system. If it appears to advocate either the doctrine of suppression or that of detachment,[11] it is merely so on the surface, for Zen as a school of general Buddhism inherits more or less the odium[12] of the Hindu ascetic discipline. The central idea, however, of the monk's life is not to waste but to make

---

(1) the massing of wealth 富を蓄積し。 (2) aggrandizement 強大。 (3) the Zen ideal 禅の理念。 (4) the Bhikshu 比丘 (びく)。僧のこと。 (5) after a fashion それに相当する。 (6) "medicinal food" 「薬石」。禅寺の夕食。 (7) rice gruel 粥。 (8) year in, year out 年が年中。 (9) asceticism 禁欲。 (10) the ultimate significance 第一義。 (11) detachment 離脱。 (12) the odium 習気 (じっけ)。くせ。悪い習慣。

hours of quiet-sitting and thus test their validity[1] in the vital field of actualities. It is my strong conviction that if the Zen monastery did not put faith in working and keeping the blood of the monks circulating, the study[2] of Zen would have sunk into the level of a mere somniferous[3] and trance-inducing system, and all the treasures garnered[4] by the masters in China and Japan would have been cast away as of no more value than heaps of rotten stuff.

The Meditation Hall, or Zendo as it is called in Japan, is a rectangular building of different sizes according to the number of monks to be accommodated. The one at Engakuji, Kamakura, is about 35×65 feet and will take in thirty or forty monks. The space allotted to each monk is one *tatami*, or a mat 3×6 feet, where he sits, meditates, and sleeps. The bedding for each never exceeds one large wadded quilt[5] about 5×6 feet, be it winter or summer. He has no regular pillow except that which is temporarily made out of his own private property. This latter, however, is next to nothing: it consists of a *kesa* (*kasaya*) and *koromo* (priestly robes), a few books, a razor, and a set of bowls, all of which are carried in a papier-maché[6] box about $13 \times 10 \times 3\frac{1}{2}$ inches. In travelling this box is carried in front, suspended from the neck with a broad sash. His entire property thus moves with its owner. "One dress and one bowl, under a tree and on a stone" graphically describes the monk's life in India. Compared with this, the modern Zen monk must be said to be abundantly supplied. Still his wants[7] are reduced to a minimum and none can fail to lead a simple, perhaps the simplest, life if he models his after the life of a Zen monk. The desire to possess is considered by Buddhism to be one of the worst passions[8] with which mortals[9] are apt to be obsessed. What, in fact, causes so much misery in the world is the universal impulse of acquisition. As power is desired, the strong always tyrannize over the weak; as wealth is coveted,[10] the rich and poor are always crossing swords of bitter enmity. International wars rage, social unrest ever increases,

(1) validity 妥当性。 (2) study 修行。 (3) somniferous 催眠的。 (4) garnered 蓄積して来た。 (5) wadded quilt 布団。 (6) papier-maché 一閑張（いっかんばり）の函。紙で貼った上に漆を塗った箱。 (7) his wants その必需品。 (8) the worst passions 最悪の煩悩（ぼんのう）。 (9) mortals 人間（たち）。 (10) as wealth is coveted 富が欲しいばかりに。

IX THE MEDITATION HALL AND THE MONK'S LIFE

Psychologically considered, this is splendid; for muscular activity is the best remedy for the dullness of mind which may grow out of the meditative habit,[1] and Zen is very apt to produce this undesirable effect. The trouble with most religious recluses[2] is that their mind and body do not act in unison; their body is always separated from their mind, and the latter from the former; they imagine that there is the body and there is the mind and forget that this separation is merely ideational,[3] and therefore artificial. The aim of the Zen discipline being to annul this most fundamental discrimination, it is always careful to avoid any practice which tends to emphasize the idea of onesidedness.[4] *Satori* in truth consists in reaching the point where all our discriminatory notions are done away with, though this is by no means a state of emptiness.[5] The sluggishness[6] of mind which is so frequently the product of quietistic[7] meditation, we can thus see, is not at all conducive to the maturing of *satori*, and those who want to advance in the study of Zen have naturally to be always on guard in this respect lest it should finally altogether stop the fluidity,[8] as it were, of mental activity. This is at least one reason why Zen followers object to the mere practice of Dhyana. The body kept busy will also keep the mind busy, and therefore fresh, wholesome, and alert.

Morally, any work involving an expenditure of physical force testifies to the soundness of ideas. Especially in Zen is this true; abstract ideas that do not reflect themselves forcibly[9] and efficiently in practical living are regarded as of no value. Conviction must be gained through experience and not through abstraction. Moral assertion ought everywhere to be over and above intellectual judgment; that is, truth ought to be based upon one's living experience. Idle reverie[10] is not their business, insist the followers of Zen. They, of course, sit quietly and practise *zazen*; that must be done if they are to assimilate whatever lessons they have gained while working. But as they are opposed to "chewing the cud"[11] all the time, they put into action whatever reflections[12] they have made during

---

(1) the meditative habit 瞑想の習慣。 (2) recluses 隠遁者。 (3) ideational 観念的なもの。 (4) onesidedness いずれか一方。 (5) emptiness 空無。 (6) sluggishness 沈滞。 (7) quietistic 寂静主義的な。 (8) fluidity 流動性。 (9) forcibly 力強く。 (10) idle reverie 怠惰な瞑想。 (11) "chewing the cud" 「反芻（はんすう）」。 (12) reflections 省察。

The Meditation Hall (*zendo*) is where Zen educates its monks.¹ To see how it is regulated is to get a glimpse into the practical and disciplinary aspect of Zen. It is a unique institution and most of the main monasteries in Japan of the Zen sect are provided with it. In the life of the Zen monks in the Meditation Hall we are reminded of the life of the Sangha⁽¹⁾ in India.

The system was founded by the Chinese Zen master, Hyakujo⁽²⁾ (Pai-chang, 720-814), more than one thousand years ago. He left a famous saying which had been the guiding principle of his life, "A day of no work is a day of no eating," which is to say, "No eating without working."² When he was thought by his devoted disciples to be too old to work in the garden, which had been his favourite occupation, they hid all his garden tools, as he would not listen to their repeated remonstrances⁽³⁾. He then refused to eat. "No work, no living." At all the Meditation Halls work, especially that which is commonly regarded as menial,⁽⁴⁾ is the vital element in the life of the monk. It thus implies a great deal of manual labour, such as sweeping, cleaning, cooking, fuel-gathering,⁽⁵⁾ tilling the farm, or going about begging in the villages far and near. No work is considered to be beneath their dignity, and a perfect feeling of brotherhood prevails among them. They believe in the sanctity⁽⁶⁾ of manual work; no matter how hard or how mean the work may be, they will not shun it, and they keep themselves in every way they can; for they are no idlers, as some of the so-called monks or mendicants⁽⁷⁾ are, as for instance in India.

1 This is fully treated in my recent work entitled *The Training of the Zen Buddhist Monk*, richly illustrated by Rev. Zenchu Sato, of Kamakura. Also see *Zen Essays*, I, p. 299 *et seq.*
2 Cf. Psalm 128 : "Thou shalt eat the labour of thine hands ; happy shalt thou be, and it shall be well with thee."

編集部注 (1) the Sangha （または Samgha） 僧伽（そうぎゃ）。仏教の教団。 (2) Hyakujo 百丈（p.61の注参照）。 (3) their repeated remonstrances 度重なる戒め（幾度諫しめても）。 (4) menial 賤しい。 (5) fuel-gathering 薪拾い。 (6) sanctity 神聖。 (7) mendicants 托鉢修道者。

IX

TEH MEDITATION HALL AND THE MONK'S LIFE

VIII THE KOAN

mentioned, and the latter is by Wanshi[1] (Hung-chih), who also poetically comments on a different collection of *koans*. Zen naturally finds its readiest expression in poetry rather than in philosophy because it has more affinity[2] with feeling than with intellect ; its poetic predilection[3] is inevitable.

(1) Wanshi　宏智正学。南宋の禅僧。　(2) affinity　親近性（親しい…）。　(3) predilection　偏倚。偏愛。

self-murdering weapon against Zen; so he committed them all to the flames.

The book, however, has survived the fire and is still in our possession as one of the most important treatises on Zen; indeed, it is a standard text and authority, to which appeal is still made to settle points of doubt in the study of Zen. The work is known in Japanese as *Hekigan-shu*[1] (*Pi-yen Chi*). To outsiders it is a sealed book; in the first place the Chinese is not after the classical model but is filled with colloquialisms of the T'ang and Sung period, which can now be traced only in Zen literature, while it is most vigorously written. Secondly, the style is peculiar to this kind of work, and its thoughts and expressions seem to be so unexpected as to stagger the reader who expects to find in it ordinary Buddhist nomenclature[2] or at least tame classicalism.[3] Besides these literary difficulties, the *Hekigan* is naturally full of Zen. However, those who want to know how *koans* are handled by Zen followers will do well to consult the book.

There are some other books dealing with the *koans* which are more or less after the style of the *Hekigan*; such are the *Shoyoroku*,[4] *Mumonkwan*,[5] *Kwaiankokugo*,[6] etc. In fact, all the Zen writings known as *Goroku* (*Wu-lu*, "sayings and dialogues") as well as the biographical histories of Zen masters, of which we have a large list, treat the *koans* in the way peculiar to Zen. Almost every master of note has left his *Goroku*, which largely constitute what is known as Zen literature. Where the philosophical study of Buddhism abounds with all sorts of annotations[7] and exegeses[8] and analyses[9] which are often very detailed and complicated, Zen offers pithy[10] remarks, epigrammatic suggestions, and ironical comments, which conspicuously[11] contrast with the former. Another characteristic of Zen literature is its partiality[12] to poetry: the *koans* are poetically appreciated or criticized. Of this the *Hekigan-shu* (*Pi-yen Chi*) or *Shoyo-roku* (*T'sung-yung Lu*) are most significant examples. The first is by Seccho, as was already

(1) *Hekigan-shu* 『碧巌集』。 (2) nomenclature 語彙（ごい）。 (3) classicalism 古典的様式。 (4) *Shoyoroku* 『従容録』。 (5) *Mumonkwan* 『無門関』。 (6) *Kwaiankokugo* 『槐安国語』（かいあんこくご）。 (7) annotations 注釈。 (8) exegeses 解釈。 (9) analyses 分析。 (10) pithy 寸鉄的な。 (11) conspicuously 著しく。 (12) its partiality 傾斜。

example, but as to understanding the old master you have just the same significantly failed." This well illustrates the fact that Zen is entirely different from being absorbed in nothingness.

The number of *koans* is traditionally estimated at 1,700, which, however, is a very generous way of counting them. For all practical purposes, less than ten, or even less than five, or just one may be sufficient to open one's mind to the ultimate truth of Zen. A thoroughgoing enlightenment, however, is attained only through the most self-sacrificing application of the mind, supported by an inflexible faith in the finality[1] of Zen. It is not to be attained by merely climbing up the gradation of the *koans* one after another, as is usually practised by followers of the Rinzai school.[2] The number really has nothing to do with it; the necessary requirements are faith and personal effort,[3] without which Zen is a mere bubble. Those who regard Zen as speculation and abstraction will never obtain the depths of it, which can be sounded only through the highest will-power. There may be hundreds of *koans*, or there may be an infinite number of them as there are infinite numbers of objects filling up the universe, but it does not necessarily concern us. Only let one gain an all-viewing and entirely satisfying insight into the living actuality of things and the *koans* will take care of themselves.

This is where lurks[4] the danger of the *koan* system. One is apt to consider it as everything in the study of Zen, forgetting the true object of Zen, which is the unfolding[5] of a man's inner life. There are many who have fallen into this pitfall and the inevitable result has been the corruption and decay of Zen. Daiye[6] (Ta-hui) was quite apprehensive of this when he burned up the book on one hundred *koans* which was compiled by his master Yengo (Yuan-wu). These one hundred *koans* were selected from Zen literature by Seccho[7] (Hsueh-ton), who commented on them with verses, one to each. Daiye was a true follower of Zen. He knew well the object which his master had in view when he made remarks upon these selections; he knew very well also that they would subsequently prove a

---

(1) the finality 窮極性。 (2) the Rinzai school 臨済宗。 (3) personal effort 人格的努力。 (4) lurk 潜んでいる。 (5) the unfolding 開発。 (6) Daiye 大慧（p.88の注参照）。 (7) Seccho 雪竇禅師。

Yisan, "I am going to tell you about my dream."

Kyosan leaned forward as if listening.

Yisan said, "You guess."

Kyosan went out and brought a basin filled with water and a towel. With the water the master washed his face, but before he had resumed his seat another monk, Kyogen,[1] came in. The master said, "We have been performing a miracle—and not a trivial one at that."

Kyogen replied, "I have been below and know all that has been going on between you."

"If so, tell me how it is," demanded the master.

Kyogen then brought him a cup of tea.

Yisan remarked: "O you two monks, what intelligent fellows you are! Your wisdom and miraculous deeds indeed surpass those of Sariputra[2] and Maudgalyayana[3]!"

Sekiso[4] (Shih-shuang) died and his followers thought that the head monk ought to succeed him. But Kyuho[5] (Chin-feng), who had been an attendant to the late master, said: "Wait, I have a question, and the successor ought to be able to answer it. The old master used to teach us thus: 'Stop all your hankerings[6]; be like cold ashes and withered plants; keep the mouth tightly closed until mould grows about it; be like pure white linen, thoroughly immaculate; be as cold and dead as a censer in a deserted shrine.' How is this to be understood?"

"This," said the head monk, "illustrates a state of absolute annihilation."

"There, you utterly fail to grasp the meaning."

"Do I? If so, have an incense-stick lighted; if I do not really understand the old master, I shall not be able to enter into a trance before the stick burns up."

So saying, the head monk fell into a state of unconsciousness from which he never arose. Stroking the back of his departed[7] fellow-monk, Kyuho said, "As to getting into a trance you have shown a splendid

---

(1) Kyogen 香厳（p.61の注参照）。 (2) Sariputra 舎利佛。シャーリプトラ。仏十大弟子の一人。 (3) Maudgalyayana 目連（もくれん）。仏十大弟子の一人。 (4) Sekiso 石霜。唐代の禅僧。 (5) Kyuho 九峯道虔。唐末五代の禅僧。 (6) hankerings あこがれ。 (7) departed 死んだ。

"cypress-tree", or the Sixth Patriarch's "original face", are all alive to the very core. Once touch the heart of it and the whole universe will rise from its grave where we have buried it with our logic and analysis.

For the benefit of students who wish to know more about the *koans* which are given to Zen students for solution, a few of them are given here. When Kyosan[1] received a mirror from Yisan,[2] he brought it out before an assemblage of monks and said: "O monks, Yisan has sent here a mirror; shall it be called Yisan's or mine? If you call it mine, how is it that it comes from Yisan? If you call it Yisan's, how do you account for its being in my hands? If you can make a statement that hits the mark, the mirror will be retained; if you cannot, it will be broken in pieces." This he declared three times and as nobody came forward to make a statement the mirror was destroyed.

Tozan[3] came to Ummon[4] for instruction; the latter asked:
"Where do you come from?"
"From Sato.[5]"
"Where have you spent the summer?"
"At Hoji of Konan."
"When did you leave there?"
"On the twenty-fifth of the eighth month."
Ummon suddenly raised his voice and said; "I spare you thirty blows. You may now retire."

In the evening Tozan went to Ummon's room and asked what his fault was, so grave as to deserve thirty blows. Said the master, "Is this the way you wander all over the country? O you rice-bag[6]!"

Yisan was having a nap, when Kyosan came in. Hearing the visitor, Yisan turned about toward the wall.

Said Kyosan, "I am your disciple; no formality is needed."

The master made a movement as if he were awakening from sleep; Kyosan started to leave the room, but the master called him back. Said

---

1 These are some of the first *koans* for Zen students.

(1) Kyosan　仰山 (p.78の注参照)。 (2) Yisan　潙山霊祐。唐代の禅僧。潙仰宗の開祖。 (3) Tozan　洞山 (p.73の注参照)。 (4) Ummon　雲門 (p.20の注参照)。 (5) Sato　査度。 (6) rice-bag　飯袋子 (ごくつぶし)。

Are these masters all asserting the same fact and pointing to the same truth? Or are they not only in words but in fact and truth contradicting one another? Let us examine more masters concerning the staff.

Suiryu[1] one day ascended the pulpit and bringing forth his staff made this confession: "My twenty years' residence in this monastery is due to the virtue of this."

A monk stepped forward and asked, "What virtue did you gain out of that?"

"Supporting myself with this, I cross the streams, I pass over the mountains; indeed, without it, what can I do?"

Later Shokei,[2] another master, hearing of this remark, said, "If I were he, I would not say that."

"What would you say?" came quickly from the monk.

Shokei now took the staff, came down to the ground, and walked away.

Ho-an now makes the observation about these two masters: "Suiryu's staff was a pretty good one, but what a pity! it has a dragon's head with a snake's tail. It makes Shokei follow him up, and the result is another pity: his was like putting speckles[3] on a painted tiger. When the monk asked what power of the staff he had got, why did he not take it out and throw it away before the congregation? Then there would have been a real dragon, a real tiger, calling forth clouds and mists."

Now let me ask, why all this—shall we say—much ado[4] about nothing? If modern Zen is a system, what kind of a system is it? It seems chaotic, and how conflicting are the masters' views! Yet from the Zen point of view there is one current running through all these confusions, and each master is supporting the others in a most emphatic manner. An apparent contradiction in no way hinders the real endorsement.[5] In thus mutually complementing each other, not indeed logically but in a fashion characteristically Zen, we find the life and truth of the *koan*. A dead statement cannot be so productive of results.[6] Hakuin's "one hand", Joshu's

(1) Suiryu 睡龍。(2) Shokei 招慶。(3) speckles 斑点。(4) ado 空騒ぎ。(5) endorsement 保証。(6) results 効果。

116

VIII THE KOAN

side of it. As has been said before, it is really a condescension,[1] an apology, a compromise, that this present work has been written; much more the whole systematization of Zen.

To outsiders this "systematization" appears to be no systematization, for it is full of contradictions, and even among the Zen masters themselves there is a great deal of discrepancy,[2] which is quite disconcerting. What one asserts another flatly denies or makes a sarcastic remark about it, so that the uninitiated[3] are at a loss what to make out of all these everlasting and hopeless entanglements. But the fact is that Zen really ought not to be considered from its surface; such terms as system, rationality, consistency, contradiction, or discordance belong to the surface of Zen; to understand Zen we are to turn up the whole piece of brocade[4] and examine it from the other side, where we can trace at a glance all the intricacies of woof and warp.[5] This reversing of the order is very much needed in Zen.

Let us quote an example to see how it is treated by different masters. Funyo,[6] a great Zen master of the T'ang dynasty, said, "If a man knows what this staff[7] is, his study of Zen comes to a close." This seems to be a simple enough *koan*. The master generally carries a long staff which is now a kind of insignia[8] of his religious authority, but in ancient days it was really a travelling stick that was useful in climbing mountains or fording streams. Being one of the most familiar objects, it is produced any time by a master before his congregation to illustrate a sermon; it is often the subject of a great discussion among the monks. Cho of Rokutan,[9] another Zen master, apparently opposed the view of the preceding master, Funyo, when he declared, "If a man knows what the staff is, he will go to hell as straight as an arrow flies." If this is the case, no one will be induced to study Zen; but what does Cho really mean? Ho-an,[10] still another Zen master, makes a statement about this staff, which is not radical; he is quite rational and innocent when he says, "If a man knows what the staff is, let him take it and put it up against the wall over there."

(1) a condescension　譲歩。　(2) discrepancy　相違。　(3) the uninitiated　門外者。　(4) brocade　金襴（きんらん）。　(5) the intricacies of woof and warp　縦糸・横糸の交錯。　(6) Funyo　汾陽。　(7) staff　拄杖（しゅじょう）。禅僧が使う杖。　(8) insignia　標識。　(9) Cho of Rokutan　瑯潭澄。唐代の禅僧。　(10) Ho-an　破庵。

hold of life in its act of living; to stop the flow of life and to look into it is not the business of Zen. The constant presence of the *koan* before our mental vision keeps the mind always occupied; that is, in full activity. *Satori* is attained in the midst of this activity and not by suppressing it, as some may imagine. How much Zen differs from "meditation" as the latter is generally understood, and practised, we now can see better from what has been said above as regards the nature of the *koan*.

The systematizing of Zen began as early as the Five Dynasties in China—that is, in the tenth century—but its completion was due to the genius of Hakuin (1683-1768) who lived in the Tokugawa era. Whatever one may say against the abuses of the *koan*, it was the *koan* that saved Japanese Zen from total annihilation. Consider how Chinese Zen is faring[1] these days; so far as we can gather it is more or less a mere name; and again notice the general tendency shown in the practice of Zen by adherents of the Soto school[2] in present-day Japan. We cannot deny that there are many good points in Soto, which ought to be carefully studied, but as to the living of Zen there is perhaps greater activity in the Rinzai, which employs the *koan* system.

One may say: "If Zen is really so far beyond the intellectual ken[3] as you claim it to be, there ought not to be any system in it; in fact, there could not be any, for the very conception[4] of a system is intellectual. To be thoroughly consistent, Zen should remain a simple absolute experience excluding all that savours of process or system or discipline. The *koan* must be an excrescence, a superfluity,[5] indeed a contradiction." Theoretically, or rather from the absolute point of view, this is quite correct; therefore, when Zen is asserted "straightforwardly" it recognizes no *koan* and knows of no round-about[6] way of proclaiming itself. Just a stick, a fan, or a word! Even when you say, "It is a stick," or "I hear a sound," or "I see the fist," Zen is no more there. It is like a flash of lightning, there is no room, no time, in Zen even for a thought to be conceived. We speak of a *koan* or a system only when we come to the practical or conventional

---

(1) …how… is faring …はどうなっているか（帰趨を辿りつつある）。 (2) the Soto school 曹洞宗。 (3) ken 範囲。 (4) the very conception 概念そのもの。 (5) an excrescence, a superfluity 贅物（ぜいぶつ）であり冗物であり。 (6) round-about 迂遠な。

VIII   THE KOAN

minds were not crammed with intellectual biases.[1] But this state of affairs could not, in the nature of things, last very long; to maintain the vitality of Zen it was necessary to find some device whereby Zen could be made more approachable and to that extent more popular; the *koan* exercise had to be established for the benefit of the rising generations and also for the coming ones. Though it is in the being of Zen that it can never be a popular religion[2] in the sense that Shin Buddhism[3] or Christianity is, yet the fact that it has kept up its line of transmission[4] unbroken for so many centuries is, in my view, principally due to the system of *koan*. In China, where Zen originated, it no longer exists in its pure form; the line of transmission is no more, so transfused[5] is it with the Pure Land[6] practice of invoking the Buddha-name.[7] It is only in Japan that Zen is still virile and still finds its orthodox exponents; and there is every reason to believe that this is due to the system of reviewing the *koans* in connection with the practice of *zazen*. There is no doubt that this system is largely artificial and harbours[8] grave pitfalls,[9] but the life of Zen runs through it when it is properly handled. To those who pursue it judiciously under a really competent master, Zen-experience is possible and a state of *satori* will surely come.

Thus we can see that this Zen-experience is something realizable by going through a certain process of training. That is, the *koan* exercise is a system definitely set up with a definite object in view. Zen is not like other forms of mysticism, entirely left to the sporadic nature or capriciousness of luck[10] for its experience. The systematization[11] of *koan* is, therefore, the one thing that is most characteristic of Zen. It is this that saves Zen from sinking into trance,[12] from becoming absorbed in mere contemplation, from turning into an exercise in tranquillization.[13] Zen attempts to take

---

(1) intellectual biases 知性的偏執。 (2) a popular religion 民衆的宗教。 (3) Shin Buddhism 真宗。 (4) its line of transmission その伝統。 (5) transfused 滲みこんでいる。 (6) Pure Land 浄土教。 (7) invoking the Buddha-name 念仏。 (8) harbour (s) …を蔵している。 (9) pitfalls 危険。 (10) left to the sporadic nature or capriciousness of luck 気まぐれな、当てにならない運まかせにする（幸運を、その偶然に来り訪れるのに委ねて）。 (11) systematization (systematizing) 組織化。 (12) trance 忘我。 (13) an exercise in tranquillization 黙照的訓練。公案禅に対し、黙々と座禅するのが黙照禅。曹洞宗の禅法。

koan becomes clear, and in the same way that one knows that ice is cold and freezing. The eye sees, the ear hears, to be sure, but it is the mind as a whole that has *satori*; it is an act of perception, no doubt, but it is a perception of the highest order. Here lies the value of the Zen discipline,[1] as it gives birth to the unshakable conviction that there is something indeed going beyond mere intellection.[2]

The wall of *koan* once broken through and the intellectual obstructions well cleared off, you come back, so to speak, to your everyday relatively constructed consciousness. The one hand does not give out a sound until it is clapped by the other. The cypress-tree stands straight before the window; all human beings have the nose vertically set and the eyes horizontally arranged. Zen is now the most ordinary thing in the world. A field that we formerly supposed to lie far beyond is now found to be the very field in which we walk, day in, day out.[3] When we come out of *satori* we see the familiar world with all its multitudinous[4] objects and ideas together with their logicalness, and pronounce them "good".

When there was as yet no system of *koan*, Zen was more natural and purer perhaps, but it was only the few elect[5] who could get into the spirit of it. Supposing you had lived in those days, what would you do if you were roughly shaken by the shoulder? How would you take it if you were called a dry dirt-scraper[6]? Or if you were simply requested to hand the cushion over there, and, when you had handed it to the master, to be struck with it? If you had a determination to fathom[7] the depths of Zen as strong as steel, and a faith in the "reasonableness"[8] of Zen which was as firm as the earth, you, after many years of meditation,[9] might succeed in mastering Zen; but such examples are rare in our modern days; we are so distracted[10] with all kinds of business that we are unable to walk all by ourselves into the labyrinthine[11] passageway of Zen. In the early days of the T'ang dynasty people were more simple-hearted and believing, their

---

(1) the Zen discipline　禅の修行。　(2) intellection　知性の作用。　(3) day in, day out　明けても暮れても。　(4) multitudinous　多種多様の。　(5) elect　選ばれたるもの。　(6) a dry dirt-scraper　乾屎橛（かんしけつ）（p.72の注参照）。　(7) fathom　…を究めよう（究める）。　(8) the "reasonableness"　「妥当性」。　(9) meditation　工夫。　(10) are so distracted　心を奪われている。　(11) labyrinthine　迷路にも似た。

VIII THE KOAN

ordinary way of talking, because whatever field of consciousness that is known to us is generally filled with conceptual riffraff,[1] and to get rid of them, which is absolutely necessary for maturing Zen experience, the Zen psychologist sometimes points to the presence of some inaccessible region in our minds. Though in actuality there is no such region apart from our everyday consciousness, we talk of it as generally more easily comprehensible by us. When the *koan* breaks down all the hindrances[2] to the ultimate truth, we all realize that there are, after all, no such things as "hidden recesses of mind" or even the truth of Zen appearing all the time so mysterious.

The *koan* is neither a riddle nor a witty remark. It has a most definite objective, the arousing of doubt and pushing it to its furthest limits. A statement built upon a logical basis is approachable through its rationality; whatever doubt or difficulty we may have had about it dissolves itself by pursuing the natural current of ideas. All rivers are sure to pour into the ocean; but the *koan* is an iron wall standing in the way and threatening to overcome one's every intellectual effort to pass. When Joshu says "the cypress-tree in the courtyard", or when Hakuin puts out his one hand, there is no logical way to get around it. You feel as if your march of thought had been suddenly cut short. You hesitate, you doubt, you are troubled and agitated, not knowing how to break through the wall which seems altogether impassable. When this climax is reached, your whole personality, your inmost will, your deepest nature,[3] determined to bring the situation to an issue, throws itself with no thought of self or no-self, of this or that, directly and unreservedly[4] against the iron wall of the *koan*. This throwing your entire being against the *koan* unexpectedly opens up a hitherto unknown region of the mind. Intellectually, this is the transcending of the limits of logical dualism, but at the same time it is a regeneration, the awakening of an inner sense which enables one to look into the actual working of things.[5] For the first time the meaning of the

---

(1) conceptual riffraff 無用の概念（概念のぼろ屑）。 (2) hindrances 邪魔物。 (3) nature 性情。 (4) unreservedly 逡巡なく。 (5) the actual working of things 物のあるがままの作用。

questioning was to see what insight this disciple of Joshu had into the meaning of the story of the cypress-tree. Therefore, the questioner further pursued Tetsu by saying, "But this is asserted by everybody, and how can you deny it?" Tetsu insisted, "My master never said it; and you will do well if you do not thus disparage[1] him." What an audacious statement! But those that know Zen know that this flat[2] denial is the irrevocable proof[3] that Tetsu thoroughly understood the spirit of his master. His Zen was beyond question. But from our common-sense point of view no amount of intellectual resourcefulness[4] can be brought upon his flat denial so that it can somehow be reconciled with the plain fact itself. Zen is, therefore, quite merciless toward those critics who take the story of the cypress-tree for an expression savouring of Mahayana pantheism.[5]

The *koans*, therefore, as we have seen, are generally such as to shut up all possible avenues to rationalization. After a few presentations of your views in the interview with the master, which is technically called *san-zen*, you are sure to come to the end of your resources,[6] and this coming to a *cul-de-sac*[7] is really the true starting point in the study of Zen. No one can enter into Zen without this experience. When this point is reached the *koans* may be regarded as having accomplished a half of the object for which they stand.

To speak conventionally—and I think it is easier for the general reader to see Zen thus presented—there are unknown recesses in our minds which lie beyond the threshold[8] of the relatively constructed[9] consciousness. To designate them as "sub-consciousness[10]" or "supra-consciousness[11]" is not correct. The word "beyond" is used simply because it is a most convenient term to indicate their whereabouts.[12] But as a matter of fact there is no "beyond", no "underneath", no "upon" in our consciousness. The mind is one indivisible whole and cannot be torn in pieces. The so-called *terra incognita*[13] is the concession of Zen to our

(1) disparage 見くびる。 (2) flat にべもない。 (3) the irrevocable proof 動かぬ証拠。 (4) resourcefulness 方便。 (5) savouring of Mahayana pantheism 大乗的汎神論を彷彿する。 (6) to come to the end of your resources 手の下しようがなくなること。 (7) a cul-de sac 窮地。 (8) the threshold 領域。 (9) relatively constructed 相対的な構造をもつ。 (10) sub-consciousness 下意識的。 (11) supra-consciousness 超意識的。 (12) their whereabouts その漠然たる所在。 (13) terra incognita 未知の領域。

VIII THE KOAN

highest principle, through which the pantheistic[1] tendency of Buddhism may be recognized. But to understand the *koan* thus intellectually is not Zen, nor is such metaphysical symbolism at all present here. Under no circumstances ought Zen to be confounded[2] with philosophy; Zen has its own reason for standing for itself, and this fact must never be lost sight of; otherwise, the entire structure of Zen falls to pieces. The "cypress-tree" is forever a cypress-tree and has nothing to do with pantheism or any other "ism". Joshu was not a philosopher even in its broadest and most popular sense; he was a Zen master through and through,[3] and all that comes forth from his lips is an utterance directly ensuing from[4] his spiritual experience. Therefore, apart from this much of "subjectivism[5]", though really there are no such dualities in Zen as subject and object, thought and the world, the "cypress-tree" utterly loses its significance. If it is an intellectual or conceptual statement, we may endeavour to understand its meaning through the ratiocinative chain[6] of ideas as contained in it, and we may come to imagine that we have finally solved the difficulty; but Zen masters will assure you that even then Zen is yet three thousand miles away from you, and the spirit of Joshu will be heard laughing at you from behind the screen, which after all you had failed to remove. The *koan* is intended to be nourished in those recesses[7] of the mind where no logical analysis can ever reach. When the mind matures so that it becomes attuned to[8] a similar frame to that of Joshu, the meaning of the "cypress-tree" will reveal itself, and without further questioning you will be convinced that you now know it all.

A disciple of Joshu called Kaku-tetsu-shi[9] (Chueh T'ieh-tzu) was asked after the death of his master whether he had really made the statement about the cypress-tree in response to the question, "What is the fundamental principle of Buddhism?" The disciple unhesitatingly declared, "My master never made that statement." This was a direct contradiction of the fact, for everybody then knew that Joshu had made it, and the one who asked Kaku-tetsu-shi about it was himself not ignorant of it. His

---

(1) pantheistic 汎神論的。 (2) be confounded 混同される。 (3) through and through どこまでも。 (4) ensuing from ～に発する。 (5) subjectivism 主観主義。 (6) the ratiocinative chain 論理的連関。 (7) those recesses 奥所。 (8) become(s) attuned to 互いに和して一つになれば（相諧和する）。 (9) Kaku-tetsu-shi 覚鉄嘴。

to open up the secret chamber of the mind, where the devotees can find numberless treasures stored. The sense of seeing or hearing has nothing to do with the essential meaning of the *koan*; as the Zen masters say, the *koan* is only a piece of brick used to knock at the gate, an index-finger pointing at the moon. It is only intended to synthesize or transcend[1]—whichever expression you may choose—the dualism of the senses.[2] So long as the mind is not free to perceive a sound produced by one hand, it is limited and is divided against itself. Instead of grasping the key to the secrets of creation, the mind is hopelessly buried in the relativity[3] of things, and, therefore, in their superficiality.[4] Until the mind is free from the fetters,[5] the time never comes for it to view the whole world with any amount of satisfaction. The sound of one hand as a matter of fact reaches the highest heaven as well as the lowest hell, just as one's original face looks over the entire field of creation even to the end of time. Hakuin and the Sixth Patriarch stand on the same platform with their hands mutually joined.[6]

To mention another instance. When Joshu was asked about the significance of Bodhidharma's coming east (which, proverbially, is the same as asking about the fundamental principle of Buddhism), he replied, "The cypress-tree in the courtyard."

"You are talking," said the monk, "of an objective symbol.[7]"

"No, I am not talking of an objective symbol."

"Then," asked the monk again, "what is the ultimate principle of Buddhism?"

"The cypress-tree in the courtyard," again replied Joshu.

This is also given to a beginner as a *koan*.

Abstractly speaking, these *koans* cannot be said to be altogether nonsensical[8] even from a common-sense point of view, and if we want to reason about them there is perhaps room[9] enough to do so. For instance, some may regard Hakuin's one hand as symbolizing the universe or the unconditioned,[10] and Joshu's cypress-tree as a concrete manifestation of the

(1) transcend 超越する。 (2) the senses 意識作用。 (3) the relativity 相対性。 (4) their superficiality 皮相性。 (5) the fetters 枷 (かせ)。 (6) with their hands mutually joined 相携えて。 (7) an objective symbol 境。 (8) nonsensical 無意味である。 (9) room 余地。 (10) the unconditioned 絶対者。

VIII THE KOAN

things was not always correct or helpful to his spiritual welfare.[1] After this is realized, the student might dwell on the statement itself and endeavour to get at its truth if it has any.[2] To force the student to assume this inquiring attitude is the aim of the *koan*. The student must then go on with his inquiring attitude until he comes to the edge of a mental precipice,[3] as it were, where there are no other alternatives but to leap over. This giving up of his last hold[4] on life will bring the student to a full view of "his original face", as desired by the statement of the Sixth Patriarch. Thus it can be seen that the *koan* is not handled now in precisely the same way that it was in those earlier days. As first proposed, it was the culmination,[5] so to speak, of all that had been working in the mind of the monk Myo, whose elaboration herein received its final finish; instead of coming at the beginning of the Zen exercise, as it does now, the Sixth Patriarch's question came at the end of the race. But in modern days the *koan* is used as a starter; it gives an initial movement to the racing for Zen experience. More or less mechanical in the beginning, the movement acquires the tone needed for the maturing of Zen consciousness; the *koan* works as a leaven. When the sufficient conditions obtain, the mind unfolds itself into the full bloom of a *satori*. To use a *koan* thus instrumentally for the opening of the mind to its own secrets is characteristic of modern Zen.

Hakuin used to produce one of his hands and demand of his disciples to hear the sound of it. Ordinarily a sound is heard only when two hands are clapped, and in that sense no possible sound can come from one hand alone. Hakuin wants, however, to strike at the root of our everyday experience, which is constructed on a so-called scientific or logical basis. This fundamental overthrowing is necessary in order to build up a new order of things on the basis of Zen experience. Hence this apparently most unnatural and therefore illogical demand made by Hakuin on his pupils. The former *koan* was about "the face", something to look at, while the latter is about "the sound", something that appeals to the sense of hearing; but the ultimate purport of both is the same; both are meant

---

(1) his spiritual welfare　安心立命。　(2) if it has any　何であれ。　(3) a mental precipice　心的断崖。　(4) hold　手懸り。　(5) the culmination　絶頂点。

needs of the disciple, more than is really good for him. This lack of soft education made the ancient Zen master all the stronger and more full of virility.[1] This was the reason why, in those early days of Zen—that is, during the T'ang dynasty—it was so active, so brilliant, so intense. When the *koan* system came into vogue during the Sung dynasty[2] the halcyon days[3] of Zen were almost over and it gradually showed signs of decline and senility.[4]

Here then is one of the first *koans* given to latter-day students. When the Sixth Patriarch was asked by the monk Myo[5] (Ming) what Zen was, he said; "When your mind is not dwelling on the dualism of good and evil, what is your original face before you were born?" (Show me this "face" and you get into the mystery of Zen. Who are you before Abraham was born? When you have had a personal, intimate interview with this personage, you will better know who you are and who God is. The monk is here told to shake hands with this original man, or, if metaphysically put, with his own inner self.)

When this question was put to the monk Myo, he was already mentally ready to see into the truth of it. The questioning is merely on the surface, it is really an affirmation meant to open the mind of the listener. The Patriarch noticed that Myo's mind was on the verge[6] of unfolding itself to the truth of Zen. The monk had been groping in the dark[7] long and earnestly; his mind had become mature, so mature indeed that it was like a ripe fruit which required only a slight shaking to cause it to drop on the ground; his mind required only a final touch by the hand of the master. The demand for "the original face" was the last finish necessary, and Myo's mind instantly opened and grasped the truth. But when this statement in the form of a question about "the original face" is given to a novice, who has had no previous discipline in Zen as Myo had, it is usually given with the intention to awaken the student's mind to the fact that what he has so far accepted as a commonplace fact, or as a logical impossibility, is not necessarily so, and that his former way of looking at

(1) virility　気力。 (2) the Sung dynasty　宋時代。 (3) the halcyon days　全盛時代。 (4) senility　衰退。 (5) the monk Myo　明上座。上座は、禅修行者の中で首位に座るもの。 (6) on the verge　触発しようとする状態にある。 (7) groping in the dark　暗中模索。

VIII   THE KOAN

of further improvement. Therefore, our grumblings generally are not very vehemently asserted.

In a similar way, the introduction of the system of *koan* into Zen, pure, natural, and elementary, is at once a deterioration and an improvement. But once brought out into existence, the system seems very hard to do away with.[1] It was, of course, quite human on the part of the Zen master to be thinking of his less fortunate brothers whose natural endowments[2] were not so rich as his own, and who, therefore, would be likely to miss opportunities to come into the truth of Zen. He wanted to impart to them, if possible, the same wonderful bliss of the understanding which he had gained through the mastery of Zen. His motherly instinct[3] made him think of some way to open or even to coerce[4] the minds of his disciples to the unknown beauties of *satori*, which, when left to their own ignorant ways, would never come upon them except by a happy rare chance. The master knew that the device of a *koan* was an artificiality and a superfluity[5]; for unless Zen grew out of a man's own inner activity it could not be truly genuine and full of creative vitality as it ought to be. But even a semblance would be a blessing when the genuine thing is so difficult and rare to have; and, moreover, it was likely, if it is left to itself, to disappear altogether out of the lore of human experience.[6] The semblance is not necessarily a mere makeshift but may have in it something quite true and full of possibilities; for the system of *koan* and *zazen*, when properly made use of, really does unfold the mind to the truth of Zen. Why then should we not adopt it and work it out to its fullness?

At the beginning, a Zen master was a kind of self-made man[7]; he had no school education, he had not been sent to college to pass through a certain course of studies, but out of an inner impelling necessity which stirred up his spirit he could not help going about and picking up whatever knowledge he needed. He was perfected by himself. Of course, he had a teacher, but the teacher did not help him in the way scholars nowadays are helped—helped too frequently, indeed, beyond the actual

---

(1) do away with　〜を廃する。 (2) natural endowments　天分。 (3) motherly instinct　母性的本能。 (4) coerce　強いて〜させる。 (5) a superfluity　余計なもの。 (6) the lore of human experience　人間の経験知。 (7) self-made man　独学の士。

came into existence, which thereafter rapidly developed so as to overshadow all the other Buddhist schools. At present there are no Buddhist monasteries in China which do not belong to the Zen sect, and most of them are of the Rinzai school of Zen.[1] One reason among others for this conquest[1] is to be found in the practice of *zazen* as the means of mastering the *koan* and thus attaining *satori*.

Ko-an literally means "a public document" or "authoritative statute[2]" —a term coming into vogue toward the end of the T'ang dynasty.[3] It now denotes some anecdote of an ancient master, or a dialogue between a master and monks, or a statement or question put forward by a teacher, all of which are used as the means for opening one's mind to the truth of Zen. In the beginning, of course, there was no *koan* as we understand it now; it is a kind of artificial instrument devised out of the fullness of heart[4] by later Zen masters, who by this means would force the evolution of Zen consciousness[5] in the minds of their less endowed[6] disciples.

The mind may grow by itself even when it is left to nature to achieve her own ends, but man cannot always wait for her, he likes to meddle for better or worse.[7] He is never patient; whenever there is a chance to put his fingers in, he is sure to do so. The interference is sometimes helpful, sometimes decidedly not. As a rule it works two ways. We welcome human interference when more is to be gained than lost and call it improvement and progress; but when it turns out otherwise we call it retrogression. Civilization is human and artificial[8]; some are not satisfied with it and want to go back to nature. Well, so-called modern progress is by no means unmitigated[9] bliss, but on the whole, at least on the material side of life, we seem to be better off these days than ever before, and we see some signs

---

1 At present Chinese Buddhism is a strange mixture of Zen and Nembutsu, though most monasteries profess to belong to the Zen sect. They recite the *Amitabha sutra* along with the *Prajnahridaya*.

(1) this conquest こうして他宗を圧倒したこと（かく他宗を圧倒した）。(2) statute 法令の如きもの。(3) the T'ang dynasty 唐朝。(4) out of the fullness of heart 黙しがたい老婆心から。(5) force the evolution of Zen consciousness 強いて禅意識を開発せしめようとした。(6) less endowed 比較的天分に恵まれぬ。(7) for better or worse 善いにつけ悪いにつけて。(8) human and artificial 人間的であり人為的である。(9) unmitigated 何等無条件の。

VIII THE KOAN

with Buddhists generally. In Zen, Dhyana or *zazen* is used as the means of reaching the solution of the *koan*. Zen does not make Dhyana an end in itself, for apart from the *koan* exercise, the practising of *zazen* is a secondary consideration.[1] It is no doubt a necessary accompaniment[2] to the mastery of Zen[3]; even when the *koan* is understood, its deep spiritual truth will not be driven home to the mind of the Zen student if he is not thoroughly trained in *zazen*. *Koan* and *zazen* are the two handmaids of Zen; the first is the eye and the second is the foot.

In the early days of Buddhism in China, philosophical discussion first attracted the attention of the earnest students of Buddhism and such sutras as the *Avatamsaka*,[4] *Pundarika*,[5] *Prajnaparamita*,[6] *Nirvana*,[7] etc., were early translated into Chinese. The deep metaphysical thoughts contained in these sacred texts interested Chinese scholars more than did other matters that were also to be found in them, and it was probably chiefly due to the incomparable Kumarajiva[8] that a great impetus[9] was given to the Chinese Buddhists to the intellectual mastery[10] of the texts. The ethical study[11] of Buddhism came next. When Bodhidharma, the First Patriarch of Zen, came to China in the sixth century, he was looked upon somewhat askance[12] as a sort of heretic.[13] Scholars of Buddhist philosophy did not understand him and disliked him. Even when Yeno (Hui-neng), the Sixth Patriarch, came out of obscurity and self-concealment[14] to announce himself as the rightful transmitter[15] of Zen, he was not very much noticed by the other practisers of Dhyana. So far Dhyana or *zazen* had been practised chiefly after the Hinayana fashion,[16] as we read in the biographical writings of earlier Buddhism in China, and also as we can infer from the sutras on Dhyana which were translated down to those days. It was a generation or two after Yeno that Zen, as we understand it now, really

---

(1) a secondary consideration 第二義的な意味。 (2) a necessary accompaniment 必須条件。 (3) the mastery of Zen 禅に精通すること。 (4) Avatamsaka 『華厳経』。 (5) Pundarika 『法華経』。 (6) Prajnaparamita 『般若経』。 (7) Nirvana 『涅槃経』。 (8) Kumarajiva 鳩摩羅什（くまらじゅう）。中国南北朝時代の僧。インド人の血を引き、『法華経』はじめ多くの経典を中国語訳した。東アジアの仏教は概ね彼によって方向づけられた。 (9) impetus 刺戟。 (10) the intellectual mastery 思想的研究。 (11) the ethical study 実修の研究。 (12) askance 猜疑。 (13) heretic 異端者。 (14) out of obscurity and self-concealment 名もなく、世に出ずにいた身から（微賤と韜晦から）。 (15) the rightful transmitter 正統を嗣ぐもの。 (16) the Hinayana fashion 小乗的様式。

> Restrictions, though mountain-high they are,
> You will attain the Six Miraculous Powers,
> And you will be able to deliver numberless beings;
> When the dust of Annoyance rises so high as to screen the heavenly sun,
> Great showers may wash it away,
> The wind of Intellectual Enlightenment may remove it,
> But it is Dhyana that will destroy it altogether.

Dhyana comes from the root *dhi*, meaning "to perceive", "to reflect upon", "to fix the mind upon"; while *dhi* etymologically may have some connection with *dha*, "to hold", "to keep", "to maintain". Dhyana thus means to hold one's thought collected, not to let thought wander away from its legitimate path[1]; that is, it means to have the mind concentrated on a single subject of thought. Therefore, when Zen or Dhyana is practised, all the outer details are to be so controlled as to bring the mind into the most favourable condition in which it will gradually rise above the turbulence of passions and sensualities.[2] For instance, eating and drinking have to be properly regulated; sleep is not to be too much indulged in; the body is to be kept in an easy and comfortable position, but straight and erect; and as to the control of breathing, the Indians are, as is well known, consummate artists. Next, the choice of the place where the Dhyana-practiser is to sit is another important consideration, and naturally such places as the market, the factory, or the business office may better be avoided. There are many more rules or suggestions relating to the control of the body and the mind, which are fully treated in Chi-sha's work on *Dhyana-Paramita*.[3]

As is evident even from this brief account of Dhyana, *zazen* as is practised by Zen devotees has not the same object in mind as is the case

---

1 As regards the practice of *zazen* in Japan, see my *Zen Essays*, II, pp. 284-7.

(1) its legitimate path 定められた通路。 (2) the turbulence of passions and sensualities 動いてやまぬ情念や官能の作用。 (3) Dhyana-Paramita 禅那波羅蜜。

VIII THE KOAN

Buddhist metaphysics. When a man lacks in any of these qualifications he cannot be said to be a very good follower of Sakyamuni. But as time went on differentiation took place, and some Buddhists came to emphasize one of the three more strongly than the others. Some were moralists more than anything else, others were students of Dhyana, and still others were devoted to the mastery of intellectual subtleties[1] implied in the teachings of Buddhism. Zen followers may be considered practisers of Dhyana, but in Zen Dhyana has ceased to be understood in its primitive sense; for Zen has now its own object in the practice of this particular Indian form of spiritual exercises.

According to the *Mahayana Sastra*[2] quoted in the *Dhyana-Paramita Systematically Expounded*[3] by Chi-sha Daishi, the founder of the T'ien-tai sect,[4] Dhyana is practised in order to fulfil the four great vows[1][5] cherished by every pious Buddhist:

> Dhyana is the storage of good wisdom,
> And the farm of blissful merits;
> Like unto water free from impurities,
> Dhyana washes all the dust of passion;
> Dhyana is the armour wrought of vajra,[6]
> Which shields the wearer from the arrows of
>   evil desires;
> Though you may not yet have attained to a
>   state of non-doing,
> You are already gaining towards Nirvana;[7]
> For you will gain the Vajra-samadhi,[8]
> You will break in pieces the Hindrances and

---

1   1. All sentient beings, however infinite, I vow to save. 2. All the passions, however inexhaustible, I vow to cut asunder. 3. All the holy teachings, however innumerable, I vow to learn. 4. All the Buddha-ways, however unsurpassable, I vow to fulfil.

(1) intellectual subtleties 精緻な知性的構造。 (2) the *Mahayana Sastra* 大乗経典。 (3) the *Dhyana-Paramita Systematically Expounded* 『釈禅波羅蜜次第法門』。 (4) the T'ien-tai sect 天台宗。 (5) the four great vows 四弘誓願（しくせいがん）。仏・菩薩が決意した四つの誓願。 (6) Dhyana is the armour wrought of vajra 禅為金剛鎧。 (7) Nirvana 涅槃。 (8) For you will gain the Vajra-samadhi 得金剛三昧。

Zen is a unique product of the Oriental mind and its uniqueness consists, so far as its practical aspect goes, in its methodical training of the mind in order to mature it to the state of *satori,* when all its secrets are revealed. Zen may be called a form of mysticism, but it differs from all other forms of it in system, in discipline, and in final attainment. By this[1] I mean principally the *koan*[1(2)] exercise and *zazen.*

Zazen, or its Sanskrit equivalent *dhyana,* means sitting cross-legged in quietude and in deep contemplation. The practice originated in India and spread all over and East. It has been going on through centuries now, and the modern followers of Zen still strictly observe it. In this respect *zazen* is the prevailing practical method of spiritual discipline in the East, but when it is used in connection with the *koan* it assumes a special feature and becomes the monopoly of Zen.

To explain fully what *zazen* or Dhyana is is not the object of this chapter, which is chiefly concerned with the *koan* as the most essential feature of Zen now practised in the Far East. Originally in Buddhism, Dhyana was one of its three branches of discipline[3]: *Sila* (moral precepts[4]), *Dhyana* (contemplation), and *Prajna* (wisdom). Good Buddhists are supposed to be morally observant of all the precepts laid down by the Buddha, to be thoroughly versed[5] in the methods for keeping their inordinate[6] passions well under control, and finally to be intellectual[2] enough to know all the intricacies of logic[7] in the advancement of

---

1 For a fuller treatment of the subject, see my *Zen Essays,* II.
2 *Prajna* is the highest power of intuition which sounds the depths of our soul-life, and is naturally much more than merely intellectual. For further information read a chapter on the Prajnaparamita in my *Zen Essays,* III.

編集部注 (1) By this　かくいうとき。(2) koan　公案。禅の問答、または問題。(3) its three branches of discipline　三学。仏道の基本的な三つの修行である戒定慧（かいじょうえ）、すなわち、戒学、定学、慧学をいう。(4) moral precepts　戒、戒学。(5) to be thoroughly versed　通暁しなければ。(6) inordinate　放恣な。(7) the intricacies of logic　複雑な論理。

VIII

THE KOAN

VII SATORI, OR ACQUIRING A NEW VIEWPOINT

now be working to a different key,⁽¹⁾ which will be more satisfying, more peaceful, and fuller of joy than anything you ever experienced before. The tone of life⁽²⁾ will be altered. There is something rejuvenating⁽³⁾ in the possession of Zen. The spring flowers look prettier, and the mountain stream runs cooler and more transparent. The subjective revolution⁽⁴⁾ that brings about this state of things cannot be called abnormal. When life becomes more enjoyable and its expanse broadens to include the universe itself, there must be something in *satori* that is quite precious and well worth one's striving after.⁽⁵⁾

---

(1) to a different key　全然別個の基調に立って。　(2) the tone of life　生の調べ。　(3) rejuvenating　活気を甦らせるもの。　(4) the subjective revolution　心境の転換。　(5) worth one's striving after　求めるに価する。

5. *Satori* is not seeing God as he is, as might be contended by some Christian mystics.[1] Zen has from the beginning made clear and insisted upon the main thesis, which is to see into the work of creation ; the creator may be found busy moulding his universe,[2] or he may be absent from his workshop, but Zen goes on with its own work. It is not dependent upon the support of a creator ; when it grasps the reason for living a life, it is satisfied. Hoyen[3] (Fa-yen, died 1104) of Go-so-san used to produce[4] his own hand and ask his disciples why it was called a hand. When we know the reason, there is *satori* and we have Zen. Whereas with the God of mysticism there is the grasping of a definite object ; when you have God, what is no-God[5] is excluded. This is self-limiting. Zen wants absolute freedom, even from God. "No abiding place"[6] means that very thing ; "Cleanse your mouth when you utter the word Buddha" amounts to the same thing. It is not that Zen wants to be morbidly unholy[7] and godless, but that it recognizes the incompleteness of a mere name. Therefore, when Yakusan (Yueh-shan, 751-834) was asked to give a lecture, he did not say a word, but instead came down from the pulpit and went off to his own room. Hyakujo merely walked forward a few steps, stood still, and then opened out his arms, which was his exposition of the great principle.

6. *Satori* is not a morbid state of mind,[8] a fit subject for the study of abnormal psychology.[9] If anything, it is a perfectly normal state of mind. When I speak of a mental upheaval, some may be led to consider Zen as something to be shunned by ordinary people. This is a most mistaken view of Zen, but one unfortunately often held by prejudiced critics. As Joshu[10] declared,"Zen is your everyday thought[11]" ; it all depends on the adjustment of the hinge whether the door opens in or opens out. Even in the twinkling of an eye the whole affair is changed and you have Zen, and you are as perfect and as normal as ever. More than that, you have acquired in the meantime something altogether new. All your mental activities will

(1) mystics　神秘家。(2) moulding his universe　宇宙形成の仕事。(3) Hoyen　法演。宋代の禅僧（p.59の注参照）。(4) produce　…を突き出して。(5) what is no-God　非神。(6) "No abiding place"　「住処はない」（「無所在」）。(7) to be morbidly unholy　病的に不敬虔である。(8) a morbid state of mind　心の病んだ状態（病態意識）。(9) abnormal psychology　異常心理。(10) Joshu　趙州従諗。南泉の弟子（p.38の注参照）。(11) everyday thought　平常心。

VII SATORI, OR ACQUIRING A NEW VIEWPOINT

pline,[1] which left the more practical Chinese at a loss as to how to grasp the central point of the doctrine of Sakyamuni. Bodhidharma,[2] the Sixth Patriarch, Baso, and other Chinese masters noticed this fact, and the proclamation and development of Zen was the natural outcome. By them *satori* was placed above sutra-learning and scholarly discussions of the sastras[3] and was identified with Zen itself. Zen, therefore, without *satori* is like pepper without its pungency.[4] But there is also such a thing as too much attachment to the experience of *satori*, which is to be detested.

4. This emphasizing of *satori* in Zen makes the fact quite significant that Zen is not a system of Dhyana[5] as practised in India and by other Buddhist schools in China. By Dhyana is generally understood a kind of meditation or contemplation[6] directed toward some fixed thought; in Hinayana Buddhism[7] it was the thought of transiency,[8] while in the Mahayana[9] it was more often the doctrine of emptiness.[10] When the mind has been so trained as to be able to realize a state of perfect void in which there is not a trace of consciousness left, even the sense of being unconscious having departed; in other words, when all forms of mental activity are swept away clean from the field of consciousness, leaving the mind like the sky devoid of every speck of cloud, a mere broad expanse of blue, Dhyana is said to have reached its perfection. This may be called ecstasy or trance, but it is not Zen. In Zen there must be *satori*; there must be a general mental upheaval[11] which destroys the old accumulations of intellection[12] and lays down the foundation for a new life; there must be the awakening of a new sense which will review the old things from a hitherto undreamed-of angle of observation. In Dhyana there are none of these things, for it is merely a quieting exercise of mind.[13] As such Dhyana doubtless has its own merit, but Zen must not be identified with it.

(1) Yoga discipline ヨーガ的修行。 (2) Bodhidharma 菩提達摩 (p.28の注参照)。 (3) sastras (Shastra または Sastra) 論釈。元来はヒンズー教の聖典をいう。 (4) pungency 辛味。 (5) Dhyana 禅那 (p.11の注参照)。 (6) contemplation 凝心 (p.23の注参照)。 (7) Hinayana Buddhism 小乗仏教 (p.8の注参照)。 (8) transiency 無常観。 (9) the Mahayana 大乗仏教 (p.8の注参照)。 (10) the doctrine of emptiness 空観。天台でいう三観の一つ。全ての存在は空であるという見方。 (11) mental upheaval 心的隆起。 (12) intellection 知性作用。 (13) a quieting exercise of mind 心を鎮静に帰する訓練。

therefore, that meditating on metaphysical and symbolical statements,[1] which are products of a relative consciousness,[2] play no part in Zen.

2. Without the attainment of *satori* no one can enter into the truth of Zen. *Satori* is the sudden flashing into consciousness of a new truth hitherto undreamed of. It is a sort of mental catastrophe[3] taking place all at once, after much piling up of matters intellectual and demonstrative.[4] The piling has reached a limit of stability and the whole edifice has come tumbling to the ground, when, behold,[5] a new heaven is open to full survey. When the freezing point is reached, water suddenly turns into ice ; the liquid has suddenly turned into a solid body and no more flows freely. *Satori* comes upon a man unawares, when he feels that he has exhausted his whole being. Religiously, it is a new birth ; intellectually, it is the acquiring of a new viewpoint. The world now appears as if dressed in a new garment, which seems to cover up all the unsightliness[6] of dualism, which is called delusion[7] in Buddhist phraseology.[8]

3. *Satori* is the *raison d'être*[9] of Zen without which Zen is no Zen. Therefore every contrivance,[10] disciplinary or doctrinal, is directed toward *satori*. Zen masters could not remain patient for *satori* to come by itself ; that is, to come sporadically[11] or at its own pleasure. In their earnestness to aid their disciples in the search after the truth of Zen their manifestly enigmatical presentations were designed to create in their disciples a state of mind which would more systematically open the way to enlightenment. All the intellectual demonstrations[12] and exhortatory persuasions[13] so far carried out by most religious and philosophical leaders had failed to produce the desired effect, and their disciples thereby had been farther and farther led astray.[14] Especially was this the case when Buddhism was first introduced into China, with all its Indian heritage of highly metaphysical abstractions[15] and most complicated systems of Yoga disci-

(1) statements 命題。 (2) products of a relative consciousness 相対的意識の産物。 (3) mental catastrophe 精神的大変動。 (4) matters intellectual and demonstrative 知性的、論証的な作為。 (5) behold 見よ。 (6) unsightliness 醜悪さ。 (7) delusion (仏教で) 無明。真実が見えないこと。 (8) in Buddhist phraseology 仏教でいう。 (9) the *raison d'être* 存在理由。 (10) every contrivance あらゆる方便。 (11) sporadically あちこちと。 (12) intellectual demonstrations 知性的弁証。 (13) exhortatory persuasions 諄諄(じゅんじゅん)たる説得。 (14) been〜 led astray 迷い出て行った。 (15) abstractions 抽象的諸観念。

VII SATORI, OR ACQUIRING A NEW VIEWPOINT

experience in things worldly, it is like a drop of water thrown into an unfathomable abyss.[1]"

One day, following the incident of the flying geese, to which reference was made elsewhere, Baso appeared in the preaching hall and was about to speak before a congregation, when Hyakujo, whose nose was literally put out of joint, came forward and began to roll up the matting which is spread before the Buddha for the master to kneel. The rolling up generally means the end of the sermon. Baso, without protesting, came down from the pulpit[2] and returned to his room. He sent for Hyakujo and asked him why he rolled up the matting before he had even uttered a word. Replied Hyakujo, "Yesterday you twisted my nose and it was quite painful." Said Baso, "Where were your thoughts wandering?" Hyakujo replied, "Today it is no longer painful." With this Baso admitted Hyakujo's understanding.

These examples are sufficient to show what changes are produced in one's mind by the attainment of *satori*. Before *satori*, how helpless those monks were! They were like travellers lost in the desert. But after *satori* they behave like absolute monarchs; they are no longer slaves to anybody, they are themselves master.

After these remarks the following points about the opening of the mind that is called *satori* may be observed and summarized.

1. People often imagine that the discipline of Zen is to produce a state of self-suggestion[3] through meditation. This entirely misses the mark, as can be seen from the various instances cited above. *Satori* does not consist in producing a certain premeditated condition[4] by intensely thinking of it. It is acquiring a new point of view for looking at things. Ever since the unfoldment of consciousness[5] we have been led to respond to the inner and outer conditions in a certain conceptual and analytical manner. The discipline of Zen consists in upsetting this ground-work[6] once for all and reconstructing the old frame on an entirely new basis. It is evident,

---

(1) an unfathomable abyss　底知れぬ淵（巨壑（きょがく））。　(2) the pulpit　壇。説教壇。
(3) self-suggestion　自己暗示。　(4) a certain premeditated condition　一定の予期された意識状態。　(5) the unfoldment of consciousness　意識の発生。　(6) ground-work　基礎工事。

describe the content of *satori*, if there is any? Your examples and statements are tentative enough, but we simply know how the wind blows; where is the port the boat finally makes for?" To this the Zen devotee may answer: As far as content goes, there is none in either *satori* or Zen that can be described or presented or demonstrated for your intellectual appreciation. For Zen has no business with ideas,[1] and *satori* is a sort of inner perception—not the perception, indeed, of a single individual object but the perception of Reality itself,[2] so to speak. The ultimate destination of *satori* is towards the Self; it has no other end but to be back within oneself. Therefore, said Joshu, "Have a cup of tea." Therefore, said Nansen, "This is such a good sickle, it cuts so well." This is the way the Self functions, and it must be caught, if at all catchable, in the midst of its functioning.

As *satori* strikes at the primary root of existence, its attainment generally marks a turning point in one's life. The attainment, however, must be thoroughgoing and clear-cut; a lukewarm *satori*, if there is such a thing, is worse than no *satori*. See the following examples:

When Rinzai (Lin-chi) was meekly[3] submitting to the thirty blows of Obaku[4] (Huang-po), he presented a pitiable sight, but as soon as he had attained *satori* he was quite a different personage. His first exclamation was, "There is not much after all in the Buddhism of Obaku." And when he again saw the reproachful Obaku, he returned his favour by giving him a slap in the face. "What arrogance! What impudence!" one may think. But there was reason in Rinzai's rudeness; no wonder Obaku was quite pleased with this treatment.

When Tokusan (Te-shan) gained an insight into the truth of Zen he immediately took out all his commentaries on the *Diamond Sutra*,[5] once so valued and considered indispensable that he had to carry them wherever he went, and set fire to them, reducing all the manuscripts to ashes. He exclaimed, "However deep one's knowledge of abstruse philosophy,[6] it is like a piece of hair flying in the vastness of space; however important one's

(1) has no business with ideas　観念とは没交渉である。　(2) Reality itself　実在そのもの。　(3) meekly　素直に。　(4) Obaku　黄檗 (p.38の注参照)。　(5) the *Diamond Sutra*　『金剛経』。　(6) abstruse philosophy　深遠な哲学。

VII SATORI, OR ACQUIRING A NEW VIEWPOINT

an unintelligent remark,[1] a blooming flower, or a trivial incident such as stumbling, is the condition or occasion that will open his mind to *satori*. Apparently, an insignificant event produces an effect which in importance is altogether out of proportion. The light touch of an igniting wire,[2] and an explosion follows which will shake the very foundation of the earth. All the causes, all the conditions of *satori* are in the mind; they are merely waiting for the maturing. When the mind is ready for some reasons or others, a bird flies, or a bell rings, and you at once return to your original home; that is, you discover your now real self.[3] From the very beginning nothing has been kept from you, all that you wished to see has been there all the time before you, it was only yourself that closed the eye to the fact. Therefore, there is in Zen nothing to explain, nothing to teach, that will add to your knowledge. Unless it grows out of yourself no knowledge is really yours, it is only a borrowed plumage.[4]

Kozankoku[5] (Huang Shan-ku), a Confucian poet[6] and statesman of the Sung,[7] came to Kwaido[8] (Hui-t'ang) to be initiated into Zen. Said the Zen master: "There is a passage in the text with which you are perfectly familiar which fitly[9] describes the teaching of Zen. Did not Confucius declare: 'Do you think I am hiding things from you, O my disciples? Indeed, I have nothing to hide from you.'" Kozankoku tried to answer, but Kwaido immediately checked him by saying, "No, no!" The Confucian scholar felt troubled in mind but did not know how to express himself. Some time later they were having a walk in the mountains; the wild laurel was in full bloom and the air was redolent with its scent. Asked the Zen master, "Do you smell it?" When the Confucian answered affirmatively, Kwaido said, "There, I have nothing to hide from you." This reminder,[10] at once led Kozankoku's mind to the opening of a *satori*.

These examples will suffice to show what *satori* is and how it unfolds itself. The reader may ask, however: "After the perusal[11] of all your explanations or indications, we are not a whit wiser. Can you not definitely

(1) an unintelligent remark　何でもない言葉。 (2) an igniting wire　導火線。 (3) your now real self　本来の面目。 (4) a borrowed plumage　借りものの晴れ着。 (5) Kozankoku　黄山谷。 (6) a Confucian poet　儒者。 (7) the Sung　宋代。 (8) Kwaido　晦堂祖心。宋代の禅僧。 (9) fitly　そっくり符合する。 (10) this reminder　この示唆。 (11) the perusal　丹念に読んだ。

disappointed and considered him unkind. Finally he came to the decision to burn up all his notes and memoranda, which seemed to be of no help to his spiritual welfare,[1] and, retiring altogether from the world, to spend the rest of his life in solitude and the simple life in accordance with Buddhist rules. He reasoned: "What is the use of studying Buddhism, which is so difficult to comprehend and which is too subtle to receive as instruction from another? I will be a plain homeless monk, troubled with no desire to master things too deep for thought." He left Yisan and built a hut near the tomb of Chu, the National Master at Nan-yang.[2] One day he was weeding and sweeping the ground when a pebble which he had swept away struck a bamboo; the unexpected sound produced by the percussion elevated his mind to a state of *satori*. His joy was boundless.[3] The question proposed by Yisan became transparent; he felt as if meeting his lost parents. Besides, he came to realize the kindness of Yisan in refusing him instruction, for now he realized that this experience could not have happened to him if Yisan had been unkind enough to explain things to him.

Cannot Zen be so explained that a master can lead all his pupils to enlightenment through explanation? Is *satori* something that is not at all capable of intellectual analysis? Yes, it is an experience which no amount of explanation or argument can make communicable to others unless the latter themselves had it previously. If *satori* is amenable to analysis[4] in the sense that by so doing it becomes perfectly clear to another who has never had it, that *satori* will be no *satori*. For a *satori* turned into a concept ceases to be itself; and there will no more be a Zen experience. Therefore, all that we can do in Zen in the way of instruction is to indicate, or to suggest, or to show the way so that one's attention may be directed towards the goal. As to attaining the goal and taking hold of the thing itself, this must be done by one's own hands, for nobody else can do it for one. As regards the indication, it lies everywhere. When a man's mind is matured for *satori* it tumbles over one everywhere. An inarticulate sound,[5]

(1) his spiritual welfare　安心。　(2) Chu, the National Master at Nan-yang　南陽忠国師 (p.80の注参照)。　(3) boundless　云い知れぬものがあった。　(4) amenable to analysis　分析を許す。　(5) an inarticulate sound　微かな音。

VII SATORI, OR ACQUIRING A NEW VIEWPOINT

or thirsty, my eating of food or drinking will not fill your stomach; you must eat and drink for yourself. When you want to respond to the calls of nature you must take care of yourself, for I cannot be of any use to you. And then it will be nobody else but yourself that will carry your body along this highway." This friendly counsel at once opened the mind of the truth-seeking monk, who was so transported with his discovery that he did not know how to express his joy. Sogen said that his work was now done and that his further companionship would have no meaning after this; so he left Doken to continue his journey all by himself. After a half year Doken returned to his own monastery. Daiye, on his way down the mountains, happened to meet Doken and at once made the following remark, "This time he knows it all." What was it, let me ask, that flashed through Doken's mind[1] when his friend Sogen gave him such matter-of-fact advice?

Kyogen[2] (Hsiang-yen) was a disciple of Hyakujo[3] (Pai-chang). After his master's death Kyogen went to Yisan (Kuei-shan), who had been a senior disciple of Hyakujo. Yisan asked him: "I am told that you have been studying under my late master, and also that you have remarkable intelligence. The understanding of Zen through this medium[4] necessarily ends in intellectual analytical comprehension, which is not of much use; but nevertheless you may have had an insight into the truth of Zen. Let me have your view as to the reason of birth and death; that is, as to your own being before your parents had given birth to you."

Thus asked, Kyogen did not know how to reply. He retired into his own room and assiduously[5] made research into the notes which he had taken of the sermons given by their late master. He failed to come across a suitable passage which he might present as his own view. He returned to Yisan and implored him to teach him in the faith of Zen, but Yisan replied: "I really have nothing to impart to you, and if I tried to do so you might have occasion to make me an object of ridicule.[6] Besides, whatever I can tell you is my own and can never be yours." Kyogen was

(1) that flashed through Doken's mind　道謙の心に閃き出たものは。 (2) Kyogen　香厳知閑。唐末の禅僧。 (3) Hyakujo　百丈 (p.61の注参照)。 (4) through this medium　そういうものを頼りにして。 (5) assiduously　熱心に。 (6) an object of ridicule　嗤いもの。

Hyakujo (Pai-chang) went out one day attending his master Baso (Ma-tsu), when they saw a flock of wild geese flying. Baso asked:

"What are they?"

"They are wild geese, sir."

"Whither are they flying?"

"They have flown away."

Baso, abruptly taking hold of Hyakujo's nose, gave it a twist. Overcome with pain, Hyakujo cried out: "Oh! Oh!"

Said Baso, "You say they have flown away, but all the same they have been here from the very first."

This made Hyakujo's back wet with perspiration; he had *satori*.

Is there any possible connection between the washing of the bowls and the blowing out of the candle and the twisting of the nose? We must say with Ummon: If there is none, how could they have all come to a realization of the truth of Zen? If there is, what is the inner relationship? What is this *satori*? What new point of view of looking at things is this?

Under Daiye[(1)] (Ta-hui),[1] the great Zen master of the Sung dynasty,[(2)] there was a monk named Doken[(3)] (Tao-ch'ien), who had spent many years in the study of Zen, but who had not as yet uncovered its secrets, if there were any. He was quite discouraged when he was sent on an errand to a distant city. A trip requiring half a year to finish would be a hindrance rather than a help to his study. Sogen[(4)] (Tsung-yuan), one of his fellow-students, was most sympathetic and said, "I will accompany you on this trip and do all I can for you; there is no reason why you cannot go on with your meditation[(5)] even while travelling." One evening Doken despairingly implored his friend to assist him in the solution of the mystery of life. The friend said, "I am willing to help you in every way I can, but there are some things in which I cannot be of any help to you; these you must look after for yourself." Doken expressed the desire to know what these things were. Said his friend: "For instance, when you are hungry

---

1 1089-1163. A disciple of Yengo.

(1) Daiye　大慧宗杲（だいえしゅこう）。南宗の禅僧。圜悟の弟子。　(2) the Sung dynasty 宋朝。　(3) Doken　道謙。　(4) Sogen　竹原宗元。南宋の禅僧。　(5) go on with your meditation　工夫を続け（る）。

VII SATORI, OR ACQUIRING A NEW VIEWPOINT

the master:

"Have you had your breakfast, or not?"

"Yes, master, I have," answered the monk.

"Go and get your bowls washed," was the immediate response. And this suggestion at once opened the monk's mind to the truth of Zen.

Later on Ummon[1] commented on the response, saying: "Was there any special instruction in this remark by Joshu, or was there not? If there was, what was it? If there was not, what *satori* was it which the monk attained?" Still later Suigan[2] had the following retort on Ummon: "The great master Ummon does not know what is what; hence this comment of his. It is altogether unnecessary; it is like painting legs to a snake, or painting a beard to the eunuch.[3] My view differs from his. That monk who seems to have attained a sort of *satori* goes to hell as straight as an arrow!"

What does all this mean—Joshu's remark about washing the bowls, the monk's attainment of *satori*, Ummon's alternatives,[4] and Suigan's assurance[5]? Are they speaking against one another, or is it much ado about nothing[6]? To my mind, they are all pointing one way and the monk may go anywhere, but his *satori* is not to no purpose.[7]

Tokusan was a great scholar of the *Diamond Sutra*.[8] Learning that there was such a thing as Zen, ignoring all the written scriptures[9] and directly laying hands on one's soul,[10] he went to Ryutan[11] to be instructed in the teaching. One day Tokusan was sitting outside trying to look into the mystery of Zen.[12] Ryutan said, "Why don't you come in?" Replied Tokusan, "It is pitch dark." A candle was lighted and held out to Tokusan. When he was at the point of taking it Ryutan suddenly blew out the light, whereupon the mind of Tokusan was opened.

(1) Ummon　雲門。唐代の禅僧。(2) Suigan　翠巖令参。中国五代の禅僧。(3) the eunuch　宦官。(4) alternatives　二者択一の問いかけ（選言命題）。(5) assurance　断案。(6) ado about nothing　空騒ぎ。(7) not to no purpose　無駄ではない。(8) the Diamond Sutra　金剛経。(9) ignoring all the written scriptures　不立文字（ふりゅうもんじ）。「不立文字、教外別伝（きょうげべつでん）、直指人心（じきしにんしん）。見性成仏（けんしょうじょうぶつ）」の四句は禅の宗義をあらわす代表的な言葉。悟りは言葉で伝えるものではなく、体験により、ひたすら座禅によって直入するものであることを言う。(10) directly laying hands on one's soul　直指人心（p.60参照）。(11) Ryutan　龍潭崇信。唐代の禅僧。(12) the mystery of Zen　禅の秘要。

The object of Zen discipline consists in acquiring a new viewpoint[1] for looking into the essence of things. If you have been in the habit of thinking logically according to the rules of dualism, rid yourself of it and you may come around somewhat to the viewpoint of Zen. You and I are supposedly living in the same world, but who can tell that the thing we popularly call a stone that is lying before my window is the same to both of us? You and I sip a cup of tea. That act is apparently alike to us both, but who can tell what a wide gap there is subjectively[(1)] between your drinking and my drinking? In your drinking there may be no Zen, while mine is brim-full[(2)] of it. The reason for it is: you move in a logical circle and I am out of it. Though there is in fact nothing new in the so-called new viewpoint of Zen, the term "new" is convenient to express the Zen way of viewing the world, but its use here is a condescension[(3)] on the part of Zen.

This acquiring of a new viewpoint in Zen is called *satori* (*wu* in C.) and its verb form is *satoru*. Without it there is no Zen, for the life of Zen begins with the "opening of *satori*". *Satori* may be defined as intuitive looking-into,[(4)] in contradistinction to intellectual and logical understanding. Whatever the definition, *satori* means the unfolding of a new world hitherto unperceived in the confusion of a dualistic mind. With this preliminary remark I wish the reader to ponder the following *mondo* (literally, "asking and answering"), which I hope will illustrate my statement.

A young monk[(5)] asked Joshu to be instructed in the faith of Zen. Said

---

1 This subject is more fully treated in my *Zen Essays*, I, pp. 215-50, and also in II, pp. 4 ff.

編集部注 (1) subjectively　心境的に。 (2) brim-full　横溢している。 (3) a condescension　一歩譲った表現。 (4) intuitive looking-into　直覚的洞察。 (5) a young monk　叢林に入って間もない一僧。

VII

SATORI, OR ACQUIRING A NEW VIEWPOINT

"When the mind is not abiding in any particular object,[1] we say that it abides where there is no abiding."

"What is meant by not abiding in any particular object?"

"It means not to be abiding in the dualism of good and evil, being and non-being, thought and matter[2]; it means not to be abiding in emptiness or in non-emptiness, neither in tranquillity nor in non-tranquillity. Where there is no abiding place, this is truly the abiding place for the mind."

Seppo[3] (Hsueh-feng, 822-908) was one of the most earnest truth-seekers in the history of Zen during the T'ang dynasty. He is said to have carried a ladle[4] throughout the long years of his disciplinary Zen peregrinations.[5] His idea was to serve in one of the most despised and most difficult positions in the monastery life—that is, as cook—and the ladle was his symbol. When he finally succeeded Tokusan (Teh-shan) as Zen master a monk approached him and asked: "What is that you have attained under Tokusan? How serene and self-contained[6] you are!" " Empty-handed I went away from home, and empty-handed I returned." Is not this a practical explanation of the doctrine of "no abiding place"? The monks wanted their master Hyakujo (Pai-chang) to give a lecture on Zen. He said, "You attend to the farming and later on I will tell you all about Zen." After they had finished the work the master was requested to fulfil his promise, whereupon he opened out both his arms, but said not a word. This was his great sermon.

---

(1) object　対象。(2) being and non-being, thought and matter　心と物。(3) Seppo 雪峯。唐代の禅僧。(4) a ladle　柄杓。(5) peregrinations　行脚。(6) How serene and self-contained　かくも悠々自在の境涯。

cow," said the pupil. "How do you attend her?" "If she goes out of the path even once, I pull her back straightway by the nose; not a moment's delay is allowed." Said the master, "You truly know how to take care of her." This is not naturalism. Here is an effort to do the right thing.

A distinguished teacher was once asked, "Do you ever make any effort to get disciplined in the truth[1]?"

"Yes, I do."

"How do you exercise yourself?"

"When I am hungry I eat; when tired I sleep."

"This is what everybody does; can they be said to be exercising themselves in the same way as you do?"

"No."

"Why not?"

"Because when they eat they do not eat, but are thinking of various other things, thereby allowing themselves to be di turbed; When they sleep they do not sleep, but dream of a thousand and one things. This is why they are not like myself."

If Zen is to be called a form of naturalism, then it is so with a rigorous discipline at the back of it.[2] It is in that sense, and not as it is understood by libertines,[3] that Zen may be designated naturalism. The libertines have no freedom of will, they are bound hands and feet by external agencies before which they are utterly helpless. Zen, on the contrary, enjoys perfect freedom; that is, it is master of itself.[4] Zen has no "abiding place",[5] to use a favourite expression in the *Prajnaparamita Sutras*.[6] When a thing has its fixed abode, it is fettered, it is no more absolute. The following dialogue will very clearly explain this point.

A monk asked, "Where is the abiding place for the mind?"

"The mind," answered the master, "abides where there is no abiding."

"What is meant by 'there is no abiding'?"

---

(1) to get disciplined in the truth　真理の習得。　(2) with a rigorous discipline at the back of it　厳しい訓練に裏打ちされた。　(3) libertines　放縦主義者。　(4) it is master of itself　随処為主。　(5) "abiding place"　住処。　(6) the *Prajnaparamita Sutras*　般若経典。

answered, "Yes!" Thus called three times, he answered three times, when the master remarked, "O you stupid fellow!" This brought Ryosui to his senses; he now understood Zen and exclaimed: "O master, don't deceive me any more. If I had not come to you I should have been miserably led astray[1] all my life by the sutras and the sastras." Later on Ryosui said to some of his fellow-monks who had been spending their time in the mastery of Buddhist philosophy, "All that you know, I know; but what I know, none of you know." Is it not wonderful that Ryosui could make such an utterance just by understanding the significance of his master's call?

Do these examples make the subject in hand any clearer or more intelligible than before? I can multiply such instances indefinitely, but those so far cited may suffice to show that Zen is after all not a very complicated affair, or a study requiring the highest faculty of abstraction and speculation. The truth and power of Zen consists in its very simplicity, directness, and utmost practicalness. "Good morning; how are you today?" "Thank you, I am well"—here is Zen. "Please have a cup of tea"—this, again, is full of Zen. When a hungry monk at work heard the dinner-gong he immediately dropped his work and showed himself in the dining-room. The master, seeing him, laughed heartily, for the monk had been acting Zen to its fullest extent. Nothing could be more natural; the one thing needful[2] is just to open one's eye to the significance of it all.

But here is a dangerous loophole[3] which the student of Zen ought to be especially careful to avoid. Zen must never be confused with naturalism or libertinism,[4] which means to follow one's natural bent without questioning its origin and value. There is a great difference between human action and that of the animals, which are lacking in moral intuition[5] and religious consciousness.[6] The animals do not know anything about exerting themselves in order to improve their conditions or to progress in the way to higher virtues. Sekkyo was one day working in the kitchen when Baso,[7] his Zen teacher, came in and asked what he was doing. "I am herding the

---

(1) led astray すかされて（迷わされて）。 (2) the one thing needful 唯一つ忘れてはならぬのは。 (3) loophole 陥穽。 (4) libertinism 放縦主義。 (5) moral intuition 道徳的直観。 (6) religious consciousness 宗教意識。 (7) Baso 馬祖道一（p.60の注参照）。（p.80の Matsu と同じ）。

Sekkyo said: "Is that the way? But after all you have not got anything."

"What then," asked the monk, "is your way?"

The master straightway took hold of the monk's nose and gave it a hard pull, which made the latter exclaim: "Oh, oh, how hard you pull at my nose! You are hurting me terribly!"

"That is the way to have good hold of empty space," said the master.

When Yenkwan[1] (Yen-kuan), one of Ma-tsu's[2] disciples, was asked by a monk who the real Vairochana Buddha[3] was, he told the monk to pass over a water-pitcher which was near by. The monk brought it to him as requested, but Yenkwan now ordered it to be taken back to its former place. After obediently following the order, the monk again asked the master who the real Vairochana Buddha was. "The venerable old Buddha is no more here," was the reply. Concerning this incident another Zen master comments, "Yes, the venerable old Buddha has long been here."

If these incidents are regarded as not entirely free from intellectual complications,[4] what would you think of the following case of Chu (Chung, died 775), the national teacher of Nan-yang,[5] who used to call his attendant three times a day, saying, "O my attendant, my attendant!" To this the attendant would respond regularly, "Yes, master." Finally the master remarked, "I thought I was in the wrong with you, but it is you that is in the wrong with me." Is this not simple enough?—just calling one by name? Chu's last comment may not be so very intelligible from an ordinary logical point of view, but one calling and another responding is one of the cmmonest and most practical affairs of life. Zen declares that the truth is precisely there, so we can see what a matter-of-fact thing Zen is. There is no mystery in it, the fact is open to all: I hail you, and you call back; one "hallo!" calls forth another "hallo!" and this is all there is to it.

Ryosui[6] (Liang-sui) was studying Zen under Mayoku[7] (Ma-ku, a contemporary of Rinzai), and when Mayoku called out, "O Ryosui!" he

---

(1) Yenkwan　塩官。 (2) Ma-tsu　馬祖道一。Baso　も同じ (p.60の注参照)。 (3) Vairochana Buddha　毘廬舎那仏。 (4) intellectual complications　知性的葛藤。 (5) Chu, the national teacher of Nan-yang　南陽忠国師。南陽慧忠。唐代の禅僧。 (6) Ryosui　寿州良遂。唐代の禅僧。 (7) Mayoku　麻谷。唐代の禅僧。

VI PRACTICAL ZEN

have? A Zen poet sings:

> How wondrously strange, and how miraculous this!
> I draw water, I carry fuel.

When Zen is said to be illogical and irrational, timid readers are frightened and may wish to have nothing to do with it, but I am confident that the present chapter devoted to practical Zen will mitigate whatever harshness and uncouthness[1] there may have been in it when it was intellectually treated. In so far as the truth of Zen is on its practical side and not in its irrationality, we must not put too much emphasis on its irrationality. This may tend only to make Zen more inaccessible to ordinary intellects, but in order to show further what a simple and matter-of-fact business[2] Zen is, and at the same time to emphasize the practical side of Zen, I will cite some more of the so-called "cases" in which appeal is made to the most naive experience one may have in life. Naive they are, indeed, in the sense of being free from conceptual demonstration[3] or from intellectual analysis You see a stick raised, or you are asked to pass a piece of household furniture, or are simply addressed by your name. Such as these are the simplest incidents of life occurring every day and being passed without any particular notice, and yet Zen is there—the Zen that is supposed to be so full of irrationalities, or, if you like to put it so, so full of the highest speculations[4] that are possible to the human understanding. The following are some more of these instances, simple, direct, and practical, and yet pregnant with meaning.

Sekkyo[5] (Shih-kung)¹ asked one of his accomplished[6] monks, "Can you take hold of empty space?"

"Yes, sir," he replied.

"Show me how you do it."

The monk stretched out his arm and clutched at empty space.

---

1 A disciple of Ma-tsu. He was a hunter before conversion, and for his interview with Ma-tsu see my *Zen Essays*, III, under "Shih-kung and San-ping", by Motonobu Kano.

(1) uncouthness　取りつきにくい印象。　(2) a simple and matter-of-fact business　単純でありきたりの事柄（単純常凡な事柄）。　(3) conceptual demonstration　概念的弁証。　(4) speculations　思弁。　(5) Sekkyo　石鞏　馬祖の弟子。　(6) accomplished　得法の。

within an enclosure called space? Zen would answer at once: "With the burning of an incense-stick the whole *triloka*[1] burns. Within Joshu's cup of tea the mermaids are dancing." So long as one is conscious of space and time, Zen will keep a respectable distance from you; your holiday is ill-spent, your sleep is disturbed, and your whole life is a failure.

Read the following dialogue between Yisan (Kuei-shan) and Kyozan[2] (Yang-shan). At the end of his summer's sojourn[3] Kyozan paid a visit to Yisan, who said, "I have not seen you this whole summer coming up this way; what have you been doing down there?"

Replied Kyozan, "Down there I have been tilling a piece of ground and finished sowing millet seeds."

Yisan said, "Then you have not wasted your summer."

It was now Kyozan's turn to ask Yisan as to his doings during the past summer, and he asked, "How did you pass your summer?"

"One meal a day and a good sleep at night."

This brought out Kyozan's comment, "Then you have not wasted your summer."

A Confucian scholar writes, "They seek the truth too far away from themselves, while it is right near them." The same thing may be said of Zen. We look for its secrets where they are most unlikely to be found, that is, in verbal abstractions and metaphysical subtleties,[4] whereas the truth of Zen really lies in the concrete things of our daily life. A monk asked the master: "It is some time since I came to you to be instructed in the holy path of the Buddha, but you have never given me even an inkling of it.[5] I pray you to be more sympathetic." To this the following answer was given: "What do you mean, my son[6]? Every morning you salute me, and do I not return it? When you bring me a cup of tea, do I not accept it and enjoy drinking it? Besides this, what more instructions do you desire from me?"

Is this Zen? It this the kind of life-experience Zen wants us to

---

(1) triloka 三界。 (2) Kyozan 仰山慧寂。唐代の禅僧。師の潙山と「潙仰宗」の開祖。 (3) his summer's sojourn 夏安居（げあんご）。仏教教団で行なわれる夏の修行。 (4) in verbal abstractions and metaphysical subtleties 抽象的な言葉や形而上学的な、哲学的な難解な表現のうちに（言語的表現や体系的精緻の上に）。 (5) an inkling of it それらしいもの。 (6) my son 弟子よ。

one hundred and twentieth year. Whatever utterances he made were like jewels that sparkled brightly. It was said of him, "His Zen shines upon his lips." A monk who was still a novice[1] came to him and asked to be instructed in Zen.

Joshu said, "Have you not had your breakfast yet?"

Replied the monk, "Yes, sir, I have had it already."

"If so wash your dishes." This remark by the old master opened the novice's eye to the truth of Zen.

One day he was sweeping the ground when a monk asked him, "You are such a wise and holy master; tell me how it is that dust ever accumulates in your yard."

Said the master, "It comes from the outside."

Another time he was asked, "Why does this holy place attract dust?" To which his reply was, "There, another particle of dust!"

There was a famous stone bridge at Joshu's monastery, which was one of the sights there. A stranger monk inquired of him, "I have for some time heard of your famous stone bridge, but I see no such thing here, only a plank."

Said Joshu, "You see a plank and don't see a stone bridge."

"Where then is the stone bridge?"

"You have just crossed it," was the prompt reply.

At another time when Joshu was asked about this same stone bridge, his answer was, "Horses pass it, people pass it, everybody passes it."

In these dialogues do we only see trivial talks about ordinary things of life and nature? Is there nothing spiritual, conducive to the enlightenment of the religious soul[2]? Is Zen, then, too practical, too commonplace? Is it too abrupt a descent from the height of transcendentalism[3] to everyday things? Well, it all depends on how you look at it. A stick of incense[4] is burning on my desk. Is this a trivial affair? An earthquake shakes the earth and Mt. Fuji topples over. Is this a great event? Yes, so long as the conception of space remains.[5] But are we really living confined

(1) a monk who was still a novice 叢林に入ったばかりの僧。 (2) conducive to the enlightenment of the religious soul 宗教的な魂の開眼に資する。 (3) transcendentalism 超越論。 (4) a stick of incense 一本の線香。 (5) so long as the conception of space remains 空間的な見方の中にある限り。

II

Those who have only read the foregoing treatment of Zen as illogical, or of Zen as a higher affirmation, may conclude that Zen is something unapproachable, something far apart from our ordinary everyday life, something very alluring but very elusive[1]; and we cannot blame them for so thinking. Zen ought, therefore, to be presented also from its easy, familiar, and approachable side. Life is the basis of all things; apart from it nothing can stand. With all our philosophy, with all our grand and enhancing ideas, we cannot escape life as we live it[2]. Star-gazers[3] are still walking on the solid earth.

What is Zen, then, when made accessible to everybody? Joshu (Chao-chou) once asked a new monk:

"Have you ever been here before?"

The monk answered, "Yes, sir, I have."

Thereupon the master said, "Have a cup of tea."

Later on another monk came and he asked him the same question, "Have you ever been here?"

This time the answer was quite opposite. "I have never been here, sir."

The old master, however, answered just as before, " Have a cup of tea."

Afterwards the Inju (the managing monk of the monastery) asked the master, "How is it that you make the same offering of a cup of tea no matter what a monk's reply is?"

The old master called out, "O Inju!" who at once replied, "Yes, master." Whereupon Joshu said, "Have a cup of tea."

Joshu (778-897) was one of the most astute[4] Zen masters during the T'ang dynasty, and the development of Zen in China owes much to him. He is said to have travelled[5] even when he was eighty years of age, his object being to perfect himself in the mastery of Zen. He died in his

---

(1) elusive 捉えどころがない。 (2) life as we live it あるがままの生。 (3) star-gazers 星を仰ぐ人。 (4) astute 機敏な。 (5) have travelled 行脚（あんぎゃ）していた。

VI PRACTICAL ZEN

taken from a treatise[1] by Daiju[1] on some principles of Zen compiled in the eighth (or ninth) century, when Zen had begun to flourish in all its brilliance and with all its uniqueness.[2] A monk asked Daiju:

"Q. Are words the Mind?

"A. No, words are external conditions[3] (*yen* in J.; *yuan* in C.); they are not the Mind.

"Q. Apart from external conditions, where is the Mind to be sought?

"A. There is no Mind independent of words. [That is to say, the Mind is in words, but is not to be identified with them.]

"Q. If there is no Mind independent of words, what is the Mind?

"A. The Mind is formless and imageless. The truth is, it is neither independent of nor dependent upon words. It is eternally serene[4] and free in its activity. Says the Patriarch, 'When you realize that the Mind is no Mind, you understand the Mind and its workings.'"

Daiju further writes: "That which produces all things is called Dharma-nature, or Dharmakaya.[5] By the so-called Dharma is meant the Mind of all beings. When this Mind is stirred up, all things are stirred up. When the Mind is not stirred up, there is nothing stirring and there is no name. The confused do not understand that the Dharmakaya, in itself formless, assumes individual forms according to conditions. The confused[6] take the green bamboo for Dharmakaya itself, the yellow blooming tree for Prajna[7] itself. But if the tree were Prajna, Prajna would be identical with the non-sentient.[8] If the bamboo were Dharmakaya, Dharmakaya would be identical with a plant. But Dharmakaya exists, Prajna exists, even when there is no blooming tree, no green bamboo. Otherwise, when one eats a bamboo-shoot, this would be eating up Dharmakaya itself. Such views as this are really not worth talking about."

---

1 Daiju Ekai, or Ta-chu Hui-hai in Chinese, was a disciple of Ma-tsu (died 788), and his work, which may be rendered "A Treatise on the Essence of Sudden Awakening", in two fascicles, gives the principal teachings of Zen as then understood.

(1) a treatise 語録。 (2) its uniqueness その特色。 (3) external conditions 縁。 (4) eternally serene 常に湛然 (たんぜん) として。 (5) Dharma-nature, or Dharmakaya 法性 もしくは法身。 (6) the confused 迷人。 (7) Prajna 般若。 (8) the non-sentient 無常の一存在。

Ummon) answered, "Three pounds of flax," to the question, "What is the Buddha ?"—which, by the way, is the same thing as asking, "What is God ?"—he did not mean that the flax he might have been handling at the time was a visible manifestation of Buddha, that Buddha when seen with an eye of intelligence could be met with in every object. His answer simply was, "Three pounds of flax." He did not imply anything metaphysical in this plain matter-of-fact utterance. These words came out of his inmost consciousness as water flows out of a spring, or as a bud bursts forth in the sun. There was no premeditation[1] or philosophy on his part. Therefore, if we want to grasp the meaning of "Three pounds of flax," we first have to penetrate into the inmost recess of Tozan's consciousness and not to try to follow up his mouth.[2] At another time he may give an entirely different answer, which might directly contradict the one already given. Logicians[3] will naturally be nonplussed[4]; they may declare him altogether out of mind. But the students of Zen will say, "It is raining so gently, see how fresh and green the grass is,"[5] and they know well that their answer is in full accord with Tozan's "Three pounds of flax."

The following will perhaps show further that Zen is not a form of pantheism, if we understand by this any philosophy that identifies the visible universe with the highest reality, called God, or Mind, or otherwise, and states that God cannot exist independent of his manifestations.[6] In fact, Zen is something more than this. In Zen there is no place for time-wasting philosophical discussion. But philosophy is also a manifestation of life-activity, and therefore Zen does not necessarily shun it. When a philosopher comes to be enlightened, the Zen master is never loath[7] to meet him on his own ground. The earlier Zen masters were comparatively tolerant toward the so-called philosophers and not so impatient as in the case of Rinzai[8] (Lin-chi, died 867) or Tokusan[9] (Te-shan, 780-865), whose dealings with them were swift and most direct.[10] What follows is

(1) premeditation 準備観念。 (2) follow up his mouth 言葉の意味を考える（その口先について廻っていく）。 (3) logicians 論理学者。 (4) be nonplussed 処置に窮する。 (5) "It is raining so gently, see how fresh and green the grass is." 雨群峯を洗って翠色を添う。 (6) independent of his manifestations こうした呼称で呼ばれるものから自由になって（この顕現の相を離れては）。 (7) never loath 快く。 (8) Rinzai 臨済（867年没）。 (9) Tokusan 徳山（780年～865年）。 (10) swift and most direct 単刀直入の。

ously[1] and without a moment's delay. A gong is struck and its vibrations instantly follow. If we are not on the alert we fail to catch them; a mere winking and we miss the mark forever. They justly compare Zen to lightning. The rapidity, however, does not constitute Zen; its naturalness, its freedom from artificialities, its being expressive of life itself, its originality—these are the essential characteristics of Zen. Therefore, we have always to be on guard not to be carried away by outward signs when we really desire to get into the core of Zen. How difficult and how misleading it would be to try and understand Zen literally and logically, depending on those statements which have been given above as answers to the question "What is the Buddha?" Of course, so far as they are given as answers they are pointers[2] by which we may know where to look for the presence of the Buddha; but we must remember that the finger pointing at the moon remains a finger and under no circumstances can it be changed into the moon itself. Danger always lurks[3] where the intellect slyly creeps in and takes the index for the moon itself.

Yet there are philosophers who, taking some of the above utterances[4] in their literary and logical sense, try to see something of pantheism[5] in them. For instance, when the master says, "Three pounds of flax," or "A dirt-scraper," by this is apparently meant, they would insist, to convey a pantheistic idea. That is to say that those Zen masters consider the Buddha to be manifesting himself[6] in everything: in the flax, in a piece of wood, in the running stream, in the towering mountains, or in works of art. Mahayana Buddhism, especially Zen, seems to indicate something of the spirit of pantheism, but nothing is in fact farther from Zen than this representation.[7] The masters from the beginning have foreseen this dangerous tendency, and that is why they make those apparently incoherent[8] statements. Their intention is to set the minds of their disciples or of scholars free from being oppressed by any fixed opinions or prejudices or so-called logical interpretations. When Tozan[9] (Tung-shan, a disciple of

(1) spontaneously 巧まずして自然に。 (2) pointers 指針。 (3) lurk ひそんでいる。 (4) the above utterances 上掲のような言葉。 (5) pantheism 汎神論。 (6) manifesting himself 顕現している。 (7) this representation この見方。 (8) incoherent 全く筋の通らぬ。 (9) Tozan 洞山良价(とうざんりょうかい)。唐代の禅僧。曹山とともに曹洞宗の開祖といわれる。

"Even the finest artist cannot paint him."
"The one enshrined[1] in the Buddha Hall."
"He is no Buddha."
"Your name is Yecho.[2]"
"The dirt-scraper all dried up."[3]
"See the eastern mountains moving over the waves."
"No nonsense here."
"Surrounded by the mountains are we here."
"The bamboo grove at the foot of Chang-lin hill.[4]"
"Three pounds of flax."[5]
"The mouth is the gate of woe.[6]"
"Lo, the waves are rolling over the plateau."
"See the three-legged donkey go trotting along."
"A reed has grown piercing through the leg."
"Here goes a man with the chest exposed and the legs all naked."

These are culled at random from a few books I am using for the purpose. When a thorough systematic search is made in the entire body of Zen literature we get quite a collection of the most strange statements ever made concerning such a simple question as, "Who is the Buddha?" Some of the answers given above are altogether irrelevant; they are, indeed, far from being appropriate so far as we judge them from our ordinary standard of reasoning. The others seem to be making sport of[7] the question or of the questioner himself. Can the Zen masters who make such remarks be considered to be in earnest and really desiring the enlightenment of their followers? But the point is to have our minds work in complete union with the state of mind in which the masters uttered these strange words. When this is done, every one of these answers appears in an altogether new light and becomes wonderfully transparent.

Being practical and directly to the point, Zen never wastes time or words in explanation. Its answers are always curt and pithy[8]; there is nothing circumlocutory[9] in Zen; the master's words come out spontane-

(1) enshrined　安置してある。 (2) Yecho　慧超。 (3) "The dirt-scraper all dried up." 乾屎橛（かんしけつ）。乾いた糞掻きべら。 (4) Chang-lin hill　杖林山。 (5) "Three pounds of flax."　麻三斤。 (6) the gate of woe　禍の門。 (7) making sport of　翻弄している。 (8) curt and pithy　簡にして迫るものがある。 (9) circumlocutory　冗長な。

VI PRACTICAL ZEN

"Have you then inherited it?"

"No," replied Yeno, "I have not."

"Why have you not?" was naturally the next question of the monk.

"Because I do not understand Buddhism," Yeno reasoned.

How hard, then, and yet how easy it is to understand the truth of Zen! Hard because to understand it is not to understand it; easy because not to understand it is to understand it. A master declares that even Buddha Sakyamuni and Bodhisattva Maitreya[1] do not understand it, where simple-minded knaves[2] do understand it.

We can now see why Zen shuns abstractions, representations, and figures of speech[3]. No real value is attached to such words as God, Buddha, the soul, the Infinite the One,[4] and suchlike words. They are, after all, only words and ideas, and as such are not conducive to[5] the real understanding of Zen. On the contrary, they often falsify and play at cross purposes. We are thus compelled always to be on our guard. Said a Zen master, "Cleanse the mouth thoroughly when you utter the word Buddha." Or, "There is one word I do not like to hear; that is, Buddha." Or, "Pass quickly on where there is no Buddha, nor stay where he is."[6] Why are the followers of Zen so antagonistic toward Buddha? Is not Buddha their Lord? Is he not the highest reality[7] of Buddhism? He cannot be such a hateful or unclean thing as to be avoided by Zen adherents. What they do not like is not the Buddha himself, but the odium[8] attached to the word.

The answers given by Zen masters to the question "Who or what is the Buddha?" are full of varieties; and why so? One reason at least is that they thus desire to free our minds from all possible entanglements and attachments[9] such as words, ideas, desires, etc., which are put up against us[10] from the outside. Some of the answers are, then, as follows:

"One made of clay and decorated with gold."

---

(1) Bodhisattva Maitreya 弥勒。 (2) simple-minded knaves 田夫野人。 (3) figures of speech 文飾。 (4) the One 一者。 (5) conducive to… ～に役立つ。 (6) "Pass quickly on where there is no Buddha, nor stay where he is." 仏のいるところはさっさと通り過ぎよ。仏のいないところにも止まっていてはならぬ。 (7) the highest reality 最高の体現者。 (8) the odium 習気(じっけ)。忌まわしさ。憎悪感。 (9) entanglements and attachments 葛藤。 (10) which are put up against us あてがわれた。

are idling your time away." "Is not idling away the time doing something?" was Yakusan's response. Sekito still pursued him. "You say you are not doing anything; who then is this one who is doing nothing?" Yakusan's reply was the same as that of Bodhidharma, "Even the wisest[1] know it not." There is no agnosticism[2] in it, nor mysticism either, if this is understood in the sense of mystification. A plain fact is stated here in plain language. If it does not seem so to the reader, it is because he has not attained to this state of mind which enabled Bodhidharma or Sekito to make the statement.

The Emperor Wu[3] of the Liang dynasty[4] requested Fu Daishi[5] (Fu-ta-shih, 497-569) to discourse on a Buddhist sutra. The Daishi taking the chair sat solemnly in it but uttered not a word. The Emperor said, "I asked you to give a discourse, and why do you not begin to speak?" Shih,[6] one of the Emperor's attendants, said, "The Daishi has finished discoursing." What kind of a sermon did this silent Buddhist philosopher deliver? Later on, a Zen master commenting on the above says, "What an eloquent sermon it was!" Vimalakirti,[7] the hero of the sutra bearing his name, had the same way of answering the question, "What is the absolute doctrine of non-duality[8]?" Someone remarked, "Thundering, indeed, is this silence of Vimalakirti." Was this keeping the mouth closed really so deafening[9]? If so, I hold my tongue now, and the whole universe, with all its hullabaloo and hurlyburly,[10] is at once absorbed in this absolute silence. But mimicry[11] does not turn a frog into a green leaf. Where there is no creative originality there is no Zen. I must say: "Too late, too late! The arrow has gone off the string."

A monk asked Yeno (Hui-neng), the Sixth Patriarch,[12] "Who has inherited the spirit of the Fifth Patriarch (Hung-jen)?"

Answered Yeno, "One who understands[13] Buddhism."

---

(1) even the wisest 千聖といえども。 (2) agnosticism 不可知論。 (3) the Emperor Wu 武帝。 (4) the Liang dynasty 中国六朝の一つ、梁。 (5) Fu Daishi 傅大士。中国南北朝の僧。梁の武帝の帰依を受けた。 (6) Shih 誌公。 (7) Vimalakirti 維摩 (p.41 参照)。 (8) doctrine of non-duality 不二法門。 (9) so deafening 耳を聾するような力をもつ。 (10) its hullabaloo and hurly-burly 喧喧囂囂 (けんけんごうごう) の騒ぎ。 (11) mimicry 猿真似では。 (12) Yeno, the Sixth Patriarch 六祖慧能 (えのう)。 (13) understand(s) 会得した。

VI PRACTICAL ZEN

When Joshu (Chao-chou) was asked what the Tao (or the truth of Zen)[1] was, he answered, "Your everyday life, that is the Tao.[2]" In other words, a quiet, self-confident, and trustful existence of your own—this is the truth of Zen, and what I mean when I say that Zen is pre-eminently practical. It appeals directly to[3] life, not even making reference to a soul or to God, or to anything that interferes with or disturbs the ordinary course of living. The idea of Zen[4] is to catch life as it flows. There is nothing extraordinary or mysterious about Zen. I raise my hand; I take a book from the other side of this desk; I hear the boys playing ball outside my window; I see the clouds blown away beyond the neighbouring woods:—in all these I am practising Zen, I am living Zen. No wordy discussion is necessary, nor any explanation. I do not know why—and there is no need of explaining, but when the sun rises the whole world dances with joy and everybody's heart is filled with bliss. If Zen is at all conceivable,[5] it must be taken hold of here.

Therefore, when Bodhidharma[6] (Daruma in J.; Ta-mo in C.) was asked who he was, he said, "I do not know."[7] This was not because he could not explain himself, nor was it because he wanted to avoid any verbal controversy,[8] but just because he did not know what or who he was, save that[9] he was what he was and could not be anything else. The reason was simple enough. When Nangaku[10] (Nan-yueh, 677-744) was approaching the Sixth Patriarch,[11] and was questioned, "What is it that thus walks toward me?" he did not know what to answer. For eight long years he pondered the question, when one day it dawned upon him, and he exclaimed, "Even to say it is something does not hit the mark.[12]" This is the same as saying, "I do not know."

Sekito once asked his disciple, Yakusan (Yueh-shan), "What are you doing here?" "I am not doing anything," answered the latter. "If so you

---

(1) the Tao (or the truth of Zen)　道教のいう「道」。 (2) Your everyday life, that is the Tao.　平常心是道。 (3) appeals…to…　…に訴える。 (4) the idea of Zen　禅の趣意。 (5) if Zen is at all conceivable　ともかくも禅というものが考えられるとすれば、 (6) Bodhidharma　菩提達摩。 (7) "I do not know."　不識。 (8) verbal controversy　言葉上の論議。 (9) save that　以外に (それを除いて)。 (10) Nangaku　南嶽。唐代の禅僧。 (11) the Sixth Patriarch　六祖。禅宗第六祖慧能のこと。 (12) not hit the mark　的を逸している。

I

So far Zen han been discussed from the intellectual point of view, in order to see that it is impossible to comprehend Zen through this channel; in fact it is not doing justice to Zen to treat it thus Philosophically. Zen abhors media,[1] even the intellectual medium; it is primarily and ultimately[2] a discipline and an experience, which is dependent on no explanation; for an explanation wastes time and energy and is never to the point; all that you get out of it is a misunderstanding and a twisted view[3] of the thing.[4] When Zen wants you to taste the sweetness of sugar, it will put the required article right into your mouth and no further words are said. The followers of Zen would say, A finger is needed to point at the moon, but what a calamity it would be[5] if one took the finger for the moon! This seems improbable,[6] but how many times we are committing this form of error we do not know. Ignorance alone often saves us from being disturbed in our self-complacency.[7] The business of a writer on Zen, however, cannot go beyond the pointing at the moon, as this is the only means permitted to him in the circumstances; and everything that is within his power will be done to make the subject in hand as thoroughly comprehensible as it is capable of being so made.[8] When Zen is metaphysically treated, the reader may get somewhat discouraged about its being at all intelligible,[9] since most people are not generally addicted to speculation[10] or introspection.[11] Let me approach it from quite a different point, which is perhaps more genuinely Zen-like.[12]

編集部注 (1) abhors media　媒介を嫌う。(2) primarily and ultimately　徹頭徹尾。(3) a twisted view　偏見。(4) the thing　実物。(5) what a calamity it would be　大変である。(6) This seems improbable, 真逆といいたいところだが、(7) in our self-complacency　好い気になって。(8) to make the subject in hand as thoroughly comprehensible as it is capable of being so made　十分に究明すべき。(9) its being at all intelligible その分りにくいのに。(10) speculation　思弁。(11) introspection　観想。(12) Zen-like　禅に相応しい。

VI

PRACTICAL ZEN

V ZEN A HIGHER AFFIRMATION

we are already quite filled up, we never realize the fact.

To conclude, here is another of the innumerable statements that abound in Zen literature, absolutely affirming the truth of Zen. Seihei[1] (Ts'ing-ping, 845-919) asked Suibi[2] (T'sui-wei) :[1]

"What is the fundamental principle of Buddhism[3]?"

"Wait," said Suibi; "when there is no one around I will tell you."

After a while Seihei repeated the request, saying, "There is no one here now; pray enlighten me."

Coming down from his chair, Suibi took the anxious inquirer into the bamboo grove,[4] but said nothing. When the latter pressed for a reply, Suibi whispered: "How high these bamboos are! And how short those over there!"

---

1 *The Transmission of the Lamp* (*Chuan-teng Lu*), Vol. XV.

(1) Seihei　清平令遵。唐末の禅僧。翠微の弟子。　(2) Suibi　翠微無学。唐代の禅僧。
(3) the fundamental principle of Buddhism　仏教の根本義（西来的的意）。　(4) the bamboo grove　竹林。

he would lift his finger. Learning of this, the master one day called the boy in and cut off his finger. The boy in fright and pain tried to run away, but was called back, when the master held up his finger. The boy tried to imitate the master, as was his wont, but the finger was no more there, and then suddenly the significance of it all dawned upon him. Copying is slavery. The letter must never be followed,[1] only the spirit is to be grasped. Higher affirmations live in the spirit. And where is the spirit? Seek it in your everyday experience, and therein lies abundance of proof for all you need.

We read in a sutra: "There was an old woman on the east side of the town who was born when the Buddha was born, and they lived in the same place throughout all their lives. The old woman did not wish to see the Buddha; if he ever approached she tried in every way to avoid him, running up and down, hiding herself hither and thither.[2] But one day, finding it impossible to flee from him, she covered her face with her hands, and lo, the Buddha appeared between each of her ten fingers. Let me ask, 'Who is this old lady?'"

Absolute affirmation is the Buddha; you cannot fly away from it, for it confronts you at every turn; but somehow you do not recognize it until you, like Gutei's little boy, lose a finger. It is strange, but the fact remains that we are like "those who die of hunger while sitting beside the rice bag", or rather like "those who die of thirst while standing thoroughly drenched in the midst of the river". One master goes a step further and says that "We are the rice itself and the water itself." If so we cannot truthfully say that we are hungry or thirsty, for from the very beginning nothing has been wanting in us. A monk came to Sozan[3] (T'sao-shan, 840-901) asking him to be charitable, as he was quite destitute.[4] Sozan called out, "O my venerable sir!" to which the monk immediately responded. Then said Sozan, "You have already had three big bowlfuls of rich home-made *chu* (liquor), and yet you insist that it has never yet wetted your lips!" Perhaps we are all like this poor opulent monk[5]; when

---

(1) the letter must never be followed 文字に囚われてはならぬ。 (2) hither and thither あちこち。 (3) Sozan 曹山。 (4) as he was quite destitute 窮乏を訴え。 (5) this poor opulent monk このみじめにも富裕な僧。

V ZEN A HIGHER AFFIRMATION

Joshu and Nansen. Unless this is apprehended, Zen is, indeed, a mere farce.[1] The cat certainly was not killed to no purpose. If any of the lower animals is ever to attain Buddhahood,[2] this cat was surely the one so destined.

The same Joshu was once asked by a monk, "All things are reducible to the One; where is this One to be reduced?" The master's reply was, "When I was in Tsin district[3] I had a monk's robe[4] made that weighed seven *chin*.[5]" This is one of the most noted sayings ever uttered by a Zen master. One may ask: "Is this what is meant by an absolute affirmation? What possible connection is there between a monk's robe and the oneness of things[6]?" Let me ask: You believe that all things exist in God, but where is the abode of God[7]? Is it in Joshu's seven-*chin* cassock[8]? When you say that God is here, he can no more be there; but you cannot say that he is nowhere, for by your definition God is omnipresent.[9] So long as we are fettered by the intellect, we cannot interview God as he is; we seek him everywhere, but he ever flies away from us. The intellect desires to have him located, but it is in his very nature that he cannot be limited. Here is a great dilemma to put to the intellect, and it is an inevitable one. How shall we find the way out? Joshu's priestly robe is not ours; his way of solution cannot be blindly followed, for each of us must beat out his own track.[10] If someone comes to you with the same question, how will you answer it? And are we not at every turn of life[11] confronted with the same problem? And is it not ever pressing for an immediate and most practical solution?

Gutei's[12] (Chu-chih)¹ favourite response to any question put to him was to lift one of his fingers. His little boy attendant imitated him, and whenever the boy was asked by strangers as to the teaching of the master

---

1 A disciple of T'ien-lung, of the ninth century.

(1) a mere farce　他愛もない道化芝居。　(2) If any of the lower animals is ever to attain Buddhahood　蠢動（しゅんどう）含霊悉く成仏するものならば。　(3) in Tsin district　青州。中国唐代の州名。　(4) a monk's robe　一領の布衫（ふさん）。　(5) seven chin　七斤。一斤は約600グラム。　(6) the oneness of things　万法帰一。　(7) the abode of God　神のありか。　(8) seven-chin cassock　七斤の布衫。　(9) omnipresent　遍在者である。　(10) beat out his own track　各自の道を打ち開かねばならぬ。　(11) at every turn of life　人生到るところで。　(12) Gutei　倶胝和尚。唐代の禅僧。

said to them, "Do not call it a pitcher but tell me what it is." The first one replied, "It cannot be called a piece of wood.[1]" The Abbot[2] did not consider the reply quite to the mark; thereupon the second one came forward, lightly pushed the pitcher down, and without making any remark quietly left the room. He was chosen to be the new abbot, who afterwards became "the master of one thousand and five hundred monks". Was this upsetting a pitcher[3] an absolute affirmation? You may repeat this act, but you will not necessarily be regarded as understanding Zen.

Zen abhors repetition or imitation of any kind, for it kills. For the same reason Zen never explains, but only affirms. Life is fact and no explanation is necessary or pertinent.[4] To explain is to apologize, and why should we apologize for living? To live—is that not enough? Let us then live, let us affirm! Herein lies Zen in all its purity and in all its nudity as well.[5]

In the monastery of Nansen monks of the eastern wing quarrelled with those of the western wing over the possession of a cat. The master seized it and lifting it before the disputing monks, said, "If any of you can say something to save the poor animal, I will let it go." As nobody came forward to utter a word of affirmation, Nansen cut the object of dispute in two, thus putting an end forever to an unproductive quarrelling over "yours" and "mine". Later on Joshu[6] (Chao-chou) came back from an outing and Nansen put the case before him, and asked him what he would have done to save the animal. Joshu without further ado[7] took off his straw sandals and, putting them on his head, went out. Seeing this, Nansen said, "If you were here at the time you would have saved the cat."

What does all this mean? Why was a poor innocent creature sacrificed? What has Joshu's placing his sandals over his head to do with the quarrelling? Did Nansen mean to be irreligious and inhuman by killing a living being? Was Joshu really a fool to play such a strange trick? And then "absolute denial" and "absolute affirmation"—are these really two? There is something fearfully earnest in both these actors,

(1) a piece of wood　木𣛺（ぼくとつ）。　(2) the Abbot　師。　(3) this upsetting a pitcher　浄瓶躍倒（じんびんやくとう）。　(4) pertinent　相応しい。　(5) in all its purity and in all its nudity as well　浄裸裸、赤灑灑（しゃくしゃしゃ）のところにこそ。　(6) Joshu　趙州（p. 38 の注参照）。　(7) without further ado　即座に……さっさと。

V ZEN A HIGHER AFFIRMATION

strange this so-called affirmation!

Riko[1] (Li K'u), a high government officer of the T'ang dynasty,[2] asked Nansen[3] (Nan-chuan): "A long time ago a man kept a goose in a bottle. It grew larger and larger until it could not get out of the bottle any more; he did not want to break the bottle, nor did he wish to hurt the goose; how would you get it out?" The master called out, "O Officer!"—to which Riko at once responded, "Yes!" "There it is out!" This was the way Nansen produced the goose out of its imprisonment. Did Riko get his higher affirmation?

Kyogen[4] (Hsiang-yen)[1] said: "Suppose a man climbing up a tree takes hold of a branch by his teeth, and his whole body is thus suspended. His hands are not holding anything and his feet are off the ground. Now another man comes along and asks the man in the tree as to the fundamental principle of Buddhism.[5] If the man in the tree does not answer, he is neglecting the questioner; but if he tries to answer he will lose his life; how can he get out of his predicament[6]?" While this is put in the form of a fable its purport is like those already mentioned. If you open your mouth trying to affirm or to negate, you are lost. Zen is no more there. But merely remaining silent will not do, either. A stone lying there is silent, a flower in bloom under the window is silent, but neither of them understands Zen. There must be a certain way in which silence and eloquence become identical, that is, where negation and assertion are unified in a higher form of statement. When we attain to this we know Zen.

What, then, is an absolute affirmative statement? When Hyakujo[7] (Pai-chang, 720-814) wished to decide who would be the next chief of Tai-kuei-shan monastery,[8] he called in two of his chief disciples, and producing a pitcher, which a Buddhist monk generally carries about him,

---

1 A younger contemporary of Kuei-shan (771-853).

(1) Riko 李翺（唐朝の高官）。 (2) T'ang dynasty 唐朝。 (3) Nansen 南泉（p. 39 の注 参照）。 (4) Kyogen 香厳。潙山の法弟。 (5) the fundamental principle of Buddhism 祖師西来意。達摩（だるま）が伝えた禅の根本精神。仏法の奥義。 (6) his predicament この窮境。 (7) Hyakujo 百丈懐海。唐の禅僧。門下から潙山や黄檗が出た。 (8) the next chief of Tai-kuei-shan monastery 大潙山の住持。住持とは、寺の長である僧。住職職。もとは、安住して仏法を持する意。

which knows no beginning or end? You cannot hesitate. Grasp the fact or let it slip—between these there is no choice. The Zen method of discipline generally consists in putting one in a dilemma, out of which one must contrive to escape, not through logic indeed, but through a mind of higher order.[1]

Yakusan[2] (Yueh-shan, 751-834) studied Zen first under Sekito[3] (Shih-t'ou, 700-790) and asked him: "As to the three divisions and twelve departments of Buddhism,[4] I am not altogether unacquainted with them, but I have no knowledge whatever concerning the doctrine of Zen as taught in the South. Its followers assert it to be the doctrine of directly pointing at the mind[5] and attaining Buddhahood through a perception of its real nature.[6] If this is so, how may I be enlightened?" Sekito replied: "Assertion prevails not, nor does denial.[7] When neither of them is to the point, what would you say?" Yakusan remained meditative,[8] as he did not grasp the meaning of the question. The master then told him to go to Badaishi (Ma Tai-shih) of Chianghsi,[9] who might be able to open the monk's eye to the truth of Zen. Thereupon, the monk Yakusan went to the new teacher with the same problem. His answer was, "I sometimes make one raise the eyebrows, or wink, while at other times to do so is altogether wrong." Yakusan at once comprehended the ultimate purport of this remark.[10] When Baso[11] asked, "What makes you come to this?" Yakusan replied, "When I was with Sekito, it was like a mosquito biting at an iron bull." Was this a satisfactory reason or explanation? How

1 Zen, in contradistinction to the other Buddhist schools, originated in the southern provinces of China.

(1) through a mind of higher order 或る高次元の心作用による。 (2) Yakusan 薬山。唐代の禅僧。 (3) Sekito 石頭希遷。唐代の禅僧。慧能の弟子。 (4) the three divisions and twelve departments of Buddhism 三乗十二分教。 (5) directly pointing at the mind 直指人心 (じきしにんしん)。 (6) attaining Buddhahood through a perception of its real nature 見性成仏 (けんしょうじょうぶつ)。直指人心、見性成仏の二句で、禅は直接人の心をとらえ、自己の仏性を自覚させて成仏させるものだという考え方を表わす言葉。 (7) Assertion prevails not, nor does denial. こうだというても駄目、こうでないというても駄目だ。 (8) remained meditative 茫然としていた。 (9) Badaishi of Chianghsi 江西の馬大師。 (10) comprehend the ultimate purport of this remark その究極の意味を理解する（契悟し（師を礼拝した。））。 (11) Baso 馬祖。馬大師も同じ。中国禅の実際上の創始者、馬祖道一のこと。

V ZEN A HIGHER AFFIRMATION

in the study of Zen.

Some examples will be given for illustration. Toku-san[1] (Teh-shan, 780-865) used to swing his big stick whenever he came out to preach in the hall,[2] saying, "If you utter a word I will give you thirty blows; if you utter not a word, just the same, thirty blows on your head." This was all he would say to his disciples. No lengthy talk on religion or morality; no abstract discourse, no hair-splitting metaphysics[3]; on the contrary, quite rough-shod riding.[4] To those who associate religion with pusillanimity[5] and sanctimoniousness[6] the Zen master must appear a terribly unpolished fellow. But when facts are handled as facts, without any intermediary, they are generally rude things.[7] We must squarely face[8] them, for no amount of winking or evading will be of any avail.[9] The inner eye is to be opened under a shower of thirty blows. An absolute affirmation must rise from the fiery crater of life itself.

Hoyen (Fa-yen, died 1104), of Gosozan[10] (Wu-tsu-shan), once asked, "When you meet a wise man[11] on your way, if you do not speak to him or remain silent, how would you interview him?" The point is to make one realize what I call an absolute affirmation. Not merely to escape the antithesis of "yes" and "no", but to find a positive way in which the opposites are perfectly harmonized—this is what is aimed at in this question. A master once pointed to a live charcoal and said to his disciples, "I call this fire, but you call it not so; tell me what it is." The same thing here again. The master intends to free his disciples' minds from the bondage of logic, which has ever been the bane of humanity.[12]

This ought not to be regarded as a riddle proposed to puzzle you. There is nothing playful about it; if you fail to answer, you are to face the consequences. Are you going to be eternally chained by your own laws of thought, or are you going to be perfectly free in an assertion of life

---

(1) Toku-san 徳山。唐代の禅僧。 (2) whenever he came out to preach in the hall 法堂に上って説法する際、いつも。 (3) hair-splitting metaphysics 精細を誇る形而上学。 (4) rough-shod riding 傍若無人な接得振り。 (5) pusillanimity 弱気。 (6) sanctimoniousness 信心振り。 (7) rude things ごつごつしている。 (8) squarely face 四つに組まねば。 (9) of any avail 役にも立つ。 (10) Hoyen of Gosozan 五祖山の法演。宋代の禅僧。五祖山に住した。 (11) a wise man 達道の人。 (12) the bane of humanity 人類の苦厄。

mere intellectual cleverness. The intellectual groove[1] of "yes" and "no" is quite accommodating when things run their regular course; but as soon as the ultimate question of life comes up, the intellect fails to answer it satisfactorily. When we say "yes", we assert, and by asserting we limit ourselves. When we say "no", we deny, and to deny is exclusion. Exclusion and limitation, which after all are the same thing, murder the soul; for is it not the life of the soul that lives in perfect freedom and in perfect unity? There is no freedom or unity in exclusion or in limitation. Zen is well aware of this. In accordance with the demands of our inner life, therefore, Zen takes us to an absolute realm[2] wherein there are no antitheses of any sort.

We must remember, however, that we live in affirmation and not in negation, for life is affirmation itself; and this affirmation must not be the one accompanied or conditioned by a negation; such an affirmation is relative and not at all absolute. With such an affirmation life loses its creative originality and turns into a mechanical process grinding forth[3] nothing but soulless flesh and bones. To be free, life must be an absolute affirmation. It must transcend all possible conditions, limitations, and antitheses that hinder its free activity. When Shuzan held forth his stick of bamboo, what he wanted of his disciples was for them to understand and realize this form of absolute affirmation. Any answer is satisfactory if it flows out of one's inmost being, for such is always an absolute affirmation. Therefore, Zen does not mean a mere escape from intellectual imprisonment, which sometimes ends in sheer wantonness.[4] There is something in Zen that frees us from conditions and at the same time gives us a certain firm foothold, which, however, is not a foothold in a relative sense. The Zen master endeavours to take away all footholds from the disciple which he has ever had since his first appearance on earth, and then to supply him with one that is really no foothold. If the stick of bamboo is not to the purpose, anything that comes handy will be made use of. Nihilism is not Zen, for this bamboo stick or anything else cannot be done away with[5] as words and logic can. This is the point we must not overlook

(1) The intellectual groove　知性的軌道。　(2) an absolute realm　絶対境。　(3) grinding forth　動かして行く。　(4) in sheer wantonness　ただの放逸に。　(5) be done away with　一緒に片附けてしまう。

V   ZEN A HIGHER AFFIRMATION

has never occurred to us that it is possible for us to escape this self-imposed intellectual limitation ; indeed, unless we break through the antithesis of "yes" and "no" we can never hope to live a real life of freedom. And the soul has always been crying for it, forgetting that it is not after all so very difficult to reach a higher form of affirmation, where no contradicting distinctions obtain between negation and assertion. It is due to Zen that this higher affirmation has finally been reached by means of a stick of bamboo in the hand of the Zen master.

It goes without saying that this stick thus brought forward can be any one of myriads of[1] things existing in this world of particulars.[2] In this stick we find all possible existences and also all our possible experiences concentrated. When we know it—this homely piece of bamboo—we know the whole story in a most thoroughgoing manner.[3] Holding it in my hand, I hold the whole universe. Whatever statement I make about it is also made of everything else. When one point is gained, all other points go with it. As the Avatamsaka (Kegon) philosophy[4] teaches : "The One embraces All, and All is merged in the One. The One is All, and All is the One. The One pervades All, and All is in the One. This is so with every object, with every existence." But, mind you, here is no pantheism, nor the theory of identity.[5] For when the stick of bamboo is held out before you it is just the stick, there is no universe epitomized in it,[6] no All, no One ; even when it is stated that "I see the stick" or that "Here is a stick," we all miss the mark.[7] Zen is no more there, much less the philosophy of the Avatamsaka.

I spoke of the illogicalness of Zen in one of the preceding chapters ; the reader will now know why Zen stands in opposition to logic, formal or informal. It is not the object of Zen to look illogical for its own sake, but to make people know that logical consistency[8] is not final, and that there is a certain transcendental statement[9] that cannot be attained by

---

(1) myriads of　数限りもない。　(2) in this world of particulars　この差別の世界に。　(3) in a most thoroughgoing manner　真に徹底した仕方で。　(4) the Avatamsaka (Kegon) philosophy　華厳哲学。　(5) the theory of identity　同一性の哲学。　(6) no universe epitomized in it　全宇宙が摂されているのでもなく。　(7) we all miss the mark　我々は皆その印を見過ごしてしまう（「箭（や）既に新羅（しんら）を過ぐ」）。　(8) logical consistency　論理との合致。　(9) transcendental statement　超越的な道（い）い方。

S huzan[1] (Shou-shan, 926-992) once held up his *shippe*[1(2)] to an assembly of his disciples and declared: "Call this a *shippe* and you assert; call it not a *shippe* and you negate. Now, do not assert nor negate, and what would you call it? Speak, speak!" One of the disciples came out of the ranks, took the *shippe* away from the master, and breaking it in two, exclaimed, "What is this?"

To those who are used to dealing with abstractions and high subjects this may appear to be quite a trivial matter, for what have they, deep learned philosophers, to do with an insignificant piece of bamboo? How does it concern those scholars who are absorbed in deep meditation, whether it is called a bamboo stick or not, whether it is broken, or thrown on the floor? But to the followers of Zen this declaration by Shuzan is pregnant with meaning. Let us really realize the state of his mind in which he proposed this question, and we have attained our first entrance into the realm of Zen. There were many Zen masters who followed Shuzan's example, and, holding forth their *shippe*, demanded of their pupils a satisfactory answer.

To speak in the abstract, which perhaps will be more acceptable to most readers, the idea is to reach a higher affirmation than the logical antithesis of assertion and denial. Ordinarily, we dare not go beyond an antithesis just because we imagine we cannot. Logic has so intimidated[3] us that we shrink and shiver whenever its name is mentioned. The mind made to work, ever since the awakening of the intellect, under the strictest discipline of logical dualism, refuses to shake off its imaginary cangue.[4] It

1 A stick about one and a half feet long, made of split bamboo bound with ratan. To be pronounced *ship-pei*.

編集部注 (1) Shuzan　首山省念。宋代初期の禅僧。(2) shippe　竹篦（しっぺい）。禅寺で体を打つのに使う道具。(3) intimidated　威圧のために。(4) its imaginary cangue　その想像上の首枷。

V

ZEN A HIGHER AFFIRMATION

to be bound by rules, but to be creating one's own rules—this is the kind of life which Zen is trying to have us live. Hence its illogical, or rather superlogical, statements.

In one of his sermons a Zen master[1] declares: "The sutras preached by the Buddha during his lifetime are said to amount to five thousand and forty-eight fascicles[(1)]; they include the doctrine of emptiness and the doctrine of being; there are teachings of immediate realization and of gradual development.[(2)] Is this not an affirmation?

"But, according to Yoka,[2(3)] 'There are no sentient beings, there are no Buddhas; sages as numerous as the sands of the Ganges are but so many bubbles in the sea; sages and worthies of the past are like flashes of lightning.' Is this not a negation?

"O you, my disciples, if you say there is, you go against Yoka; if you say there is not, you contradict our old master Buddha. If he were with us, then how would he pass through the dilemma? If you know, however, just exactly where we are, we shall be interviewing Buddha in the morning and saluting him in the evening. If, on the other hand, you confess your ignorance, I will let you see into the secret. When I say there is not, this does not necessarily mean a negation; when I say there is, this also does not signify an affirmation. Turn eastward and look at the Western Land; face the south and the North Star is pointed out there!"

1 Goso Hoyen (Fa-yen of Wu-tsu-shan).
2 Yung-chia in his "Song of Enlightenment".

(1) fascicles （経の）巻。 (2) teachings of immediate realization and of gradual development　頓を説くものもあれば、漸を説くものもある。 (3) Yoka　永嘉玄覚。唐代の禅僧。

IV ILLOGICAL ZEN

A few more words : the reason why Zen is so vehement[1] in its attack on logic, and why the present work treats first of the illogical aspect of Zen, is that logic has so pervasively entered[2] into life as to make most of us conclude that logic is life and without it life has no significance. The map of life has been so definitely and so thoroughly delineated[3] by logic that what we have to do is simply to follow it, and that we ought not to think of violating the laws of thought, which are final. Such a general view of life has come to be held by most people, though I must say that in point of fact they are constantly violating what they think inviolable. That is to say, they are "holding a spade and yet not holding it", they are making the sum of two and two sometimes three, sometimes five ; only they are not conscious of this fact and imagine that their lives are logically or mathematically regulated. Zen wishes to storm[4] this citadel of topsy-turvydom[5] and to show that we live psychologically or biologically and not logically.

In logic there is a trace of effort and pain ; logic is self-conscious. So is ethics, which is the application of logic to the facts of life. An ethical man performs acts of service[6] which are praiseworthy, but he is all the time conscious of them, and moreover, he may often be thinking of some future reward. Hence we should say that his mind is tainted[7] and not at all pure, however objectively or socially good his deeds are. Zen abhors[8] this. Life is an art, and like perfect art it should be self-forgetting ; there ought not to be any trace of effort or painful feeling. Life, according to Zen, ought to be lived as a bird flies through the air or as a fish swims in the water. As soon as there are signs of elaboration,[9] a man is doomed, he is no more a free being. You are not living as you ought to live, you are suffering under the tyranny of circumstances ; you are feeling a constraint of some sort, and you lose your independence. Zen aims at preserving your vitality, your native freedom, and above all the completeness of your being.[10] In other words, Zen wants to live from within. Not

---

(1) vehement　急である。　(2) pervasively entered　滲み亘っている。　(3) delineated　描かれており。　(4) storm　…を襲って。　(5) this citadel of topsy-turvydom　この転倒の砦を。　(6) acts of service　奉仕の行。　(7) is tainted　汚れ、腐敗している。　(8) abhor(s)　…を忌む。　(9) signs of elaboration　作為（エラボレーション）の萌し。　(10) the completeness of your being　存在としての全一性。

kinds of invalids, how would they treat them? The blind cannot see even if a stick or a mallet[1] is produced; the deaf cannot hear however fine the preaching may be; and the dumb cannot talk however much they are urged to do so. But if these people severally suffering cannot somehow be benefited,[2] what good is there after all in Buddhism?" The explanation does not seem to explain anything after all. Perhaps Butsugen's[3] (Fo-yen) comment may throw more light on the subject. He said to his disciples: "You each have a pair of ears; what have you ever heard with them? You each have one tongue; what have you ever preached with it? Indeed, you have never talked, you have never heard, you have never seen. From whence then do all these forms, voices, odours, and tastes come?" (That is to say, where does this world come from?)

If this remark still leaves us where we were before, let us see whether Ummon[4] (Yun-men, died 966), one of the greatest of Zen masters who ever lived, can help us. A monk came to Ummon and asked to be enlightened upon the above remark by Gensha. Ummon ordered him first to salute him in the formal way. When the monk stood up after prostrating himself on the ground,[5] Ummon pushed him with his stick, and the monk stepped back. The master said, "You are not blind, then." He now told the monk to come forward, which he did. The master said, "You are not deaf, then." He finally asked the monk if he understood what all this was about, and the latter replied, "No, sir." Ummon then concluded, "You are not dumb, then."

With all these comments and gestures, are we still travelling through a *terra incognita*[6]? If so, there is no other way but to go back to the beginning and repeat the stanza:

> Empty-handed I go, and behold the spade is
>   in my hands;
> I walk on foot, and yet on the back of an ox
>   I am riding;

(1) a mallet 槌。 (2) cannot somehow be benefited どうも得することができない（接化から洩れるようなことがある）。 (3) Butsugen 仏眼。仏が諸法実相を照見する眼。 (4) Ummon 雲門。唐代末期の禅僧。雲門宗を開いた (p.20の注参照)。 (5) after prostrating himself on the ground 拝伏して。 (6) a terra incognita 五里霧中の態で。

IV ILLOGICAL ZEN

and all things in it and out of it are understood. In Zen the spade is the key to the whole riddle. How fresh and full of life it is—the way Zen grapples with[1] the knottiest questions of philosophy[2]!

A noted Christian Father of the early Middle Ages once exclaimed: "O poor Aristotle! Thou who has discovered for the heretics the art of dialectics, the art of building up and destroying, the art of discussing all things and accomplishing nothing!" So much ado about nothing, indeed! See how philosophers of all ages contradict one another[3] after spending all their logical acumen[4] and analytical ingenuity on the so-called problems of science and knowledge. No wonder the same old wise man, wanting to put a stop once for all to all such profitless discussions, has boldly thrown the following bomb right into the midst of those sand-builders[5]: "*Certum est quia impossible est*"[6]; or, more logically, "*Credo quia absurdum est.*"[7] I believe because it is irrational; is this not an unqualified[8] confirmation of Zen?

An old master brought out his stick before an assemblage of monks and said: "O monks, do you see this? If you see it, what is it you see? Would you say, 'It is a stick'? If you do you are ordinary people, you have no Zen. But if you say, 'We do not see any stick,' then I would say, 'Here I hold one, and how can you deny the fact?'" There is no trifling in Zen. Until you have a third eye opened to see into the inmost secret of things, you cannot be in the company of the ancient sages. What is this third eye that sees the stick and yet sees it not? Where does one get this illogical apprehension of things?

Zen says, "Buddha preached forty-nine years and yet his 'broad tongue' (*tanujihva*) never once moved." Can one talk without moving one's tongue? Why this absurdity? The explanation given by Gensha[9] (Hsuan-sha, 831-908) follows: "All those piously inclined profess to bless others in every possible way[10]; but when they come across three

---

(1) grapples with …と取り組む。 (2) the knottiest questions of philosophy 哲学のもっとも入り組んだ問題（盤根錯節する哲学の諸問題）。 (3) contradict one another 相矛盾する（互いに撞著し合う）。 (4) logical acumen 論理の鋭さ。 (5) those sand-builders これら砂上建築者。 (6) "*Certum est quia impossible est*" 「不可能なるが故に確実なのだ」。 (7) "*Credo quia absurdum est*" 「不合理なるが故に信ずるのだ」。 (8) unqualified 無条件に。 (9) Gensha 玄沙。 (10) profess to bless others in every possible way 接物利生を主張している。利生とは、仏菩薩（ぶつぼさつ）が衆生を救うこと。

before it. The result will be to acknowledge a spade to be a spade and at the same time not to be a spade. To recognize the first only is a common-sense view, and there is no Zen until the second is also admitted along with the first. The common-sense view is flat and tame,[1] whereas that of Zen is always original and stimulating. Each time Zen is asserted[2] things get vitalized; there is an act of creation.

Zen thinks we are too much of slaves to words and logic. So long as we remain thus fettered[3] we are miserable and go through untold[4] suffering. But if we want to see something really worth knowing, that is conducive to[5] our spiritual happiness, we must endeavour once for all to free ourselves from all conditions; we must see if we cannot gain a new point of view from which the world can be surveyed in its wholeness and life comprehended inwardly.[6] This consideration has compelled one to plunge oneself deep into the abyss of the "Nameless" and take hold directly of the spirit as it is engaged in the business of creating the world. Here is no logic, no philosophizing; here is no twisting of facts to suit our artificial measures[7]; here is no murdering of human nature in order to submit it to intellectual dissections; the one spirit stands face to face with the other spirit like two mirrors facing each other, and there is nothing to intervene between their mutual reflections.

In this sense Zen is pre-eminently practical. It has nothing to do with abstractions or with subtleties of dialectics.[8] It seizes the spade lying in front of you, and holding it forth, makes the bold declaration, "I hold a spade, yet I hold it not." No reference is made to God or to the soul; there is no talk about the infinite[9] or a life after death. This handling of a homely[10] spade, a most ordinary thing to see about us, opens all the secrets we encounter in life. And nothing more is wanted. Why? Because Zen has now cleared up[11] a new approach to the reality of things. When a humble flower in the crannied wall[12] is understood, the whole universe

(1) tame　無気力である。　(2) Each time Zen is asserted　禅の挙揚されるところ。　(3) fettered　足枷を嵌められている。　(4) untold　数知れぬ。　(5) conducive to　打ち開くに足る。　(6) life comprehended inwardly　生の秘義（秘儀）をその内から捉える。　(7) our artificial measures　人為の尺度。　(8) subtleties of dialectics　弁証法の狡智。　(9) the infinite　無限者。　(10) homely　見栄えもせぬ。　(11) cleared up　疑問を解いた（豁開（かつかい）した）。　(12) in the crannied wall　石垣の隙間に。

IV ILLOGICAL ZEN

life are lost sight of. Now, however, we have the key to the whole situation ; we are master of realities ; words have given up their domination over us. If we are pleased to call a spade not a spade, we have the perfect right to do so ; a spade need not always remain a spade ; and, moreover, this, according to the Zen master, expresses more correctly the state of reality which refuses to be tied up to names.

This breaking up of the tyranny of name and logic is at the same time spiritual emancipation[1] ; for the soul is no longer divided against itself.[2] By acquiring the intellectual freedom the soul is in full possession of itself ; birth and death no longer torment it ; for there are no such dualities anywhere ; we live even through death.[3] Hitherto[4] we have been looking at things in their contradicting and differentiating aspect,[5] and have assumed an attitude toward them in accordance with that view, that is, more or less antagonistic.[6] But this has been revolutionized,[7] we have at last attained the point where the world can be viewed, as it were, from within. Therefore, "the iron trees are in full bloom" ; and "in the midst of pouring rain I am not wet". The soul is thus made whole, perfect, and filled with bliss.

Zen deals with facts and not with their logical, verbal, prejudiced, and lame representations.[8] Direct simplicity[9] is the soul of Zen ; hence its vitality, freedom, and originality. Christianity speaks much of simplicity of heart, and so do other religions, but this does not always mean to be simple-hearted or to be a Simple Simon.[10] In Zen it means not to get entangled in intellectual subtleties,[11] not to be carried away by philosophical reasoning that is so often ingenuous and full of sophistry.[12] It means, again, to recognize facts as facts and to know that words are words and nothing else. Zen often compares the mind to a mirror free from stains. To be simple, therefore, according to Zen, will be to keep this mirror always bright and pure and ready to reflect simply and absolutely whatever comes

(1) spiritual emancipation　精神的解放。 (2) against itself　その本然に反して。 (3) we live even through death　我々は死をすら生きるのである。 (4) hitherto　これまでは。 (5) aspect　相。 (6) antagonistic　敵対的な。 (7) this has been revolutionized　これが一回転して。 (8) lame representations　いびつな表現。 (9) direct simplicity　単刀直入（ダイレクト・シンプリシティ）。 (10) to be a Simple Simon　シモンの如く初心であること。 (11) intellectual subtleties　知性的穿鑿。 (12) sophistry　詭弁。

We generally think that "A is A" is absolute, and that the proposition[1] "A is not-A" or "A is B" is unthinkable. We have never been able to break through these conditions of the understanding[2]; they have been too imposing. But now Zen declares that words are words and no more. When words cease to correspond with facts it is time for us to part with words and return to facts. As long as logic has its practical value it is to be made use of; but when it fails to work, or when it tries to go beyond its proper limits, we must cry, "Halt!" Ever since the awakening of consciousness we have endeavoured to solve the mysteries of being and to quench our thirst[3] for logic through the dualism of "A" and "not-A"; that is, by calling a bridge a bribge, by making the water flow, and dust arise from the earth; but to our great disappointment we have never been able to obtain peace of mind, perfect happiness, and a thorough understanding of life and the world. We have come, as it were, to the end of our wits.[4] No further steps could we take which would lead us to a broader field of reality. The inmost agonies of the soul could not be expressed in words, when lo! light comes over our entire being. This is the beginning of Zen. For we now realize that "A is not-A" after all, that logic is onesided, that illogicality so-called is not in the last analysis[5] necessarily illogical; what is superficially irrational[6] has after all its own logic, which is in correspondence with the true state of things.[7] "Empty-handed I go, and behold the spade is in my hands!" By this we are made perfectly happy, for strangely this contradiction is what we have been seeking for all the time ever since the dawning of the intellect. The dawning of the intellect did not mean the assertion of the intellect but the transcending of itself. The meaning of the proposition "A is A" is realized only when "A is not-A". To be itself is not to be itself—this is the logic of Zen, and satisfies all our aspirations.

"The flower is not red, the willow is not green." This is regarded by Zen devotees as most refreshingly satisfying. So long as we think logic final we are chained, we have no freedom of spirit, and the real facts of

(1) the proposition 命題。 (2) these conditions of the understanding こうした悟性の諸条件。 (3) quench our thirst 渇望を医(いや)そう。 (4) come to the end of our wits 途方に暮れた。 (5) in the last analysis 究め来れば。 (6) what is superficially irrational 一見非合理的と見えるもの。 (7) the true state of things 存在の実相。

IV ILLOGICAL ZEN

seem, Zen insists that the spade must be held in your empty hands, and that it is not the water but the bridge that is flowing under your feet.

These are not, however, the only irrational statements Zen makes. There are many more equally staggering[1] ones. Some may declare Zen irrevocably[2] insane or silly. Indeed, what would our readers say to such assertions[3] as the following?

"When Tom drinks, Dick gets tipsy."

"Who is the teacher of all the Buddhas, past, present, and future? John the cook."

"Last night a wooden horse neighed[4] and a stone man cut capers.[5]"

"Lo, a cloud of dust is rising from the ocean, and the roaring of the waves is heard over the land."

Sometimes Zen will ask you such questions as the following:

"It is pouring now; how would you stop it?"

"When both hands are clapped a sound is produced: listen to the sound of one hand."

"If you have heard the sound of one hand, can you make me hear it too?"

"When we see about us mountains towering high and seas filling hollow places, why do we read in the sacred sutras that the Dharma is sameness,[6] and there is nothing high, nothing low?"

Have the followers of Zen lost their senses? Or are they given up to deliberate mystification? Have all these statements no inner meaning, no edifying signification[7] except to produce confusion in our minds? What is Zen through these apparent trivialities and irrationalities[8] really driving us to comprehend? The answer is simple. Zen wants us to acquire an entirely new point of view whereby to look into[9] the mysteries of life and the secrets of nature. This is because Zen has come to the definite conclusion that the ordinary logical process of reasoning is powerless to give final satisfaction to our deepest spiritual needs.

(1) staggering 人をまごつかせるような。 (2) irrevocably 何とも手の施し様がない。 (3) assertions 主張。 (4) neigh いななく。 (5) cut capers 舞を舞うた。 (6) the Dharma is sameness 法は平等なり（是法平等）。 (7) edifying signification 啓発するところある意義。 (8) through these apparent trivialities and irrationalities これらの暇潰しとも非合理とも見える言葉を通じて。 (9) look into 洞見せよ。

> Empty-handed I go, and behold the spade is
>   in my hands;
> I walk on foot, and yet on the back of an ox
>   I am riding;
> When I pass over the bridge,
> Lo, the water floweth not, but the bridge doth
>   flow.

This is the famous gatha[1] of Jenye[2] (Shan-hui, A. D. 497-569), who is commonly known as Fudaishi (Fu-tai-shih) and it summarily gives the point of view as entertained by the followers of Zen. Though it by no means exhausts all that Zen teaches, it indicates graphically the way toward which Zen tends. Those who desire to gain an intellectual insight, if possible, into the truth of Zen, must first understand what this stanza[3] really means.

Nothing can be more illogical and contrary to common-sense than these four lines. The critic will be inclined to call Zen absurd, confusing, and beyond the ken of ordinary reasoning.[4] But Zen is inflexible and would protest that the so-called common-sense way of looking at things is not final, and that the reason why we cannot attain to a thoroughgoing comprehension of the truth is due to our unreasonable adherence to a "logical" interpretation of things. If we really want to get to the bottom of life, we must abandon our cherished syllogisms,[5] we must acquire a new way of observation whereby we can escape the tyranny of logic and the one-sidedness of our everyday phraseology.[6] However paradoxical it may

編集部注 (1) gatha　偈（げ）。偈とは、仏の徳や教えをたたえる韻文。 (2) Jenye　善慧大士。婺州善慧。通称傅大士。南北朝時代の禅僧。 (3) this stanza　この短詩。 (4) beyond the ken of ordinary reasoning　普通の考え方では頓と分からぬものだ。 (5) our cherished syllogisms　用いなれた推論式（シロジズム）。 (6) the one-sidedness of our everyday phraseology　我々日常語法の一面性。

IV

ILLOGICAL ZEN

III IS ZEN NIHILISTIC?

Let me conclude this chapter with the following quotation[1] from one of the earliest Zen writings. Doko[(1)] (Tao-kwang), a Buddhist philosopher and a student of the Vijnaptimatra (absolute idealism),[(2)] came to a Zen master and asked:

"With what frame of mind[(3)] should one discipline oneself in the truth?"

Said the Zen master, "There is no mind to be framed, nor is there any truth in which to be disciplined."

"If there is no mind to be framed and no truth in which to be disciplined, why do you have a daily gathering of monks who are studying Zen and disciplining themselves in the truth?"

The master replied: "I have not an inch of space to spare, and where could I have a gathering of monks? I have no tongue, and how would it be possible for me to advise others to come to me?"

The philosopher then exclaimed, "How can you tell me a lie like that to my face?"

"When I have no tongue to advise others, is it possible for me to tell a lie?"

Said Doko despairingly, "I cannot follow your reasoning."

"Neither do I understand myself," concluded the Zen master.

---

1 This is taken from a work by Daiju Yekai (Tai-chu Huihai), disciple of Baso (Ma-tsu, died 738). For other quotations see elsewhere.

(1) Doko 道光。 (2) a student of the Vijnaptimatra (absolute idealism) 唯識学者。
(3) with what frame of mind 何の心を用いて。

you have left behind and what you see before. A monk may come out of the assembly and say, 'I see the Buddha-hall and the temple gate before me, my sleeping cell and living room behind.' Has this man an inner eye opened? When you can discriminate him, I will admit that you really have had a personal interview with the ancient sages."

When silence does not avail, shall we say, after Yengo, "The gate of Heaven opens above, and an unquenched fire[1] burns below"? Does this make clear the ultimate signification of Zen, as not choked by the dualism of "yes" and "no"? Indeed, so long as there remains the last trace of consciousness as to this and that, *meum et tuum*, none can come to a fuller realization of Zen, and the sages of old will appear as those with whom we have nothing in common. The inner treasure will remain forever unearthed.[2]

A monk asked, "According to Vimalakirti, one who wishes for the Pure Land[3] ought to have his mind purified; but what is the purified mind?" Answered the Zen master: "When the mind is absolutely pure, you have a purified mind, and a mind is said to be absolutely pure when it is above purity and impurity. You want to know how this is to be realized? Have your mind thoroughly void[4] in all conditions, then you will have purity. But when this is attained, do not harbour any thought of it, or you get non-purity. Again, when this state of non-purity is attained, do not harbour any thought of it, and you are free of non-purity. This is absolute purity." Now, absolute purity is absolute affirmation, as it is above purity and non-purity and at the same time unifies them in a higher form of synthesis.[5] There is no negation in this, nor any contradiction. What Zen aims at is to realize this form of unification in one's everyday life of actualities, and not to treat life as a sort of metaphysical exercise. In this light all Zen "Questions and Answers"[6] (*Mondo*) are to be considered. There are no quibblings,[7] no playing at words, no sophistry[8]; Zen is the most serious concern in the world.

(1) an unquenched fire　劫火（ごうか）。世界を焼き尽す大火。 (2) remain forever unearthed　永久に持ち腐れとなる。 (3) the Pure Land　浄土。 (4) thoroughly void　徹底的にむなしく。 (5) in a higher form of synthesis　より高い綜合の立場に於て。 (6) all Zen "Questions and Answers"　すべての禅「問答」。 (7) quibblings　地口。 (8) sophistry　詭弁。

III IS ZEN NIHILISTIC?

it and yet it is not talked about; we know it and yet it is not known. Let me ask, How does it so happen?"

Is this an interrogation as it apparently is? Or, in fact, is it an affirmative statement describing a certain definite attitude of mind?

Therefore, when Zen denies, it is not necessarily a denial in the logical sense. The same can be said of an affirmation. The idea is that the ultimate fact of experience must not be enslaved by any artificial or schematic laws of thought,[1] nor by any antithesis of "yes" and "no", nor by any cut and dried formulae[2] of epistemology.[3] Evidently Zen commits absurdities and irrationalities[4] all the time; but this only apparently. No wonder it fails to escape the natural consequences—misunderstandings, wrong interpretations, and ridicules[5] which are often malicious. The charge of nihilism[6] is only one of these.

When Vimalakirti[7] asked Manjusri[8] what was the doctrine of non-duality as realized by a Bodhisattva,[9] Manjusri replied: "As I understand it, the doctrine is realized when one looks upon all things as beyond every form of expression and demonstration and as transcending knowledge and argument.[10] This is my comprehension; may I ask what is your understanding?" Vimalakirti, thus demanded, remained altogether silent. The mystic response—that is, the closing of the lips—seems to be the only way one can get out of the difficulties in which Zen often finds itself involved, when it is pressed hard for a statement. Therefore, Yengo (Yuan-wu), commenting on the above, has this to say:

"I say, 'yes', and there is nothing about which this affirmation is made; I say, 'no', and there is nothing about which this is made. I stand above 'yes' and 'no', I forget what is gained and what is lost. There is just a state of absolute purity, a state of stark nakedness.[11] Tell me what

---

(1) artificial or schematic laws of thought　構成的もしくは図式的な思惟法則。 (2) any cut and dried formulae　曖昧の失せた構造式。 (3) epistemology　認識論。 (4) absurdities and irrationalities　背理・非合理。 (5) ridicules　揶揄。 (6) the charge of nihilism　虚無主義を非難すること。 (7) Vimalakirti　維摩。維摩経の主人公の名。富豪で高度の学識を持つ者。 (8) Manjusri　文殊。文殊菩薩のこと。仏の智慧を象徴する。 (9) the doctrine of non-duality as realized by a Bodhisattva　菩薩不二の法門。法門は、仏教の教え、仏門。 (10) as beyond every form of expression and demonstration and as transcending knowledge and argument　無言・無説・無示・無識にして。 (11) a state of absolute purity, a state of stark nakedness　浄裸裸、赤灑灑（しゃくしゃしゃ）。

They have a certain firm basis of truth obtained from a deep personal experience. There is in all their seemingly crazy performances a systematic demonstration[1] of the most vital truth. When seen from this truth, even the moving of the whole universe is of no more account than the flying of a mosquito or the waving of a fan. The thing is to see one spirit working throughout all these, which is an absolute affirmation, with not a particle of nihilism in it.

A monk asked Joshu, "What would you say when I come to you with nothing?"

Joshu said, "Fling it down to the ground."

Protested the monk, "I said that I had nothing; what shall I let go?"

"If so, carry it away," was the retort of Joshu.

Joshu has thus plainly exposed the fruitlessness[2] of a nihilistic philosophy. To reach the goal of Zen, even the idea of "having nothing" ought to be done away with.[3] Buddha reveals himself when he is no more asserted; that is, for Buddha's sake Buddha is to be given up. This is the only way to come to the realization[4] of the truth of Zen. So long as one is talking of nothingness or of the absolute one is far away from Zen, and ever receding from Zen. Even the foothold of Sunyata[5] must be kicked off. The only way to get saved is to throw oneself right down into a bottomless abyss. And this is, indeed, no easy task.

"No Buddhas," it is boldly asserted by Yengo[6] (see p. 27), "have ever appeared on earth; nor is there anything that is to be given out as a holy doctrine. Bodhidharma, the First Patriarch of Zen,[7] has never come east,[8] nor has he ever transmitted any secret doctrine through the mind; only people of the world, not understanding what all this means, seek the truth outside of themselves. What a pity that the thing they are so earnestly looking for is being trodden under their own feet! This is not to be grasped by the wisdom of all the sages. However, we see the thing and yet it is not seen; we hear it and yet it is not heard; we talk about

---

(1) a systematic demonstration　脈絡一貫した証示（デモンストレーション）。　(2) the fruitlessness　むなしさ。　(3) be done away with　捨て去られる（掃蕩しなければ）。　(4) the realization　体得する。　(5) the foothold of Sunyata　空（シューニャター）の足場。　(6) Yengo　圜悟（かんご）。　(7) Bodhidharma, the First Patriarch of Zen　中国禅宗の初祖達摩（だるま）。　(8) come east　西来した。

ed by Shoju.

Zen is not all negation, leaving the mind all blank as if it were pure nothing; for that would be intellectual suicide. There is in Zen something self-assertive, which, however, being free and absolute, knows no limitations and refuses to be handled in abstraction. Zen is a live fact,[1] it is not like an inorganic rock[2] or like an empty space. To come into contact with this living fact—nay, to take hold of it in every phase of life—is the aim of all Zen discipline.

Nansen[3] (Nan-chuan, 748-834) was once asked by Hyakujo[4] (Pai-chang, 720-814), one of his brother monks,[5] if there was anything he dared not talk about to others. The master answered, "Yes."

Whereupon the monk continued, "What then is this something you do not talk about?"

The master's reply was, "It is neither mind, nor Buddha, nor matter.[6]"

This looks to be the doctrine of absolute emptiness, but even here again we observe a glimpse of something showing itself through the negation. Observe the further dialogue that took place between the two. The monk said:

"If so, you have already talked about it."

"I cannot do any better. What would you say?"

"I am not a great enlightened one," answered Hyakujo.

The master said, "Well, I have already said too much about it."

This state of inner consciousness,[7] about which we cannot make any logical statement, must be realized before we can have any intelligent talk on Zen. Words are only an index to this state[8]; through them we are enabled to get into its signification, but do not look to words for absolute guidance. Try to see first of all in what mental state the Zen masters are so acting. They are not carrying on all those seeming absurdities,[9] or, as some might say, those silly trivialities,[10] just to suit their capricious moods.[11]

---

(1) a live fact 一箇の生き物。 (2) an inorganic rock 生命のない巌石。 (3) Nansen 南泉普願。中国唐代の禅僧。 (4) Hyakujo 百丈。 (5) one of his brother monks 法弟。 (6) It is neither mind, nor Buddha, nor matter. 不是心、不是仏、不是物。 (7) inner consciousness 内的自覚。 (8) this state この自覚の一境。 (9) all those seeming absurdities こうした荒唐無稽。 (10) those silly trivialities 馬鹿げ切った暇潰し。 (11) just to suit their capricious moods 恣意のもよおすままに。

"How rude you are!"

"Do you know where you are," exclaimed the master; "here I have no time to consider for your sake what rudeness or politeness means.[1]" With this another slap was given.

Intelligent readers will see in this attitude of Obaku something he is anxious to communicate in spite of his apparent brusqueness to his disciple. He forbids outwardly, and yet in the spirit he is affirming. This must be comprehended if Zen is to be at all understood.

The attitude of Zen towards the formal worship of God[2] may be gleaned more clearly from Joshu's[3] (Chao-chou, 778-897) remarks given to a monk who was bowing reverently before Buddha. When Joshu slapped the monk, the latter said, "Is it not a laudable thing[4] to pay respect to Buddha?" "Yes," answered the master, "but it is better to go without even a laudable thing." Does this attitude savour of anything nihilistic and iconoclastic[5]? Superficially, yes; but let us dive deep into the spirit of Joshu out of the depths of which this utterance comes, and we will find ourselves confronting an absolute affirmation quite beyond the ken of our discursive understanding.[6]

Hakuin[7] (1685-1768), the founder of modern Japanese Zen, while still a young monk eagerly bent on the mastery of Zen, had an interview with the venerable Shoju.[8] Hakuin thought that he fully comprehended Zen and was proud of his attainment, and this interview with Shoju was in fact intended to be a demonstration of his own high understanding. Shoju asked him how much he knew of Zen. Hakuin answered disgustingly, "If there is anything I can lay my hand on, I will get it all out of me." So saying, he acted as if he were going to vomit. Shoju took firm hold of Hakuin's nose and said: "What is this? Have I not after all touched it?" Let our readers ponder with Hakuin over this interview and find out for themselves what is that something which is so realistically demonstrat-

(1) what rudeness or politeness means　細とか麤(そ)とか。(2) the formal worship of God　形の上の礼拝。(3) Joshu　趙州従諗(じょうしゅうじゅうしん)。中国唐代の禅僧。南泉に師事した。(4) a laudable thing　讃むべきこと。(5) savour of anything nihilistic and iconoclastic　虚無主義的な或は偶像破壊的なところがある。(6) beyond the ken of our discursive understanding　分別的理解を越えた。(7) Hakuin　白隠。江戸時代の臨済禅中興の祖。(8) the venerable Shoju　正受老人。

III IS ZEN NIHILISTIC?

(*avidya*), which tenaciously clings to the mind as wet clothes do to the body. "Ignorance"[1] is all very well as far as it goes, but it must not go out of its proper sphere. "Ignorance" is another name for logical dualism.[(1)] White is snow and black is the raven. But these belong to the world and its ignorant way of talking. If we want to get to the very truth of things, we must see them from the point where this world has not yet been created, where the consciousness of this and that has not yet been awakened and where the mind is absorbed in its own identity, that is, in its serenity and emptiness. This is a world of negations but leading to a higher or absolute affirmation—an affirmation in the midst of negations. Snow is not white, the raven is not black, yet each in itself is white or black. This is where our everyday language fails to convey the exact meaning as conceived by Zen.

Apparently Zen negates; but it is always holding up before us something which indeed lies right before our own eyes; and if we do not pick it up by ourselves, it is our own fault. Most people, whose mental vision[(2)] is darkened by the clouds of ignorance, pass it by and refuse to look at it. To them Zen is, indeed, nihilism just because they do not see it. When Obaku[(3)] (Huang-po, died 850) was paying reverence to the Buddha in the sanctuary,[(4)] a pupil of his approached and said, "When Zen says not to seek it through the Buddha, nor through the Dharma,[(5)] nor through the Sangha,[(6)] why do you bow to the Buddha as if wishing to get something by this pious act?"

"I do not seek it," answered the master, "through the Buddha, nor through the Dharma, nor through the Sangha; I just go on doing this act of piety to the Buddha.[(7)]"

The disciple grunted, "What is the use, anyway, of looking so sanctimonious[(8)]?"

The master gave him a slap in the face, whereupon the disciple said,

1 This may be regarded as corresponding to Heraclitus' *Enantiodromia*, the regulating function of antithesis.

(1) logical dualism　論理的二元論。　(2) mental vision　心眼。　(3) Obaku　黄檗。中国唐代の禅僧。　(4) in the sanctuary　仏殿にあって。　(5) through the Dharma　法に著いて。　(6) through the Sangha　僧に著いて。　(7) doing this act of piety to the Buddha　こうやって礼拝する。　(8) looking so sanctimonious　礼拝して。

knowledge of Nirvana,[1] no obtaining of it, no not-obtaining of it. Therefore, O Sariputra, as there is no obtaining of Nirvana, a man who has approached the Prajnaparamita of the Bodhisattvas dwells unimpeded in consciousness.[2] When the impediments of consciousness are annihilated,[3] then he becomes free of all fear, is beyond the reach of change,[4] enjoying final Nirvana."

Going through all these quotations, it may be thought that the critics are justified in charging Zen with advocating a philosophy of pure negation, but nothing is so far from Zen as this criticism would imply. For Zen always aims at grasping the central fact of life, which can never be brought to the dissecting table[5] of the intellect. To grasp this central fact of life, Zen is forced to propose a series of negations. Mere negation, however, is not the spirit of Zen, but as we are so accustomed to the dualistic way of thinking, this intellectual error must be cut at its root. Naturally[6] Zen would proclaim, "Not this, not that, not anything." But we may insist upon asking Zen what it is that is left after all these denials, and the master will perhaps on such an occasion give us a slap in the face, exclaiming, "You fool, what is this?" Some may take this as only an excuse to get away from the dilemma, or as having no more meaning than a practical example of ill-breeding. But when the spirit of Zen is grasped in its purity, it will be seen what a real thing that slap is. For here is no negation, no affirmation, but a plain fact, a pure experience, the very foundation[7] of our being and thought. All the quietness and emptiness one might desire in the midst of most active mentation[8] lies therein. Do not be carried away by anything outward or conventional. Zen must be seized with bare hands, with no gloves on

Zen is forced to resort to negation because of our innate ignorance[9]

---

(1) Knowledge of Nirvana　涅槃の智。 (2) dwells unimpeded in consciousness　無礙（むげ）の心境の住する。 (3) when the impediments of consciousness are annihilated　無礙である故に。 (4) beyond the reach of change　一切の転倒妄想を遠離して。 (5) the dissecting table　解剖台。 (6) naturally　然るべきところである。 (7) the very foundation　依拠そのもの。 (8) in the midst of most active mentation　動いてやまぬ心の只中に。 (9) our innate ignorance　我々の生れもつ無明。無明とは、煩悩にとらわれ、仏法の真理に暗いこと。真如に対する無知。

III IS ZEN NIHILISTIC?

of Buddhism.[1] The sage is reported to have answered, "Vast emptiness and nothing holy in it.[2]"

These are passages taken at random from the vast store of Zen literature, and they seem to be permeated with the ideas of emptiness (*sunyata*), nothingness (*nasti*), quietude (*santi*), no-thought[3] (*acinta*), and other similar notions, all of which we may regard as nihilistic or as advocating negative quietism.

A quotation from the *Prajnaparamita-Hridaya Sutra*[1][4] may prove to be more astounding than any of the above passages. In fact, all the sutras belonging to this Prajna class of Mahayana literature[5] are imbued thoroughly with the idea of Sunyata,[6] and those who are not familiar with this way of thinking will be taken aback and may not know how to express their judgment. This sutra, considered to be the most concise and most comprehensive of all the Prajna sutras, is daily recited in the Zen monasteries; in fact it is the first thing the monks recite in the morning[7] as well as before each meal.

"Thus, Sariputra,[8] all things have the character of emptiness, they have no beginning, no end, they are faultless and not faultless, they are not perfect and not imperfect. Therefore, O Sariputra, here in this emptiness there is no form, no perception, no name, no concepts, no knowledge. No eye, no ear, no nose, no tongue, no body, no mind. No form, no sound, no smell, no taste, no touch, no objects.[9] . . . There is no knowledge, no ignorance, no destruction of ignorance. . . . There is no decay nor death; there are no four truths, viz. there is no pain, no origin of pain, no stoppage of pain, and no path to the stoppage of pain. There is no

---

1 See also the quotation from Sekiso, *supra*, often misunderstood as expressly advocating the doctrine of annihilation. For the original Sanskrit, Hsuan-chuang's Chinese translation, and a more literary and accurate English rendering, see my *Zen Essays*, Series III, pp. 190-206, where the author gives his own interpretation of the signification of this important sutra.

(1) the ultimate and holiest principle of Buddhism 仏教の第一義。 (2) "Vast emptiness and nothing holy in it." 「廓然無聖」（かくねんむしょう）。 (3) emptiness, nothingness, quietude, no-thought 空、無、寂静、不思議。 (4) the *Prajnaparamita-Hridaya Sutra* 『般若波羅蜜多心経』。 (5) this Prajna class of Mahayana literature 般若系大乗経典。 (6) the idea of Sunyata 空の思想。 (7) in the morning 晨朝（じんちょう）。晨朝とは、朝の勤行（ごんぎょう）。朝のおつとめ。 (8) Sariputra 舎利弗（しゃりほつ）。舎利弗とは、釈尊の十大弟子の一人。 (9) no objects …法も（すべて）ない。

have nothing to give you, and what truth of Buddhism do you desire to find in my monastery? There is nothing, absolutely nothing."

A master would sometimes say: "I do not understand Zen. I have nothing here to demonstrate; therefore, do not remain standing so, expecting to get something out of nothing. Get enlightened by yourself, if you will. If there is anything to take hold of, take it by yourself."

Again: "True knowledge (*bodhi*) transcends[1] all modes of expression. There has been nothing from the very beginning which one can claim as having attained towards enlightenment."

Or: "In Zen there is nothing to explain by means of words, there is nothing to be given out as a holy doctrine. Thirty blows whether you affirm or negate.[2] Do not remain silent; nor be discursive.[3]"

The question "How can one always be with Buddha?" called forth the following answer from a master: "Have no stirrings in your mind[4]; be perfectly serene toward the objective world.[5] To remain thus all the time in absolute emptiness and calmness[6] is the way to be with the Buddha."

Sometimes we come across the following: "The middle way[7] is where there is neither middle nor two sides. When you are fettered by the objective world, you have one side; when you are disturbed in your own mind, you have the other side. When neither of these exists, there is no middle part, and this is the middle way."

A Japanese Zen master who flourished several hundred years ago used to say to his disciples, who would implore him to instruct them in the way to escape the fetters of birth-and-death, "Here is no birth-and-death."

Bodhidharma (Daruma, J.; Tamo, C.), the First Patriarch of the Zen sect in China, was asked by Wu, the first Emperor (reigned A. D. 502-549) of the Liang dynasty,[8] as to the ultimate and holiest principle

---

(1) transcends 超越している。 (2) Thirty blows whether you affirm or negate. 道（い）い得るも三十棒、道（い）い得ざるも三十棒だ。 (3) be discursive 言説に亘る。 (4) have no stirrings in your mind 念を動かすな。 (5) toward the objective world 境に対して。 (6) emptiness and calmness 空寂。 (7) the middle way 中道。 (8) Wu, the first Emperor of the Liang dynasty 梁の武帝。

III IS ZEN NIHILISTIC?

master of the signification of the first stanza by Yeno stamps it[1] as the orthodox expression of Zen faith. As it seems to breathe[2] the spirit of nothingness, many people regard Zen as advocating nihilism. The purpose of the present chapter is to refute this.[3]

It is true there are many passages in Zen literature which may be construed as conveying a nihilistic doctrine; for example, the theory of Sunyata (emptiness).¹[4] Even among those scholars who are well acquainted with the general teaching of Mahayana Buddhism,[5] some still cling to the view that Zen is the practical application of the "Sanron" (*san-lun*) philosophy,[6] otherwise known as the Madhyamika school.[7] *Sanron* means the "three treatises", which are Nagarjuna's *Madhyamika Sastra* and *The Discourse of Twelve Sections*,[8] and Deva's *Discourse of One Hundred Stanzas*.[9] They comprise all the essential doctrines of this school. Nagarjuna is thought to be its founder, and as the Mahayana sutras classified under the head of Prajnaparamita[10] expound more or less similar views, the philosophy of this school is sometimes designated as the Prajna doctrine.[11] Zen, therefore, they think, practically belongs to this class; in other words, the ultimate signification of Zen would be the upholding of the Sunyata system.

To a certain extent, superficially at least, this view is justifiable. For instance, read the following:

"I come here to seek the truth of Buddhism," a disciple asked a master.

"Why do you seek such a thing here?" answered the master. "Why do you wander about, neglecting your own precious treasure at home? I

---

1 What the theory of Sunyata really means is explained somewhat in detail in my *Essays in Zen Buddhism*, Series III, under "The philosophy and Religion of the Prajnaparamita-Sutra" (pp. 207–88).

(1) stamp(s) it 印可した（する）。印可とは、指導者が修行者の悟境を認めること。
(2) it seems to breathe 気息に感じさせる。 (3) to refute this その論駁。 (4) the theory of Sunyata (emptiness) 空説。 (5) Mahayana Buddhism 大乗仏教 (p.8の注を参照)。 (6) the "Sanron" philosophy 三論哲学。 (7) the Madhyamika school 中観派教説。中観派はインド大乗仏教の学派。 (8) Nagarjuna's *Madhyamika Sastra* and *The Discourse of Twelve Sections* 龍樹の『中論』・『十二門論』。 (9) Deva's *Discourse of One Hundred Stanzas* 提婆の『百論』。 (10) the Mahayana sutras classified under the head of Prajnaparamita 般若系大乗経典。 (11) the Prajna doctrine 般若系教説。

In the history of Zen, Yeno[1] (Hui-neng,[1] 638-713), traditionally considered the Sixth Patriarch[2] of the Zen sect in China, cuts a most important figure. In fact, he is the founder of Zen as distinguished from the other Buddhist sects then existing in China. The standard set up by him as the true expression of Zen faith[3] is this stanza:

> The Bodhi (True Wisdom) is not like the tree;
> The mirror bright is nowhere shining:
> As there is nothing from the first,
> Where does the dust itself collect?

This was written in answer to a stanza composed by another Zen monk who claimed to have understood[4] the faith in its purity. His lines run thus:

> This body is the Bodhi-tree;
> The soul is like the mirror bright;
> Take heed[5] to keep it always clean,
> And let no dust collect upon it.

They were both the disciples of the Fifth Patriarch, Gunin[6] (Hung-jen, died 675); and he thought that Yeno rightly comprehended the spirit of Zen, and, therefore, was worthy of wearing his mantle and carrying his bowl as his true successor in Zen. This recognition by the

---

1 Hui-neng is pronounced Wei-lang in Shanghai dialect.

編集部注 (1) Yeno 慧能（えのう）。中国の禅宗第六祖。中興の祖といわれる。(2) the Sixth Patriarch 第六祖。(3) Zen faith 禅的信。(4) have understood 体得した。(5) take heed …に心して。(6) the Fifth Patriarch, Gunin 第五祖弘忍。

III

IS ZEN NIHILISTIC?

they not, however multitudinous, all possessions obtainable within the original being of yourself? Every treasure there is but waiting your pleasure and utilization. This is what is meant by 'Once gained, eternally gained, even unto the end of time.'[1] Yet really there is nothing gained; what you have gained is no gain, and yet there is something truly gained in this."

---

(1) 'Once gained, eternally gained, even unto the end of time.' 「一得永得尽未来際」。ひと度得たものは永久に身について離れないという意味。

of immaculate silk[1]; let your one thought be eternity; let yourself be like dead ashes, cold and lifeless; again let yourself be like an old censer[2] in a deserted village shrine!'

"Putting your simple faith in this, discipline yourself accordingly; let your body and mind be turned into an inanimate object of nature like a stone or a piece of wood; when a state of perfect motionlessness and unawareness is obtained all the signs of life[3] will depart and also every trace of limitation will vanish. Not a single idea will disturb your consciousness, when lo! all of a sudden you will come to realize a light abounding in full gladness. It is like coming across a light in thick darkness; it is like receiving treasure in poverty. The four elements and the five aggregates[4] are no more felt as burdens; so light, so easy, so free you are. Your very existence has been delivered from all limitations; you have become open, light, and transparent. You gain an illuminating insight into the very nature of things, which now appear to you as so many fairylike flowers[5] having no graspable realities. Here is manifested the unsophisticated self[6] which is the original face of your being; here is shown all bare the most beautiful landscape of your birthplace.[7] There is but one straight passage open and unobstructed through and through. This is so[8] when you surrender all—your body, your life, and all that belongs to your inmost self. This is where you gain peace, ease, non-doing,[9] and inexpressible delight. All the sutras and sastras[10] are no more than communications of this fact; all the sages, ancient as well as modern, have exhausted their ingenuity and imagination[11] to no other purpose than to point the way to this. It is like unlocking the door to a treasury; when the entrance is once gained, every object coming into your view is yours, every opportunity that presents itself is available for your use; for are

(1) immaculate silk 白練（しろねり）。 (2) censer 香炉。 (3) all the signs of life あらゆる生の徴。 (4) the four elements and the five aggregates 四大五蘊のこの身も。五蘊は、人間を成り立たせている五要素。色蘊（しきうん）、受蘊（じゅうん）、想蘊（そううん）、行蘊（ぎょううん）、識蘊（しきうん）を言い、それぞれ肉体、感覚、想像、心の作用、それに意識を意味する。 (5) so many fairylike flowers 数々の空華。 (6) the unsophisticated self 詭弁に惑わされない自己（戯論の瞞著し得ない自己）。 (7) your birthplace おんみの本地。 (8) This is so そこにその道があるのだ。 (9) non-doing 無作（むさ）。無作は、悟り。涅槃の異称。 (10) all the sutras and sastras 一切の経論（きょうろん）。 (11) exhausted their ingenuity and imagination その能を尽し構想の妙を尽した。

1566-1642) may answer, to a certain extent, the question asked in the beginning of this chapter, "What is Zen?"

"It is presented right to your face, and at this moment the whole thing is handed over to you. For an intelligent fellow, one word should suffice[1] to convince him of the truth of it, but even then error has crept in. Much more so when it is committed to paper and ink, or given up to wordy demonstration or to logical quibble,[2] then it slips farther away from you. The great truth of Zen is possessed by everybody. Look into your own being and seek it not through others. Your own mind is above all forms[3]; it is free and quiet and sufficient; it eternally stamps itself in your six senses and four elements.[4] In its light all is absorbed. Hush[5] the dualism of subject and object, forget both, transcend the intellect, sever yourself from the understanding,[6] and directly penetrate deep into the identity of the Buddha-mind; outside of this there are no realities. Therefore, when Bodhidharma[7] came from the West, he simply declared, 'Directly pointing to one's own soul, my doctrine is unique, and is not hampered by the canonical teachings[8]; it is the absolute transmission[9] of the true seal.[10]' Zen has nothing to do with letters, words, or sutras.[11] It only requests you to grasp the point directly and therein to find your peaceful abode. When the mind is disturbed, the understanding is stirred, things are recognized, notions are entertained, ghostly spirits are conjured,[12] and prejudices grow rampant. Zen will then forever be lost in the maze.[13]

"The wise Sekiso[14] (Shih-shuang) said, 'Stop all your hankerings[15]; let the mildew[16] grow on your lips; make yourself like unto a perfect piece

---

(1) should suffice できる筈だ。 (2) given up to wordy demonstration or to logical quibble 言詮に渉る時。 (3) above all forms あらゆる形相を超え。 (4) in your six senses and four elements 六根（ろっこん）四大に。六根とは、眼（げん）、耳（に）、鼻（び）、舌（ぜつ）、身（しん）、意（い）の六種の根を言う。根は能力の意で、またその能力をもつ器官を意味する。 (5) hush 沈黙せしめよ。 (6) sever yourself from the understanding 悟性を離れ。 (7) Bodhidharma 菩提達摩（ぼだいだるま）。菩提は、あらゆる煩悩から解放された、迷いのない状態。仏陀の正しい悟りの智。達摩は禅宗の始祖。 (8) the canonical teachings いわゆる教え。 (9) the absolute transmission 正しく…単伝するもの。単伝とは正法を純粋に独り伝えること。 (10) the true seal 心印。心印とは、仏祖から伝えられた永遠不変の悟りの核心。 (11) sutra(s) 経典。 (12) ghostly spirits are conjured 妄想を逞しうし。 (13) be lost in the maze 片影すらも見当らない。 (14) the wise Sekiso 賢者石霜。 (15) hankerings 心の喘ぎ。 (16) the mildew 黴。

II WHAT IS ZEN?

being biased by anything.

As has been said before, what makes Zen unique as it is practised in Japan is its systematic training of the mind. Ordinary mysticism has been too erratic[1] a product and apart from one's ordinary life; this Zen has revolutionized. What was up in the heavens, Zen has brought down to earth. With the development of Zen, mysticism has ceased to be mystical; it is no more the spasmodic[2] product of an abnormally endowed mind[3]. For Zen reveals itself in the most uninteresting and uneventful life[4] of a plain man of the street, recognizing the fact of living in the midst of life as it is lived. Zen systematically trains the mind to see this; it opens a man's eye to the greatest mystery as it is daily and hourly performed; it enlarges the heart to embrace eternity of time and infinity of space in its every palpitation[5]; it makes us live in the world as if walking in the garden of Eden; and all these spiritual feats[6] are accomplished without resorting to any doctrines but by simply asserting in the most direct way the truth that lies in our inner being.

Whatever else Zen may be, it is practical and commonplace and at the same time most living. An ancient master, wishing to show what Zen is, lifted one of his fingers, another kicked a ball, and a third slapped the face of his questioner. If the inner truth that lies deep in us is thus demonstrated, is not Zen the most practical and direct method of spiritual training ever resorted to by any religion? And is not this practical method also a most original one? Indeed, Zen cannot be anything else but original and creative because it refuses to deal with concepts but deals with living facts of life. When conceptually understood, the lifting of a finger is one of the most ordinary incidents in everybody's life. But when it is viewed from the Zen point of view it vibrates with divine[7] meaning and creative vitality. So long as Zen can point out this truth in the midst of our conventional and concept-bound existence[8] we must say that it has its reason of being.

The following quotation from a letter of Yengo[9] (Yuan-wu in C.

---

(1) erratic　その赴くままに。　(2) spasmodic　発作的な。　(3) an abnormally endowed mind　異常な天分を有するもの。　(4) in the most uninteresting and uneventful life　最も目に立たぬありふれた生活の裡に。　(5) in its every palpitation　その一鼓動毎に。　(6) feats　離れ業。　(7) divine　霊妙な。　(8) our conventional and concept-bound existence　我々の因襲的な概念に縛られた生活。　(9) Yengo　圜悟（かんご）。

inner being. For whatever authority there is in Zen, all comes from within. This is true in the strictest sense of the word. Even the reasoning faculty[1] is not considered final[2] or absolute. On the contrary, it hinders the mind from coming into the directest communication with itself. The intellect accomplishes its mission when it works as an intermediary,[3] and Zen has nothing to do with an intermediary except when it desires to communicate itself to others. For this reason all the scriptures are merely tentative and provisory[4]; there is in them no finality. The central fact of life as it is lived is what Zen aims to grasp, and this in the most direct and most vital manner. Zen professes itself[5] to be the spirit of Buddhism, but in fact it is the spirit of all religions and philosophies. When Zen is thoroughly understood, absolute peace of mind is attained, and a man lives as he ought to live.[6] What more may we hope?

Some say that as Zen is admittedly a form of mysticism it cannot claim to be unique in the history of religion. Perhaps so; but Zen is a mysticism of its own order.[7] It is mystical in the sense that the sun shines, that the flower blooms, that I hear at this moment somebody beating a drum in the street. If these are mystical facts, Zen is brim-full[8] of them. When a Zen master was once asked what Zen was, he replied, "Your everyday thought."[9] Is this not plain and most straightforward? It has nothing to do with any sectarian spirit. Christians as well as Buddhists can practise Zen just as big fish and small fish are both contentedly living in the same ocean. Zen is the ocean, Zen is the air, Zen is the mountain, Zen is thunder and lightning, the spring flower, summer heat, and winter snow; nay,[10] more than that, Zen is the man. With all the formalities, conventionalisms,[11] and superadditions that Zen has accumulated in its long history, its central fact is very much alive. The special merit of Zen[12] lies in this: that we are still able to see into this ultimate fact without

(1) the reasoning faculty　知性のはたらき。　(2) final　窮極のもの。　(3) as an intermediary　媒介的に。　(4) provisory　条件つきのもの。　(5) profess(es) itself　表明する。　(6) a man lives as he ought to live　人は計らずして如法（にょほう）の生を生きるのである。如法とは、仏の教え（法）のとおりに行うこと。　(7) a mysticism of its own order　自己自身の秩序をもつ神秘主義。　(8) brim-full　充ち溢れんばかり。　(9) "Your everyday thought."　「平常心」（びょうじょうしん）。　(10) nay　否。　(11) the formalities, conventionalisms　形式的行為・因襲。　(12) the special merit of Zen　禅独特の長所。

II WHAT IS ZEN?

nothing more!" A minute's hesitation and Zen is irrevocably lost.[1] All the Buddhas of the past, present, and future[2] may try to make you catch it once more, and yet it is a thousand miles away. "Mind-murder" and "self-intoxication", forsooth![3] Zen has no time to bother itself with such criticisms.

The critics may mean that the mind is hypnotized[4] by Zen to a state of unconsciousness, and that when this obtains, the favourite Buddhist doctrine of emptiness[5] (*sunyata*) is realized,[6] where the subject[7] is not conscious of an objective world[8] or of himself, being lost in one vast emptiness, whatever this may be. This interpretation again fails to hit Zen aright. It is true that there are some such expressions in Zen as might suggest this kind of interpretation, but to understand Zen we must make a leap here. The "vast emptiness" must be traversed.[9] The subject must be awakened from a state of unconsciousness if he does not wish to be buried alive. Zen is attained only when "self-intoxication" is abandoned and the "drunkard" is really awakened to his deeper self. If the mind is ever to be "murdered", leave the work in the hand of Zen; for it is Zen that will restore the murdered and lifeless one into a state of eternal life. "Be born again, be awakened from the dream, rise from the death, O ye drunkards!" Zen would exclaim. Do not try, therefore, to see Zen with the eyes bandaged; and your hands are too unsteady to take hold of it. And remember I am not indulging in figures of speech.

I might multiply many such criticisms if it were necessary but I hope that the above have sufficiently prepared the reader's mind for the following more positive statements concerning Zen. The basic idea of Zen is to come in touch with the inner workings of our being, and to do this in the most direct way possible, without resorting to anything external or superadded.[10] Therefore, anything that has the semblance of[11] an external authority is rejected by Zen. Absolute faith[12] is placed in a man's own

---

(1) irrevocably lost　失われて取り返す術もない。 (2) All the Buddhas of the past, present, and future　三世（さんぜ）の諸仏。 (3) forsooth!　…も結構だが、 (4) is hypnotized　引入れられる。 (5) emptiness　空。 (6) is realized　体験される。 (7) the subject　主体。 (8) an objective world　客体的世界。 (9) be traversed　横断されなければ。 (10) to anything external or superadded　何等外部的、追加的存在に。 (11) the semblance of　…を思わせるようなもの。 (12) absolute faith　絶対信。

that Zen is "mystical self-intoxication".[1] Does he mean that Zen is intoxicated in the "Greater Self"[2]; so called, as Spinoza was intoxicated in God? Though Mr. Reischauer is not quite clear as to the meaning of "intoxication", he may think that Zen is unduly absorbed in the thought of the "Greater Self" as the final reality in this world of particulars.[3] It is amazing to see how superficial some of the uncritical observers of Zen are! In point of fact, Zen has no "mind" to murder; therefore, there is no "mind-murdering" in Zen. Zen has again no "self" as something to which we can cling as a refuge; therefore, in Zen again there is no "self" by which we may become intoxicated.

The truth is, Zen is extremely elusive as far as its outward aspects are concerned; when you think you have caught a glimpse of it, it is no more there; from afar it looks so approachable, but as soon as you come near it you see it even further away from you than before. Unless, therefore, you devote some years of earnest study to the understanding of its primary principles,[4] it is not to be expected that you will begin to have a fair grasp of Zen.

"The way to ascend unto God is to descend into one's self";—these are Hugo's words. "If thou wishest to search out the deep things of God, search out the depths of thine own spirit";—this comes from Richard of St. Victor. When all these deep things are searched out there is after all no "self". Where you can descend, there is no "spirit", no "God" whose depths are to be fathomed. Why? Because Zen is a bottomless abyss. Zen declares, though in a somewhat different manner: "Nothing really exists throughout the triple world[5]; where do you wish to see the mind (or spirit = $hsin$)? The four elements[6] are all empty in their ultimate nature[7]; where could the Buddha's abode be?—but lo![8] the truth is unfolding itself right before your eye. This is all there is to it—and indeed

(1) "mystical self-intoxication" 神秘的自己陶酔。 (2) "Greater Self" 「大我」(たいが)。 (3) in this world of particulars 個別の世界に於ける。 (4) its primary principles その根本原理。 (5) the triple world 三界(さんがい)。三界は、欲界(よくかい)、色界(しきかい)、無色界(むしきかい)の三つの総称。 (6) The four elements 四大(しだい)。四大とは、四つの粗大な実在。物質を作り上げる地、水、火、風の四元素のこと。 (7) in their ultimate nature 畢竟。 (8) but lo! しかも見よ。

II WHAT IS ZEN?

perceives or feels, and does not abstract nor meditate. Zen penetrates and is finally lost in the immersion.[1] Meditation, on the other hand, is outspokenly dualistic and consequently inevitably superficial.

One critic[1] regards Zen as "the Buddhist counterpart of the 'Spiritual Exercises'[2] of St. Ignatius Loyala". The critic shows a great inclination to find Christian analogies for things Buddhistic, and this is one of such instances. Those who have at all a clear understanding of Zen will at once see how wide of the mark[3] this comparison is. Even superficially speaking,[4] there is not a shadow of similitude between the exercises of Zen and those proposed by the founder of the Society of Jesus. The contemplations[5] and prayers of St. Ignatius are, from the Zen point of view, merely so many fabrications of the imagination elaborately woven for the benefit of the piously minded; and in reality this is like piling tiles upon tiles on one's head, and there is no true gain in the life of the spirit. We can say this, however, that those "Spiritual Exercises" in some ways resemble certain meditations of Hinayana Buddhism,[6] such as the Five Mind-quieting Methods,[7] or the Nine Thoughts on Impurity,[8] or the Six or Ten Subjects of Memory.[9]

Zen is sometimes made to mean "mind-murder and the curse of idle reverie[10]". This is the statement of Griffis, the well-known author of *Religions of Japan*.[2] By "mind-murder" I do not know what he really means, but does he mean that Zen kills the activities of the mind by making one's thought fix on one thing, or by inducing sleep? Mr. Reischauer in his book[3] almost endorses this view of Griffis by asserting

---

1 Arthur Lloyd: *Wheat Among the Tares*, p. 53.　**2** p. 255.　**3** *Studies of Buddhism in Japan*, p. 118.

(1) Zen penetrates and is finally lost in the immersion.　禅は徹底してはたらきそのものであり、そこにはもはや見るものも見られるものも存しない。　(2) 'Spiritual Exercises' 霊的訓練。　(3) how wide of the mark　見当はずれも甚しい。　(4) Even superficially speaking　外見からして。　(5) the contemplations　凝心。心を一つにして考えること。熟慮。　(6) Hinayana Buddhism　小乗仏教 (p. 8 の注 参照)。　(7) the Five Mind-quieting Methods　五停心観。邪心を停止する五つの方法。　(8) the Nine Thoughts on Impurity　九不浄観。不浄観とは肉体や外界の不浄な様を観じて煩悩を取り除く法。　(9) the Six or Ten Subjects of Memory　六随念・十徧処。　(10) idle reverie　無為の瞑想。

We may say that Christianity is monotheistic,[1] and the Vedanta[2] pantheistic[3]; but we cannot make a similar assertion about Zen. Zen is neither monotheistic nor pantheistic; Zen defies all such designations. Hence there is no object in Zen upon which to fix the thought. Zen is a wafting cloud in the sky. No screw fastens it, no string holds it; it moves as it lists.[4] *No amount of meditation will keep Zen in one place.* Meditation is not Zen. Neither pantheism nor monotheism provides Zen with its subjects of concentration. If Zen is monotheistic, it may tell its followers to meditate on the oneness of things where all differences and inequalities, enveloped in the all-illuminating brightness of the divine light, are obliterated.[5] If Zen were pantheistic it would tell us that every meanest flower in the field reflects the glory of God. But what Zen says is "After all things are reduced to oneness, where would that One be reduced?" Zen wants to have one's mind free and unobstructed; even the idea of oneness or allness is a stumbling-block and a strangling snare[6] which threatens the original freedom of the spirit.

Zen, therefore, does not ask us to concentrate out thought on the idea that a dog is God, or that three pounds of flax are divine. When Zen does this it commits itself to a definite system of philosophy, and there is no more Zen. Zen just feels fire warm and ice cold, because when it freezes we shiver and welcome fire. The feeling is all in all, as Faust declares; all our theorization fails to touch reality. But "the feeling" here must be understood in its deepest sense or in its purest form. Even to say that "This is the feeling" means that Zen is no more there. Zen defies all concept-making. That is why Zen is difficult to grasp.

Whatever meditation Zen may propose, then, will be to take things as they are, to consider snow white and the raven black. When we speak of meditation we in most cases refer to its abstract character; that is, meditation is known to be the concentration of the mind on some highly generalized proposition, which is, in the nature of things, not always closely and directly connected with the concrete affairs of life. Zen

---

(1) monotheistic 一神論的。 (2) the Vedanta ヴェーダンタ。インド哲学の主流をなす思想体系。 (3) pantheistic 汎神論的。 (4) as it lists おのが好むままに。 (5) are obliterated 取り除かれる（亡ぼられる）。 (6) a strangling snare 陥穽（かんせい）。

have struck him dead with one blow and thrown the corpse into the maw[1] of a hungry dog." What unbelievers would ever think of making such raving remarks[2] over a spiritual leader? Yet one of the Zen masters[3] following Ummon says: "Indeed, this is the way Ummon desires to serve the world, sacrificing everything he has, body and mind! How grateful he must have felt for the love of Buddha!"

Zen is not to be confounded with a form of meditation as practised by "New Thought" people, or Christian Scientists, or Hindu Sannyasins,[4] or some Buddhists. Dhyana, as it is understood by Zen, does not correspond to the practice as carried on in Zen. A man may meditate on a religious or philosophical subject while disciplining himself[5] in Zen, but that is only incidental; the essence of Zen is not there at all. Zen purposes to discipline the mind itself, to make it its own master, through an insight into its proper nature. This getting into the real nature of one's own mind or soul is the fundamental object of Zen Buddhism. Zen, therefore, is more than meditation and Dhyana in its ordinary sense. The discipline of Zen consists in opening the mental eye in order to look into the very reason of existence.

To meditate, a man has to fix his thought on something; for instance, on the oneness of God, or his infinite love, or on the impermanence of things.[6] But this is the very thing Zen desires to avoid. If there is anything Zen strongly emphasizes it is the attainment of freedom; that is, freedom from all unnatural encumbrances.[7] Meditation is something artificially put on; it does not belong to the native activity of the mind. Upon what do the fowl of the air[8] meditate? Upon what do the fish in the water meditate? They fly; they swim. Is not that enough? Who wants to fix his mind on the unity of God and man,[9] or on the nothingness of this life[10]? Who wants to be arrested in the daily manifestations of his life-activity by such meditations as the goodness of a divine being or the everlasting fire of hell?

(1) maw　胃袋。　(2) such raving remarks　かかる狂気の批評。　(3) Zen masters　禅匠。　(4) Hindu Sannyasins　印度教の遊行僧。　(5) while disciplining himself　修行中。　(6) the impermanence of things　存在の無常。　(7) unnatural encumbrances　不自然な絆。　(8) the fowl of the air　空飛ぶ鳥。　(9) the unity of God and man　神と人との一者性。　(10) the nothingness of this life　現在のむなしさ。

and other beings that one comes across in Zen temples, they are like so many[1] pieces of wood or stone or metal ; they are like the camellias, azaleas, or stone lanterns in my garden. Make obeisance to the camellia now in full bloom, and worship it if you like, Zen would say. There is as much religion in so doing as[2] in bowing to the various Buddhist gods,[3] or as sprinkling holy water, or as participating in the Lord's Supper.[4] All those pious deeds considered to be meritorious or sanctifying[5] by most so-called religiously minded people are artificialities[6] in the eyes of Zen. It boldly declares that "the immaculate Yogins[7] do not enter Nirvana[8] and the precept-violating monks[9] do not go to hell". This, to ordinary minds, is a contradiction of the common law[10] of moral life, but herein lies the truth and life of Zen. Zen is the spirit of a man. Zen believes in his inner purity and goodness.[11] Whatever is superadded[12] or violently torn away, injures the wholesomeness of the spirit. Zen, therefore, is emphatically against all religious conventionalism.[13]

Its irreligion,[14] however, is merely apparent. Those who are truly religious will be surprised to find that after all there is so much of religion in the barbarous declaration of Zen. But to say that Zen is a religion, in the sense that Christianity or Mohammedanism[15] is, would be a mistake. To make my point clearer, I quote the following. When Sakyamuni was born, it is said that he lifted one hand toward the heavens and pointed to the earth with the other, exclaiming, "Above the heavens and below the heavens, I alone am the Honoured One![16]" Ummon (Yun-men),[17] founder of the Ummon School of Zen, comments on this by saying, "If I had been with him at the moment of his uttering this, I would surely

---

(1) so many そこばくの。 (2) There is as much religion in so doing as… …の宗教味も（この一揖一拝を出づる）ものではないのだ。 (3) the various Buddhist gods 諸天諸神。 (4) the Lord's Supper 聖餐式。 (5) to be meritorious or sanctifying 功徳あり神聖である。 (6) artificialities 余計なわざ。 (7) the immaculate Yogins 清浄の行者。 (8) Nirvana 涅槃（ねはん）。 (9) precept-violating monks 破戒の比丘。 (10) the common law 不文律。 (11) his inner purity and goodness その本来清浄であり本来善であること。 (12) superadded 附加せられたり。 (13) religious conventionalism 宗教的因習。 (14) irreligion 非宗教性。 (15) Mohammedanism マホメット教。 (16) I alone am the Honoured One！ 唯我独尊。 (17) Ummon (Yun-men) 雲門文偃。唐末から五代の頃の禅僧。雲門宗の祖。

II WHAT IS ZEN?

fundamental philosophy.

Zen claims to be Buddhism, but all the Buddhist teachings as propounded in the sutras and sastras[1] are treated by Zen as mere waste paper whose utility consists in wiping off the dirt of intellect and nothing more. Do not imagine, however, that Zen is nihilism. All nihilism is self-destructive, it ends nowhere. Negativism[2] is sound as method, but the highest truth is an affirmation. When it is said that Zen has no philosophy, that it denies all doctrinal authority, that it casts aside all so-called sacred literature as rubbish, we must not forget that Zen is holding up in this very act of negation[3] something quite positive and eternally affirmative. This will become clearer as we proceed.

Is Zen a religion? It is not a religion in the sense that the term is popularly understood; for Zen has no God to worship, no ceremonial rites to observe, no future abode[4] to which the dead are destined, and, last of all, Zen has no soul whose welfare is to be looked after by somebody else and whose immortality is a matter of intense concern with some people. Zen is free from all these dogmatic and "religious" encumbrances.[5]

When I say there is no God in Zen, the pious reader may be shocked, but this does not mean that Zen denies the existence of God; neither denial nor affirmation concerns Zen. When a thing is denied, the very denial involves something not denied. The same can be said of affirmation. This is inevitable in logic. Zen wants to rise above logic, Zen wants to find a higher affirmation where there are no antitheses.[6] Therefore, in Zen, God is neither denied nor insisted upon; only there is in Zen no such God as has been conceived by Jewish and Christian minds. For the same reason that Zen is not a philosophy, Zen is not a religion.

As to all those images of various Buddhas and Bodhisattvas and Devas[7]

---

(1) all the Buddhist teachings as propounded in the sutras and sastras [shastras]　経論（きょうろん）所説底にたいしては。経論とは、仏陀の説法を集成した経と経を注釈した論。
(2) negativism　否定の立場に立つこと。　(3) in this very act of negation　外ならぬこの否定を通じて。　(4) future abode　未来の国土。　(5) encumbrances　羈絆。　(6) antitheses　対立。　(7) Buddhas and Bodhisattvas and Devas　仏・菩薩・天人（てんにん）。菩薩とは、悟りを求める人々と悟りをそなえた人々の意味から、大乗ではことに後者を言う。菩薩は悟り（仏）の世界から人間界に降りてきて、人々と共歓同苦しながら衆生救済に努める存在。天人――道を治めた人。仏典では天に住んでいる神々。

B efore proceeding to expound the teaching of Zen at some length in the following pages, let me answer some of the questions which are frequently raised by critics concerning the real nature of Zen.

Is Zen a system of philosophy, highly intellectual and profoundly metaphysical, as most Buddhist teachings are?

I have already stated that we find in Zen all the philosophy of the East crystallized, but this ought not to be taken as meaning that Zen is a philosophy in the ordinary application of the term.[1] Zen is decidedly not a system founded upon logic and analysis. If anything, it is the antipode to logic, by which I mean the dualistic mode of thinking. There may be an intellectual element in Zen, for Zen is the whole mind,[2] and in it we find a great many things; but the mind is not a composite thing[3] that is to be divided into so many faculties, leaving nothing behind when the dissection[4] is over. Zen has nothing to teach us in the way of intellectual analysis; nor has it any set doctrines[5] which are imposed on its followers for acceptance. In this respect Zen is quite chaotic if you choose to say so. Probably Zen followers may have sets of doctrines, but they have them on their own account, and for their own benefit[6]; they do not owe the fact to Zen. Thereore, there are in Zen no sacred books or dogmatic tenets,[7] nor are there any symbolic formulae through which an access might be gained into the signification of Zen. If I am asked, then, what Zen teaches, I would answer, Zen teaches nothing. Whatever teachings there are in Zen, they come out of one's own mind. We teach ourselves; Zen merely points the way. Unless this pointing is teaching, there is certainly nothing in Zen purposely[8] set up as its cardinal doctrines[9] or as its

編集部注 (1) in the ordinary application of the term 一般にいわれているような意味で。(2) the whole mind 全心情。(3) a composite thing 集合体。(4) dissection 解剖。(5) any set doctrines 型にはまった教義。(6) on their own account, and for their own benefit 各人の好尚と便宜による。(7) dogmatic tenets 教理。(8) purposely ことさらに。(9) its cardinal doctrines 基礎教義。

II

WHAT IS ZEN?

I PRELIMINARY

life stand in remarkable contrast to the other Buddhist sects. Undoubtedly the main ideas of Zen are derived from Buddhism, and we cannot but consider it a legitimate development of the latter ; but this development has been achieved in order to meet the requirements peculiarly characteristic of the psychology of the Far-Eastern people.[1] The spirit of Buddhism has left its highly metaphysical superstructure in order to become a practical discipline of life. The result is Zen. Therefore I make bold to say that in Zen are found systematized,[2] or rather crystallized, all the philosophy, religion, and life itself of the Far-Eastern people, especially of the Japanese.

---

(1) the psychology of the Far-Eastern people　極東民衆の心情。　(2) systematized　体系的に統摂されている。

Oriental culture. And I can affirm that the cultivation[1] of this kind of mysticism is principally due to the influence of Zen. If Buddhism were to develop in the Far East so as to satisfy the spiritual cravings[2] of its people, it had to grow into Zen. The Indians are mystical, but their mysticism is too speculative, too contemplative, too complicated, and, moreover, it does not seem to have any real, vital relation with the practical world of particulars in which we are living.[3] The Far-Eastern mysticism, on the contrary, is direct, practical, and surprisingly simple. This could not develop into anything else but Zen.

All the other Buddhist sects in China as well as in Japan bespeak[4] their Indian origin in an unmistakable manner. For their metaphysical complexity, their long-winded phraseology,[5] their highly abstract reasoning, their penetrating insight into the nature of things,[6] and their comprehensive interpretation[7] of affairs relating to life, are most obviously Indian and not at all Chinese or Japanese. This will be recognized at once by all those who are acquainted with Far-Eastern Buddhism. For instance, look at those extremely complex rites as practised by the Shingon sect, and also at their elaborate systems[8] of "Mandala", by means of which they try to explain the universe. No Chinese or Japanese mind would have conceived such an intricate net-work of philosophy without being first influenced by Indian thought. Then observe how highly speculative is the philosophy of the Madhyamika,[9] the Tendai (*T'ien-tai* in C.), or Kegon (*Avatamsaka* or *Gandavyuha* in Sanskrit). Their abstraction and logical acumen[10] are truly amazing. These facts plainly show that those sects of Far-Eastern Buddhism are at bottom foreign importations.

But when we come to Zen, after a survey of the general field of Buddhism, we are compelled to acknowledge that its simplicity, its directness, its pragmatic tendency, and its close connection with everyday

---

(1) cultivation 教養。 (2) the spiritual carvings 霊的渇望。 (3) the practical world of particulars in which we are living 我々のすむ実際的な個個特殊の世界。 (4) bespeak 示している。 (5) long-winded phraseology 冗長な措辞。 (6) their penetrating insight into the nature of things 存在の実相についての深遠な洞察。 (7) comprehensive interpretation 抱擁力に富む解釈。 (8) elaborate systems 彫琢(ちょうたく)をこらした諸体系。 (9) the Madhyamika 中観（派）。中観（派）——極端な考えかたを離れて、物事を自由に見る視点。 (10) logical acumen 論理の鋭さ。

I PRELIMINARY

for a comprehensive grasp of the whole, and this intuitively. Therefore the Eastern mind, if we assume its existence, is necessarily vague and indefinite, and seems not to have an index which at once reveals the contents to an outsider. The thing is there before our eyes, for it refuses to be ignored; but when we endeavour to grasp it in our own hands in order to examine it more closely or systematically, it eludes and we lose its track. Zen is provokingly[1] evasive. This is not due of course to any conscious or premeditated artifice[2] with which the Eastern mind schemes to shun the scrutiny of others[3]. The unfathomableness is in the very constitution[4], so to speak, of the Eastern mind. Therefore, to understand the East we must understand mysticism; that is, Zen.

It is to be remembered, however, that there are various types of mysticism, rational and irrational, speculative and occult[5], sensible and fantastic[6]. When I say that the East is mystical, I do not mean that the East is fantastic, irrational, and altogether impossible to bring within the sphere of intellectual comprehension. What I mean is simply that in the working of the Eastern mind there is something calm, quiet, silent, undisturbable[7], which appears as if always looking into eternity. This quietude[8] and silence, however, does not point to mere idleness or inactivity. The silence is not that of the desert shorn of all vegetation[9], nor is it that of a corpse forever gone to sleep and decay. It is the silence of an "eternal abyss" in which all contrasts and conditions are buried; it is the silence of God who, deeply absorbed in contemplation of his works past, present, and future, sits calmly on his throne of absolute oneness and allness[10]. It is the "silence of thunder" obtained in the midst of the flash and uproar of opposing electric currents. This sort of silence pervades all things[11] Oriental. Woe[12] unto those who take it for decadence and death, for they will be overwhelmed by an overwhelming outburst of activity out of the eternal silence. It is in this sense that I speak of the mysticism of

(1) provokingly 腹立たしいほど。 (2) premeditated artifice 計画的な術策。 (3) shun the scrutiny of others 他者の穿鑿の眼ざしを避ける。 (4) the very constitution 本質そのもの。 (5) occult 秘儀的な。 (6) fantasitc 怪奇的な。 (7) undisturbable 擾(みだ)すことのできぬ。 (8) quietude 静寂。 (9) the desert shorn of all vegetation 如何なる植物も育たぬ砂漠。 (10) absolute oneness and allness 絶対的一即全。 (11) all things 事事物物 (じじぶつぶつ)。 (12) woe 禍である。

A few words must be said here in regard to the systematic training by Zen of its followers in the attainment of the spiritual insight which has been referred to before as the foundation-experience of Zen. For this is where Zen pre-eminently distinguishes itself from other forms of mysticism. To most mystics such spiritual experience, so intensely personal, comes as something sporadic,[1] isolated, and unexpected. Christians use prayer, or mortification,[2] or contemplation[3] so called, as the means of bringing this on themselves, and leave its fulfilment to divine grace. But as Buddhism does not recognize a supernatural agency in such matters, the Zen method of spiritual training is practical and systematic. From the beginning of its history in China there has been such a tendency well marked ; but, as time went on, a regular system has finally come into existence, and the Zen school at present has a thoroughgoing[4] method for its followers to train themselves in the attainment of their object. Herein lies the practical merit of Zen. While it is highly speculative[5] on the one hand, its methodical discipline on the other hand produces most fruitful and beneficial results on moral character.[6] We sometimes forget its highly abstract character when it is expressed in connection with the facts of our everyday practical life ; but here it is where we have to appreciate the real value of Zen, for Zen finds an inexpressibly deep thought even in holding up a finger, or in saying a "good morning" to a friend casually met on the street. In the eye of Zen the most practical is the most abstruse,[7] and *vice versa*. All the system of discipline adopted by Zen is the outcome of this fundamental experience.

I said that Zen is mystical. This is inevitable, seeing that Zen is the keynote of Oriental culture ; it is what makes the West frequently fail to fathom[8] exactly the depths of the Oriental mind, for mysticism in its very nature defies the analysis of logic, and logic is the most characteristic feature of Western thought. The East is synthetic in its method of reasoning ; it does not care so much for the elaboration of particulars[9] as

(1) sporadic　散発的。　(2) mortification　苦行。　(3) contemplation　凝心。　(4) thoroughgoing　周到な。　(5) speculative　思弁的。　(6) moral character　品性。　(7) the most abstruse　最も深いもの。　(8) fathom　測る。　(9) elaboration of particulars　細部の精究。

I PRELIMINARY

thing is concerned with life itself, personal experience is an absolute necessity. Without this experience nothing relative to its profound working will ever be accurately and therefore efficiently grasped. The foundation of all concepts is simple, unsophisticated experience. Zen places the utmost emphasis upon this foundation-experience, and it is around this that Zen constructs all the verbal and conceptual scaffold which is found in its literature known as "Sayings[(1)]" (*goroku*, J.; *yu-lu*, Ch.). Though the scaffold affords a most useful means to reach the inmost reality, it is still an elaboration and artificiality. We lose its whole significance when it is taken for a final reality.[(2)] The nature of the human understanding[(3)] compels us not to put too much confidence in the superstructure.[(4)] Mystification is far from being the object of Zen itself, but to those who have not touched the central fact of life Zen inevitably appears as mystifying. Penetrate through the conceptual superstructure and what is imagined to be a mystification will at once disappear, and at the same time there will be an enlightenment[(5)] known as *satori*.[1]

Zen, therefore, most strongly and persistently insists on an inner spiritual experience.[(6)] It does not attach any intrinsic importance to the sacred sutras[(7)] or to their exegeses[(8)] by the wise and learned.[(9)] Personal experience is strongly set against authority and objective revelation,[(10)] and as the most practical method of attaining spiritual enlightenment[(11)] the followers of Zen propose the practice of Dhyana,[(12)] known as *zazen*[2] in Japanese.

1 See below.
2 *Za* means "to sit", and *zazen* may be summarily taken as meaning "to sit in meditation". What it exactly signifies will be seen later in connection with the description of "The Meditation Hall" (*zendo*, J.; *ch'an-t'ang*, Ch.).

(1) "Sayings" 「語録」。 (2) a final reality 窮極の実在。 (3) the human understanding 人間的悟性。悟性（ごせい）は知性・知力・論理的思惟能力の意。感性・理性に対する語。特に理性と区別して、経験界に属する知性。 (4) the superstructure 上部構造。 (5) an enlightenment 心機開発、すなわち悟り。心機——心の動き、心の働き。 (6) an inner spiritual experience 内的な霊的経験。 (7) the sacred sutras 聖典（sutra 経典）。 (8) exegeses (a exegesis) 論釈。 (9) the wise and learned 賢哲。 (10) objective revelation 外的啓示。 (11) spiritual enlightenment 霊的知見。 (12) Dhyana 禅那（ディヤーナ）、すなわち座禅。

11

This school is unique in various ways in the history of religion. Its doctrines, theoretically stated, may be said to be those of speculative mysticism,[1] but they are presented and demonstrated in such a manner that only those initiates who, after long training, have actually gained an insight into the system can understand their ultimate signification. To those who have not acquired this penetrating knowledge, that is, to those who have not experienced Zen in their everyday active life—its teachings, or rather its utterances, assume quite a peculiar, uncouth,[2] and even enigmatical aspect. Such people, looking at Zen more or less conceptually, consider Zen utterly absurd and ludicrous, or deliberately making itself unintelligible in order to guard its apparent profundity against outside criticism. But, according to the followers of Zen, its apparently paradoxical statements are not artificialities contrived[3] to hide themselves behind a screen of obscurity; but simply because the human tongue[4] is not an adequate organ for expressing the deepest truths of Zen, the latter cannot be made the subject of logical exposition[5]; they are to be experienced in the inmost soul when they become for the first time intelligible. In point of fact, no plainer and more straightforward expressions than those of Zen have ever been made by any other branch of human experience. "Coal is black"—this is plain enough; but Zen protests, "Coal is not black." This is also plain enough, and indeed even plainer than the first positive statement when we come right down to the truth of the matter.[6]

Personal experience, therefore, is everything in Zen. No ideas are intelligible to those who have no backing of experience. This is a platitude.[7] A baby has no ideas, for its mentality is not yet so developed as to experience anything in the way of ideas. If it has them at all, they must be something extremely obscure and blurred and not in correspondence with realities. To get the clearest and most efficient understanding[8] of a thing, therefore, it must be experienced personally. Especially when the

---

(1) speculative mysticism　思弁的神秘主義。思弁——経験によらず、純粋に思惟によって認識を構成すること。　(2) peculiar, uncouth　奇異・奇矯（な）。　(3) artificialities contrived　作為。　(4) the human tongue　人間の言葉（言語）。　(5) logical exposition　論理的解明。　(6) the truth of the matter　這箇（しゃこ）の消息。這箇は、禅宗で、一切の事物の根源をさす言葉。禅の極致。　(7) a platitude　分り切った話。　(8) the clearest and most efficient understanding　最も明確で充実した理解。

more primitive type. At present the Mahayana form may be said not to display, superficially at least, those features most conspicuously characteristic of original Buddhism.

For this reason there are people who would declare that this branch of Buddhism is in reality no Buddhism in the sense that the latter is commonly understood. My contention, however, is this: anything that has life in it is an organism,[1] and it is in the very nature of an organism that it never remains in the same state of existence. An acorn is quite different, even as a young oak with tender leaves just out of its protective shell is quite different from a full-grown tree so stately and gigantic and towering up to the sky. But throughout these varying phases of change there is a continuation of growth and unmistakable marks of identity, whence we know that one and the same plant has passed through many stages of becoming. The so-called primitive Buddhism[2] is the seed; out of it Far-Eastern Buddhism has come into existence with the promise of still further growth. Scholars may talk of historical Buddhism, but my subject here is to see Buddhism not only in its historical development but from the point of view of its still vitally concerning us as a quickening spiritual force in the Far East.

Among the many sects of Buddhism that have grown up, especially in China and Japan, we find a unique order claiming to transmit the essence and spirit of Buddhism directly from its author, and this not through any secret document or by means of any mysterious rite. This order is one of the most significant aspects of Buddhism, not only from the point of view of its historical importance and spiritual vitality, but from the point of view of its most original and stimulating manner of demonstration. The "Doctrine of the Buddha-heart (*buddhahridaya*[3])" is its scholastic name, but more commonly it is known as "Zen". That Zen is not the same as Dhyana,[4] though the term *Zen* is derived from the Chinese transliteration (*ch'an-na*; *zenna* in Japanese) of the original Sanskrit, will be explained later on.

(1) an organism　生き物。(2) primitive Buddhism　原始仏教。(3) Doctrine of the Buddha-heart (*buddhahridaya*)　仏心宗。すなわち、一般にいう禅。(4) Dhyana　このサンスクリットの原語を漢語に移したのが「禅那」で、言葉としては「禅」はこれに由来する。しかし、Dhyana と「禅」とは同じではない。

B uddhism in its course of development has completed a form which distinguishes itself from its so-called primitive or original type—so greatly, indeed, that we are justified in emphasizing its historical division into two schools, Hinayana and Mahayana, or the Lesser Vehicle and the Greater Vehicle of salvation.[1] As a matter of fact, the Mahayana, with all its varied formulae, is no more than a developed form of Buddhism and traces back its final authority to its Indian founder, the great Buddha Sakyamuni.[2] When this developed form of the Mahayana was introduced into China and then into Japan, it achieved further development in these countries. This achievement was no doubt due to the Chinese and Japanese Buddhist leaders, who knew how to apply the principles of their faith to the ever-varying conditions of life and to the religious needs of the people. And this elaboration and adaptation on their part has still further widened the gap that has already been in existence between the Mahayana[1] and its

1 To be accurate, the fundamental ideas of the Mahayana are expounded in the Prajnaparamita group of Buddhist literature, the earliest of which must have appeared at the latest within three hundred years of the Buddha's death. The germs are no doubt in the writings belonging to the so-called primitive Buddhism. Only their development, that is, a conscious grasp of them as most essential in the teachings of the founder, could not be effected without his followers' actually living the teachings for some time through the variously changing conditions of life. Thus enriched in experience and matured in reflection, the Indian Buddhists came to have the Mahayana form of Buddhism as distinguished from its primitive or original form. In India two Mahayana schools are known: the Madhyamika of Nagarjuna and the Vijnaptimatra or Yogacara of Asanga and Vasubandhu. In China more schools developed: the Tendai (*t'ien-tai*), the Kegon (*avatamsaka*), the Jodo (*ching-t'u*), the Zen (*ch'an*), etc. In Japan we have besides these the Hokke, the Shingon, the Shin, the Ji, etc. All these schools or sects belong to the Mahayana wing of Buddhism.

編集部注 (1) Hinayana または the Lesser Vehicle (of salvation) 小乗仏教。サンスクリット原語では「劣った乗り物」の意味。小乗仏教——後期仏教の二大流派の一つ。「大乗」を称した者たちが他派に対し「自利を図ることしかしない」と名づけた貶称。現在、インド、タイの仏教はこれに属する。Mahayana または the Greater Vehicle (of salvation) 大乗仏教。「小乗」に対する語。「大乗」とは、「あらゆる衆生を乗せて悟りに導く大きな乗り物 (教え)」の意味。利他主義の立場で、人間の救済に関する教義を説く。
(2) Sakyamuni 釈迦牟尼 (しゃかむに)。仏陀のこと。

I

PRELIMINARY

PREFACE

The articles collected here were originally written for the *New East*, which was published in Japan during the 1914 War under the editorship of Mr. Robertson Scott. The editor suggested publishing them in book-form, but I did not feel like doing so at that time. Later, they were made the basis of the First Series of my *Zen Essays* (1927),[1] which, therefore, naturally cover more or less the same ground.

Recently, the idea came to me that the old papers might be after all reprinted in book-form. The reason is that my *Zen Essays* is too heavy for those who wish to have just a little preliminary knowledge of Zen. Will not, therefore, what may be regarded as an introductory work be welcomed by some of my foreign friends?

With this in view I have gone over the entire MS., and whatever inaccuracies I have come across in regard to diction as well as the material used have been corrected. While there are quite a few points I would like to see now expressed somewhat differently, I have left them as they stand, because their revision inevitably involves the recasting of the entire context. So long as they are not misrepresenting, they may remain as they were written.

If the book really serves as a sort of introduction to Zen Buddhism, and leads the reader up to the study of my other works, the object is attained. No claim is made here for a scholarly treatment of the subject-matter.

The companion book, *Manual of Zen Buddhism*,[2] is recommended to be used with this *Introduction*.

D. T. S.

Kamakura, August 1934

編集部注 (1) *Zen Essays* (1927) 『禅論』第一巻（1927年刊）。(2) *Manual of Zen Buddhism* (1935) 邦訳は『禅学便覧』（1935年刊）。参考：The Training of the Zen Buddhism Monk (1934)（邦訳版『禅堂の修行と生活』。岩波全集第十七巻所収では『禅堂生活』となっている）本書とこれら二書を合わせて、禅入門の三部書として併用するとよい。

CONTENTS

	Author's Preface	5
I	Preliminary	7
II	What Is Zen?	17
III	Is Zen Nihilistic?	31
IV	Illogical Zen	45
V	Zen a Higher Affirmation	55
VI	Practical Zen	67
VII	Satori, or Acquiring a New Viewpoint	85
VIII	The Koan	99
IX	The Meditation Hall and the Monk's Life	123

An Introduction to Zen Buddhism
DAISETZ T. SUZUKI

Art Days